For women whose sexua[...] this book is like a warm hug that gives you the courage and strength to move forward! It's the book I've been looking for as I hear, day in and day out, from women who have been left broken, their arousal maps distorted, while they try to navigate sex, desire, and relationships. Tabitha shows bottomless empathy without shying away from the truths about what healing work looks like. You'll end this book with a sigh of relief and a road map to wholeness.

SHEILA WRAY GREGOIRE, founder of Bare Marriage and coauthor of *The Great Sex Rescue*

A necessary resource for those in the survivor community. With gentleness and expert guidance, Tabitha Westbrook brings readers on a journey to wholeness and peace.

BOB GOFF, *NYT* bestselling author of *Love Does, Everybody Always, Dream Big,* and *Undistracted*

Tabitha Westbrook offers a pathway to healing that is deeply compassionate and rooted in biblical truth. *Body & Soul, Healed & Whole* is a lifeline for women who have been wounded and silenced, longing to break free from the chains of abuse and embrace the abundant life Jesus offers.

CHRIS MOLES, pastor and author of *The Heart of Domestic Abuse*

I'm so thankful for the work Tabitha Westbrook does and the way she pours out her life for those who are vulnerable or have been silenced. She's a friend to and defender of women, and she knows what she's talking about. Listen to her, for she is wise.

ELYSE FITZPATRICK, coauthor of *Worthy*

Body & Soul, Healed & Whole is the message our hearts have needed all along. What a powerful resource. This book is for you. It's for your mother, your sister, your friend. It's for a world of women who, for far too long, have had to carry the burden of their physical, emotional, and sexual trauma alone. You are not alone.

YOLANDA HARPER, LCSW, trauma and relationship therapist, TEDx speaker, author of *Soul Sabbatical*

My friend Tabitha Westbrook's work, as well as her own personal story, grants her deep empathy and qualifies her to point the way toward healing and wholeness—in both body and soul. This book is a practical and essential guide for those whose sexuality has been shattered and for those of us who care for them.

GREG WILSON, DEDMIN, LPC-S, coauthor of *When Home Hurts*

Tabitha Westbrook combines her own story of survival with her vast knowledge and experience as a Christian therapist to help survivors of abuse engage with the difficult topics of sex and sexuality. This book is deeply compassionate and handles a difficult topic with straightforward but careful language. Any female abuse survivor who struggles to find a healthy and God-honoring view of sexuality will find hope and practical guidance from this book.

BETH M. BROOM, LPC-S, executive director of Christian Trauma Healing Network and contributing author in *Caring for Families Caught in Domestic Abuse*

I have had the privilege of watching Tabitha Westbrook enjoy the Lord and seek to serve others for the last several years. Her heart and expertise come through in the pages of this book. There is healing for the deep trauma of our souls found in Jesus Christ. This book is a good guide.

MATT CHANDLER, lead pastor of The Village Church

In a world of clichés and sound bites, Tabitha Westbrook has written something that is both authentic and substantial. Tabitha has spent years of her life restoring the health of people who have been crushed by abuse. In this book, she combines her years of experience with academic rigor and biblical truth. Pastors who love their congregations should have multiple copies of this book to hand out as needed, but more than that, I pray that all leaders will spend thoughtful time in these pages. No book released this year will be as beneficial as this one.

MICHAEL RAMSEY, PhD, pastor, Hillsborough, NC

Body & Soul, Healed & Whole is truly an *invitation* to examine the messages and events that have impacted our relationship with our body, as well as the ability to heal those to again become sexual beings in the way that God intended. Tabitha Westbrook does a superior job of blending the elements of research, psychological knowledge, biblical references, and story, resulting in a book that will draw you in. Her gentle, healing nature and presence come through the words on the page as she guides and opens the reader to very direct and honest discussion about the impact of abuse as well as the ways God's Word is sometimes manipulated when applied to sexual relationships. I highly recommend this book as a part of your healing!

CYNDI DOYLE, LPC-S, NCC, CDWF, creator of Code4Couples

In *Body & Soul, Healed & Whole*, Tabitha Westbrook gently lifts the heavy weight of shame that has burdened too many women as they seek to heal and reclaim their sexuality after the devastation of sexual assault and sexual abuse. Her fresh insights and practical strategies offer genuine hope for anyone living with the pain of such hurt.

GEORGIA SHAFFER, professional certified coach, PA licensed psychologist, author of *Taking Out Your Emotional Trash*, founder of ReBUILD after Divorce

Tabi Westbrook combines the unflinching story of her own experiences of trauma with her wisdom and extensive healing knowledge in this important book. Despite the difficult subject matter, the chapters are engaging and readable, offering the reader exercises and nurturing. Tabi's voice is genuine and professional, taking readers through what can be a tough journey with humor and a comforting tone. The book combines clinical expertise with wise insight and practical guidance, and is highly recommended for anyone who has experienced trauma, abuse, or coercive control as well as for professionals working with such clients.

LYNN M. McLEAN, LCSW-S, Houston Family Therapy Associates

This book gives voice to those who have intimately known oppression, guiding readers into a gentle path toward healing. Courageously sharing her own story, Tabitha creates a space where survivors can feel truly seen and heard in experiences that are often beyond words. With a compassionate blend of scriptural wisdom and clinical expertise, this book is a powerful resource for both survivors seeking healing and clinicians striving to deepen their understanding of trauma recovery. Tabitha reveals profound strength and grace of spirit, and she inspires hope in those who encounter her journey.

DAN HUNT, PhD, marriage and family therapist, Arkansas Family Therapy & Consulting

Body & Soul, Healed & Whole brings together trauma theory and the lived experiences of survivors in an understandable, relatable, conversational style that highlights the struggles and victories paving the road to healing and health. Tabi's warmth and compassion wrap around you from page one and carry you through the practical exercises and mindset shifts she lays out in each chapter. Highly recommended for anyone who has experienced trauma.

GINA AGUAYO, PhD, founder and CEO of Blue Square Counseling and Wellness

Finally, a bold and unflinching Christian guide for survivors of sexual abuse. This book doesn't shy away from the toughest of topics about healing from sexual trauma. Part memoir, part practical guide, *Body & Soul, Healed & Whole* will not disappoint. Tabi knows this topic because she has lived it. Both as a survivor of abuse who is traveling on the road to her own recovery and as a seasoned guide on the front lines of recovery, Tabi is leading countless women to healing and connection. This will be a trusted resource for years to come.

RYAN RUSS, LPC, CSAT, BSP, EMDR I & II, CTTc, CTCYM, cofounder of The Finding Place Counseling and Recovery

I have known and loved Tabitha Westbrook, and her ministry to abuse survivors, since God providentially brought us together in 2017. As a survivor herself, she can speak firsthand to the unique challenges of healing from abuse and trauma, and that is why this book is so powerful. Throughout it, you will find parts of Tabitha's own healing journey alongside practical exercises to help soothe both body and soul. Those seeking to heal from sexual abuse and to understand God's design for healthy sexuality will find this book a treasure.

JOY FORREST, founder and executive director of Called to Peace Ministries, author of *Called to Peace*

BODY & SOUL,

*An Invitational Guide to Healthy Sexuality
after Trauma, Abuse & Coercive Control*

HEALED & WHOLE

TABITHA K. WESTBROOK

LMFT-S, LCMHC-QS, LPC-S, LPC

TYNDALE
REFRESH®

Think Well. Live Well. Be Well.

Visit Tyndale online at tyndale.com.

Visit Tabitha at tabithawestbrook.com.

Tyndale, Tyndale's quill logo, *Tyndale Refresh*, and the Tyndale Refresh logo are registered trademarks of Tyndale House Ministries. Tyndale Refresh is a nonfiction imprint of Tyndale House Publishers, Carol Stream, Illinois.

Body & Soul, Healed & Whole: An Invitational Guide to Healthy Sexuality after Trauma, Abuse, and Coercive Control

Designed by Lindsey Bergsma

Published in association with Don Gates of the literary agency The Gates Group; www.the-gates-group.com.

For information about special discounts for bulk purchases, please contact Tyndale House Publishers at csresponse@tyndale.com, or call 1-855-277-9400.

The URLs in this book were verified prior to publication. The publisher is not responsible for content in the links, links that have expired, or websites that have changed ownership after that time.

The case examples in this book are fictional composites based on the author's years of professional interactions with hundreds of clients, as a speaker, and from her experience in women's ministry. All names are invented, and any resemblance between these fictional characters and real people is coincidental.

Library of Congress Cataloging-in-Publication Data

A catalog record for this book is available from the Library of Congress.

ISBN 978-1-4964-9066-7

Printed in the United States of America

31	30	29	28	27	26	25
7	6	5	4	3	2	1

This book is dedicated to all the survivors of sexual abuse and assault. Those experiences can shatter our sexuality, but healing is possible. I hope you find at least a bit of that in this book.

Contents

Foreword

I can't think of a better time for *Body & Soul, Healed & Whole* to come into your hands. I'm excited for you to read it and begin the work of healing.

When I was growing up in the church, we never had conversations about our physical body, other than that it was the temple of the Holy Spirit (whatever that meant). I do remember our youth group leader warning the girls that our maturing bodies could cause boys and men to "stumble." The message was clear: "Girls, cover your body from neck to knees, lest you cause your brother to sin." Being told I was responsible for someone else's thoughts and behaviors made emerging into womanhood feel daunting. Too many women, myself included, have experienced another person using, misusing, and abusing our bodies for sinful, selfish reasons. Sadly, Christian women often carry the physical, emotional, spiritual, sexual, and psychological fallout of blame, guilt, and shame from someone else's sin against them.

As a Christian counselor and coach, I've journeyed with countless women who have never healed from their sexual trauma. They've sat for years in the rubble of silence and shame, never telling another human being what happened. Recently a woman shared with me that she had been sexually abused while dating. She was well into middle age but, until now, had stayed quiet. Why? She said she felt responsible, even though she was asleep when he violated her. She swallowed the lie that she was damaged goods and God was disappointed in her. She believed God wanted her to marry her abuser. What kind of God is that? The harm inflicted wasn't just sexual, physical, or emotional. It was spiritual.

Healing from that harm is a process and takes time. How do we begin to change the way we see and relate to our own body? Our self? Our God? Or even our abuser? How do we learn to banish the self-hatred we've felt and lived with and learn to feel compassion toward the parts of us that have been misused, broken, and damaged by others? How do we bring that kindness and compassion to the part of ourselves that contributed to our own harm in our awkward attempts to soothe or comfort our pain?

How do we begin to feel our feelings when our practice has been to stuff them down and shut them out? How do we dial down the intensity of our emotions when they get too strong or out of control, scaring ourselves or others? How do we heal what feels eternally broken? We wonder, *Will I ever feel sexually whole again? Are sexual feelings okay for a good Christian woman to feel? To express? To enjoy?* And what do we do with those sexual feelings when there is no safe or biblically sanctioned partner (i.e., husband) to express them with?

Today most women can find information about their bodies, sexual abuse, trauma, and what's normal and not. But information alone does not bring wisdom, healing, or growth. We also need to be safely welcomed into healthy conversations with God, ourselves, and other women so we can better understand how our bodies impact our sense of self and our relationships.

Tabitha's book is a rare gift for those who have experienced sexual trauma. Much like a lullaby, Tabi's words will soothe your hypersensitive nervous system as she sings over you with biblically and psychologically sound wisdom. She gently sprinkles truth with compassionate practices that will help you take that long journey from head to heart and from body to soul. There's no rush. Take your time as you savor each chapter. Do the exercises again and again if you need to. Linger as long as you like. Stop when it becomes too much and rest. Stopping and resting are part of your healing and intentional care for yourself. Each step forward creates a sturdy base, providing a sense of safety and trust in yourself that will help you heal and bring you into alignment with the woman God designed you to be.

I know Tabitha. She has the heart of a teddy bear and the soul of a warrior. She is gentle and she is fierce. You can trust her to walk this journey of healing and wholeness with you.

Leslie Vernick, MSW
relationship coach, speaker, author of
The Emotionally Destructive Relationship
and The Emotionally Destructive Marriage

Author's Note

Please note that this book is direct, and I don't mince words. We're going to talk about all the hard things here, so parts of it may feel brutal or heavy. If you find that to be true for you, I encourage you to consider partnering with a licensed therapist who can help you process your experiences. I believe the information and exercises here will assist you in your healing journey, but this book doesn't replace counseling or other mental health care.

Please take care of yourself as you read. I tell all my clients, clinicians, and students the same thing: You are the only you that you have. You are created in the image and likeness of God Himself, and you deserve good care. Please pay attention to your body; it tells you so much. And as you're reading, if the experience becomes overwhelming, step away. Take a walk, read another book, listen to a lighthearted podcast, watch a funny movie, play with your kids, or get a hug from someone you trust.

All the stories in this book are compilations from my counseling clients and from women I've met while speaking or teaching in women's ministry. Names have been changed, and I've been careful to be sure there are no identifying details. Situations like these are so common in abusive relationships that you may see aspects of yourself in these pages. My hope is that they bring healing to your soul.

If you are in a dangerous situation

Please consider reaching out for help. You can contact the National Domestic Violence Hotline (thehotline.org) as a starting point. If you need an advocate, you can contact your local domestic violence shelter or reach out to a ministry like Called to Peace (calledtopeace.org). If you are in immediate danger, call 911 or go to the nearest police station for help. If you are struggling with suicidal thoughts, please reach out to the Suicide and Crisis Lifeline by calling or texting 988. Someone is there to support you twenty-four hours a day, seven days a week.

Take care of you. The information will be here when you're ready.

Grace upon grace upon grace to you as we journey together.

MY INVITATION TO YOU

Sex has the power to touch the deepest dimension of what it means to be human and alive to God; therefore, it stands to reason that it is hated more than any other dimension of humanity by a kingdom that opposes the glory of God.

DAN ALLENDER, *Healing the Wounded Heart*

While driving around town one day in 2008, I noticed a blinking light on my dash, warning me that I needed to fill up my tank or I'd soon be pushing my SUV rather than driving it. I made a quick right-hand turn into a familiar gas station. I stepped out by the pump under a clear sky that was a brilliant Carolina blue. I was enjoying the gentle breeze that carried little humidity—a rarity in the Southern summer—when I noticed a fellow next to me who was filling up his Jeep. He smiled at me as I pumped gas. I smiled back. We made small talk as we filled our vehicles. This was nothing strange for me. Those who know me would tell you that I can basically talk to a brick wall. I will talk to nearly anyone because I really like people. This guy seemed nice, and he was handsome with a good sense of humor. After our tanks were full, he and I stood and chatted for a few more minutes. Then he asked for my phone number. I felt my pulse quicken and my palms begin to sweat. I panicked. I agreed but gave

1

him a fake number. I felt suddenly disoriented, though I'd been to this gas station many times. We got in our vehicles and drove away.

I felt nauseated and even forgot where I was headed. I pulled into a neighborhood nearby and parked, my whole body trembling, sweat pouring off me. What was happening? I had enjoyed the conversation; what was the harm in giving this man my phone number? Images flashed through my mind of my ex-husband's treatment of me. My body shook harder as I was flooded with horrific memories. I sat in my SUV until the flashback passed.

As my body and mind settled, I cried. I felt hated, broken, used, and destroyed. No way could I think about having another relationship. Ever.

I'd love to say I have only intellectual knowledge of the impact of sexual abuse and assault, but sadly my knowledge is experiential and runs deep. I was sexually abused as a child and sexually assaulted repeatedly in my abusive marriage. My sexuality was utterly shattered so early in life I didn't even know at the time that something had been stolen by the kingdom of darkness. By the time I understood the implications of what happened to me, I was left standing in what felt like a barren wasteland full of toppling buildings and burned-out ruins, like some dystopian novel. Except this was my very real life.

The confusion and brokenness I felt is common among women. Our stories may not be exactly alike. Maybe your innocence also was stripped away in childhood. Maybe you were sexually assaulted as a young college student while living away from home for the first time. Even if you were harmed in an abusive marriage, where you were never permitted to say no and your needs and desires were never considered, the circumstances and aftermath may have been quite different from mine. No matter how your sense of sexuality and sense of self were shattered, it created deep wounding and confusion. You wonder if you were damaged beyond repair. You wonder whether God can even love you. You wonder whether or not you even want God to love you; after all, where was He when it was happening?

You want to know if it can ever be healed or different. I wondered all that too.

Before we really dive in, I want you to know that I feel the weight of this topic. Like many women who have been sexually abused, I spent years grappling with the fallout—everything from shame and sorrow to a distorted view of my sexuality. But it wasn't until I finally escaped my controlling, coercive, abusive marriage that I was determined to find healing and wholeness. My healing journey wasn't quick and easy—my experiences had left me shattered, both physically and emotionally. It has taken me a long time to work through my own story. In fact, I continue to do this repair work. Though the journey can be tough and is often not linear or nearly as fast as we'd like, I want to promise you it is possible to heal. It's a lot like climbing a mountain with rock scrambles and switchbacks amid the fog and rain. Some moments you hurt all over, your knees are scraped up from slipping and falling on hidden roots and rocks, and you wonder why you can no longer see the trail. But when you finally hit the summit and look out over the epic views, you realize that the journey was worth it.

This isn't an easy topic for me, even though I now regularly talk with women about sex and sexuality as a certified sex addiction therapist (CSAT) and trauma-specialized therapist.[1] Not only have I experienced the helplessness and hopelessness as an abuse survivor, but I've also sat across from hundreds of hurting people and felt the heaviness of their stories. These women often bring questions with no easy answers, and despite the alphabet soup of letters after my name, I don't claim to be an expert who has everything figured out. I'm a fellow journeyer, and I hope you'll give me grace as I travel this road with you.

You may be reading this as you're just beginning to think about the harm that's been done to you, or you may be further along in this process. Wherever you are, I invite you to care for yourself. Together, we will examine the damage done by abuse and assault, step onto a pathway to healing, and address a whole bunch of questions that many women are too afraid to ask. Along the way, you'll discover that sexuality does not have to be a minefield or permanently broken.

Much has been written about sex in both secular and religious spaces, but I have yet to see many specialists really look at how sexuality is shattered after abuse, especially domestic abuse and coercive control. There is a particular lack of resources for women who are single. More importantly, women need to know how to put those pieces back together. Even if the abuse ends, our sexuality doesn't suddenly reemerge intact. Our vision of healthy sex has been distorted.

The women I talk with often end up in one of two places—either shutting down their sexuality altogether or engaging in sexual behaviors that don't match their values. They may even alternate between those two responses or slide back and forth on the continuum.

Some women vow to never touch a man again and become celibate, though they may have a deep longing to find a true partner and companion. Others decide the way they'd been taught to "be pure" must have been wrong, and they're going to sleep with or do whatever with whomever they want, married or otherwise. They say, "I played by the rules, and I was played by the rules. Now I'm going to do what I want." They lament that they did the "right" things—waited for their first kiss at the altar or for sex on their wedding night—and then found themselves in the torture of an abusive marriage with no hope of escape. They cry, "No more," in their attempt to make sense of the harm they endured.

Maybe you can relate to the woman who has begun using pornography because it was forced on her in her marriage and she now feels she needs it for sexual arousal. Or perhaps you understand the single woman who turns to masturbation for comfort or who is frightened by her sexual urges. Or maybe you understand another woman's fixation on erotic fiction because that's the only sexual outlet that feels safe to her. Possibly you relate to the woman who has pushed down her longings so far that she insists she feels no sexual desire whatsoever. Women in each of these situations have questions—but where and with whom can they even broach them?

These pages are a safe place to bring these questions. As we begin, let's take a look at the road map we'll follow in the coming chapters.

FINDING THE FOOTPATH

Sexual abuse and assault can be scary subjects. Sometimes the signs are unmistakable, but many victims wonder whether their experience qualifies because they've been told over and over that it's all in their heads or that they just need to be more submissive or it "wasn't that bad." We start the first chapter, then, with a frank discussion of what constitutes abuse and assault, as well as coercive control. What are the signs, and how do they affect us?

When we've been harmed, we may be tempted to seek safety in solitude. But as we'll discover, God created us to need healthy relationships—with Him, with ourselves, and with others. And that includes people of the opposite sex. In chapters 2 and 3, we'll explore how to build these relationships as we heal our sexual selves. We'll learn about important boundaries, safety, and self-care, and how we can incorporate them into our relationships.

Another key to a healthy relationship with ourselves is to acknowledge that we live in bodies and that our faith is never separated from them. When our bodies have been violated through abuse, our faith and our connection to our bodies both take a massive hit. In chapter 4, we'll learn to reconnect to the very good bodies God gave us. As we do, we will shore up our faith too.

We've all heard, at some point, the research that says babies who get no touch fail to thrive. Did you know that, as adults, we need touch just as much? Did you know that loneliness is actually physically deadly? Touch is vital, so giving and receiving healthy, nonsexual touch is critical. During this stop on our journey in chapters 5 and 6, we will explain that type of touch and consider ways to begin incorporating it into our daily life.

What turns you on? Do you know? Do you know how your preferences were formed? Our next two chapters, 7 and 8, explore this important topic. Arousal structures are key to understanding our bodies and our healing, so we'll look at what they are, how they're formed and distorted by abuse, and how to begin reframing them when needed to help us heal our sexual selves.

When we've been abused, we often find ourselves agreeing with things the abuser said to or over us—and then we live out those beliefs, which we assume we created ourselves. Worse yet, we often think they reflect the way God sees us. Growing up, we may have been told (or even said), "Sticks and stones may break my bones, but words will never hurt me," only to realize that they sure do hurt. (In fact, emotional pain causes the same areas of the brain to light up as physical pain, so those words that feel like a gut punch are basically a gut punch.) Chapter 9 will help us break the vows (lies we've come to believe about our identity) because of curses spoken over us (the stuff our abusers said about who we are) and explore what God actually says about us.

Once we have addressed some of those complicated topics, we will engage in a discussion of healthy sex in chapter 10. You may be thinking, *Wow, it will take us a long time to get to the point!* I appreciate that. We have to lay the foundation for our complete sexuality, which is far more than just sex itself. If we jump into this topic too soon, we may be left lacking and hurting. Chapter 10 will apply to all of us, whether we're married or single. We don't have to have a partner to be healthy sexual beings.

Assault and abuse can affect not only our thought processes, but also our sexual behavior and preferences. My clients often bring their toughest questions to therapy. These are the ones they're too afraid to walk up to their women's ministry leader and ask—but they need answers. Chapter 11 poses the hard questions—the ones that often hold the most shame—and provides answers.

Finally, we'll bring it all home in the final chapter by shining a light on the path ahead of us. Though we will reach the end of our journey together here, we will now have the tools we need to continue to heal and move forward.

I want to be very clear about something. While faith guides my steps, I am well aware that Scripture has been a weapon used by many abusers. I am not a take-two-verses-and-call-me-in-the-morning girlie. I have no patience for trite use of Scripture that is used to spiritually bypass the destruction of abuse. Because you can't hear my voice or see my face as you read these words, I want to unequivocally say I get madder than a hornet when God's Word is misused to silence victims and prevent justice. Anywhere I use Scripture or talk about God, I've tried to be especially careful and consider how it could be heard. Please know, above all else, your pain is real, it matters, and you never should have been harmed.

Engaging with this book takes enormous courage, and I applaud you for that. As I mentioned earlier, I know these are weighty topics with multiple layers that affect people differently. For that reason, I invite you to work through these chapters at your own pace. Also, to give you opportunities to pause, rest, and reflect along the way, I've included Mindful Moments journaling prompts and self-care practices to help you do exactly that.

And if you come across some exercises that you think are cheesy, I encourage you to give them a whirl anyway. Some may be simple, but they're not easy. Your brain and body have done a great job of protecting you—often through avoidance, dissociation, and busyness. Doing something new can feel really weird and uncomfortable. I can't even tell you how often I've said during my own therapy, "I don't like how this feels!" the first few times I've tried something. Those practices are now the ones my clients and I have grown to love and embrace.

You will also notice sidebars in some chapters. Many of these take a closer look at the vocabulary we use around sex. I know it can be tempting to read right around sidebars in books, but I encourage you not to do that. Words often hold more power than we realize. What we say and how we speak to ourselves and other people matter. Words are often used as weapons against survivors, and it's time to destigmatize and desexualize terms that hold much more meaning than we may realize.

As we expand our vocabulary and talk about restoring healthy sexuality, noticing what we feel and where those feelings are in our bodies can help us process harm and embrace difficult sensations and thoughts. As you begin this work, it may even be helpful to see where you can incorporate some of these words into your overall context of life.

All of these additional helps—journaling, body practices, and even vocabulary expansion—are designed to help all of you—body, mind, and spirit—participate in the healing process. Think of these self-care skills as taking time to sit beside still waters, restoring your soul. We will do so much heavy lifting together that I encourage you to find the rest stops you need along the way.

You've got this. You are worth healing. You are worth wholeness.

ASSAULT ON THE SOUL

Recognizing the Signs That Something Isn't Right

*Whether we realize it or not, it is our woundedness, or how we
cope with it, that dictates much of our behavior, shapes our
social habits, and informs our ways of thinking about the world.*

GABOR MATÉ, *The Myth of Normal*

Natalie sat across from me on the couch in my office, her eyes puffy
and tears streaming down her face. Sunlight poured in from the window, casting a warm light in the room. The room didn't feel bright in
that moment though. The room felt heavy. Though unseen, a thick
darkness seemed to swirl around us, despite the sunlight.

I listened intently as Natalie told me about a "bad sexual experience" she'd had with her husband earlier in the week.

"I'd been looking forward to sitting down to dinner with Bill
and the kids, but my heart sank as soon as he walked in the door
after work," she said, knotting the tissue in her hand. "He didn't
even bother to say hello. He just gave me a weird smirk and said, 'I
had a hard day at work today, so you'd better be ready for me later,
baby.'

"The thing is, I had a migraine that morning after being up with
our four-month-old most of the night. During the day I made sure

the laundry was done and the house was vacuumed. I was looking forward to finally having a quiet night after the kids went to bed so I could try to get rid of the pounding in my head.

"Bill made it abundantly clear that was not going to happen. He kept after me as I got the table set for dinner. I told him no; I wasn't feeling well. I told him the baby had been up all night. I asked if we could just rest that evening. I offered to cuddle with him. None of that mattered.

"When the oven timer went off, I turned to head into the kitchen, but he yanked me back by my arm. He told me it was my duty as his wife. I got a brief break during dinner with the kids, but he was right back at it while I was loading the dishwasher. I found myself begging him to please let me rest, to wait till the next day when I would feel better. He told me I'd been resting all day as a stay-at-home mom. When I tried again to tell him all I did during the day—caring for the kids, getting all the chores done, and making sure dinner was ready when he walked in—he yelled at me." Natalie used her tissue to dab at the tears sliding down her cheeks.

"Late that night, after the kids went to bed, Bill and I watched TV. During a commercial, he told me that the Bible says he owns the rights to my body. I was to be ready for him whenever he asked. If I failed to do so, I was worthless as a wife. Then he asked me if I was sleeping with someone else! After hours of his ranting, I finally gave him what he wanted so I could go to sleep. My head was splitting, and I was barely able to see. I just needed to get some rest."

"What did I do wrong?" she asked me, putting her head down in her hands. "I love Bill, so why did I feel so broken, used, and dirty afterward?"

When she looked up at me, I saw a mix of shame, fear, and a bit of hope. My heart was heavy, knowing the words I'd have to use.

I leaned forward and softly said, "You told him no. You were sick and had cared for the kids all day. He called you worthless and wouldn't take no for an answer. He badgered you for hours. Then he accused you of having sex with some other man since you were telling

ASSAULT ON THE SOUL

him no. And in the end, when you were too weary and too tired to fight anymore, he took what he wanted."

I paused, noticing my own body's heaviness, and took a deep breath. Then I said, "The word for what happened is *rape*." I paused to let that register with her.

She looked at me with wide eyes and stammered, "N-No. No. It can't be. I'm married. I gave my forever 'yes' at the altar. I don't have any rights to my body. The Bible says so. I should have said yes. I sinned against him." She put her head down again and began to sob.

Every day I listen to women like Natalie tell me the details about how they became sexually shattered.

And like her, they think they are responsible for the pain they're in.

AFTERSHOCKS

So many women I've worked with have experienced echoes of Natalie's story. Sexual abuse and assault are far more prevalent than many believe: One in five women is raped in her lifetime; one in three of those women experienced rape between the ages of eleven and seventeen. Half of female rape victims were assaulted by an intimate partner.[1] Some were abused as children by someone they should have been able to trust. Others were assaulted in high school or college (or childhood, high school, and college). Some were sexually abused in their marriage. At times, women are forced to watch and reenact pornography with their spouses. Some have been forced to share their beds with others—even animals. I'm so sorry to be so direct, but if this is part of your story, I want you to know it's safe to bring that here.

Perhaps by now you recognize that someone did harm you in some way. You may be tempted, though, to minimize it or to "pull up those bootstraps" and just keep going. After all, what's done is done, right? The truth, however, is that violence done to your body, mind, and spirit doesn't simply evaporate. If not dealt with, it will remain lodged inside, a silent but unwelcome guest that leaves several distinct calling cards. It may not be obvious that your body is reckoning with the harm, but it is.

Shame

Shame is prevalent in women who've been violated. In my therapy room, it also shows up in words that can barely be uttered and often come out in a whisper, while women sit with red faces, wet with tears, eyes cast down at the floor. What is healthy sex? What is a real, consented yes? For those grappling with sexuality after being sexually abused or assaulted (including being assaulted in marriage), it's so confusing and unclear.

Often women have been exposed to teaching in the church that says men simply cannot control their sexual urges. Wives must comply with their demands; otherwise, their husbands will use pornography. (Spoiler alert: Lots of men turn to porn even if their wives never say no. It's not about the women or even about sex—but that's a whole other book.)

Shame may also show up in our reaction to our body's sensations. Some women are lured into the web of pornography or erotic fiction themselves because they don't know what to do with what they feel in their bodies. In fact, women's use of pornography has skyrocketed in recent years. While it's hard to find good statistics around this, one Barna study reported that about 15 percent of Christian women admit to using pornography at least once a month.[2] As a practitioner, I'd say that statistic is likely low. Many women I work with struggle to admit to using pornography due to shame.

Grief

When bodies and souls have been abused, grief wells up. While it is uncomfortable, grief is also healing. It's often the first indicator some-one has that what happened to them was not okay, and feeling sad is both natural and a signal that pain and loss need to be addressed.

When processing grief, it's vital that we orient ourselves kindly

LET'S HAVE A WORD

Sexuality

The language we use around sex matters. In our society, so many terms
have been overly sexualized. When we hear many rich and beautiful
words—think *sensuality, alluring,* and *intimacy*—we are likely to think of
their sexual implications first. When we've been harmed, that leads to a lot
of activation in the body. We may feel our hearts race, breathing increase,
and muscles tighten. Because those are unpleasant sensations, we push
them away. But what if some of these words have a fuller and broader
context? What if, as we enter into embracing our sexuality, we were able to
appreciate the vibrancy that our senses and relationships were designed to
add to our lives? With that goal, I've sprinkled "Let's Have a Word" sidebars
throughout the book, which are designed to help you reclaim the power of
words that may have been cheapened or limited for you.

Let's start with the "big one." Perhaps when you hear the word *sexuality,*
you think only of sexual activity. I'd like to push back on that for two reasons:
First, it feels so narrow. Second, I don't think we should define words by
their root (thank you, sixth grade English class, for instilling that fierce belief
in my soul).

For our purposes, I define sexuality as the aspects of sexual expression,
sexual interest, and sexual activity that God created in us. This definition is
consistent with those used by certified sex addiction therapists (CSATs), who
help clients return to healthy sexuality either because they battle addiction or
compulsion or because they've been betrayed by someone who struggles in
that arena.

How do we express our sexual selves? Is your heart racing right now
because you can't even imagine *having* a sexual self? Or does the term
alone totally freak you out? I hear you. Yet this might be a concept to consider. *We are sexual beings.* We were created this way. We'll talk more
about being embodied and our embodied sexuality elsewhere, but for now
just allow yourself to be open to the possibility that you have a sexual self.

What about your sexual interest? If you've been abused or otherwise
violated, you may be thinking, *I have no sexual interest, thanks.* And that
may be true now. Or maybe you're simply afraid to talk about it. I mean,
where in the church can we go to have these conversations? You may not
be in a congregation where you can walk up to the women's leadership
team and say, "I'd like to have a frank discussion about sexual interest. Is
there a time next Tuesday that would work for you? I'll bring coffee and
donuts." But these conversations really do need to be had—and we will,
throughout this book.

toward the little girl or woman who had so much stolen from her. We can bless all that little girl or woman experienced. And if you recoil at the thought of blessing these hard places, stick with me. We're going to talk more about this. I know this concept of blessing can be disorienting if you've never considered it. We are also going to talk more about grief as we journey together.

Isolation

Abusers often isolate us from healthy community. Actually, they often isolate victims from *any* community! They may insist that you celebrate holidays alone or prevent you from signing up for a neighborhood book club. But they don't always forbid you to interact with family and friends; some abusers are much more subtle. When you have a girls' night out planned, your husband may call a few minutes before he was supposed to be home to watch the kids to tell you he now has to work late. Or he might use looks or body language to warn you implicitly against going to avoid some sort of future punishment.

Sometimes abusers so thoroughly distort our self-perception that we believe no one would even want to be our friend. This isn't true at all, but that belief makes taking the risk of community incredibly hard. If our faith community was weaponized against us, finding good, godly community may be a terrifying thought. This is an example of an area where we can combat the lies we've been fed even if they *feel* so true.

Normalization

Our neural pathways are shaped by what we're exposed to. The more often something is presented to us, the more normal it becomes to us. This is called *habituation*, which means that something that was once novel or new becomes normal. This is why exposure to sexualized ads, pornography, and violence makes it seem more normal to our senses.

Our very own brain can convince us that something is normal as well. When we tell ourselves in the thick of an abusive situation that

everything is fine, okay, and normal, we may inadvertently habitu-
ate ourselves to harm. So many survivors have been told that their
husbands have headship and the final say that they come to believe
they must submit no matter the cost. These women may believe that
this is just what a normal, godly marriage looks like—even though
it's often nothing like what the Bible says marriage should be. Many
evangelical women were raised in a purity culture that insisted they
were wholly responsible for a man's lust issues. Again, that is a significant distortion. Because of normalization, however, by the time they
wonder whether a particular behavior is proper or a certain viewpoint
is true, they've been drinking poison for a long time.

If you're reading this and thinking, *Oh, no! This sounds way too
familiar!*, don't fret. This is how it is for so many people, and we can
only know what we know when we know. In some ways our brains
normalizing things is how we survive the awfulness of it all. And now
that you know, you can make shifts toward a healthier and healed
place. As I've said a few times and will say again: Once a woman is
free from abuse, her sexuality doesn't somehow suddenly emerge or
reemerge intact. Her vision of what is healthy has been distorted and
needs healing.

PAINFULLY SKEWED

I had a really good meal in Arkansas recently, and it was a sign of
healing. Let me explain.

I was thoroughly traumatized when I landed in Arkansas on a
warm, spring day. The weather was perfect: not too hot or cold or
humid. The landscape was lush and green with all the newness of
spring. But a storm was raging inside me that made everything feel
topsy-turvy. Though I had been free from my abuser for more than a
decade, the aftermath of the abuse in our family was still playing out.
I've mentioned this and will continue to mention it—the body keeps
the score.[3] And that's true for our kids too.

So after I had lived in North Carolina for thirty-four years, life as I knew it ended. In thirty days I'd sold everything we owned—our house, its contents, literally anything with value—and moved to Arkansas to get my son needed medical care. Though I realize Arkansas is not the place people think of as a medical bastion, what we needed was not offered in North Carolina but weirdly was available in Arkansas. Since I'm a mama who would do anything to help her kiddo, we relocated. And any mama with a kiddo who is in a life-and-death struggle knows the toll that takes on your own soul.

As we settled into an apartment just off the Arkansas River, I tried to get my soul to settle in. There was no settling. I deeply grieved all I had lost but was hopeful that this move could lead to something good. Yet in the days that followed, Arkansas did not seem kind to me. The people were nice enough. Our medical providers were helpful and skilled. But I couldn't see *goodness*. I could see only *struggle*. I couldn't even find a good meal. A round of early-days COVID had sabotaged my taste and smell. When they finally returned, I could not seem to find a decent restaurant anywhere, and I was often too tired to cook. Back then, my son and I agreed that the best restaurant in Arkansas was our kitchen.

Despite my hopelessness, something was happening. It just goes to show what I've learned over the years: Jesus is sneaky. To be clear, He knows what He's doing; I just don't know what He's up to. That's why, when I see His hand move, I often refer to Him as "sneaky Jesus."

Looking back now, what I thought was meant to be a brief pit stop actually became a major hub for my personal healing. By the time my son's medical treatment had finished and we prepared to move to Texas, I had begun connecting with community. Because I now spend time at both our Texas and North Carolina counseling offices, God has ordered my life to include trips back to or through Arkansas frequently. To avoid having to drive through Atlanta traffic, I take what I call the "northern route" between Texas and North Carolina—and that takes me right through Arkansas every time.

As the years have progressed, God has given me a beautiful and kind community in Arkansas, and I'm grateful to be able to spend time with them often. This hit me one night while I was out with friends at a restaurant and realized that I was savoring an excellent meal. I was also enjoying the space and presence of people I love. And it was good. Arkansas was no longer a dark place full of turmoil and fear—it was a place of precious relationships—and also some good meals. Though I remain an excellent cook, I can officially say that if I ever moved back to Arkansas, my kitchen would not be the only good place to eat.

But what had changed?

The only thing different was my healing. I was able to see and experience *goodness* where I had seen only *darkness* before.

EXPLORING THE DICHOTOMY

When we've experienced sexual harm, it really messes up our whole sexual system. We don't know what we believe. Like I felt in Arkansas at first, we see nothing good at all. We sense only a wasteland in our souls, like something out of the movie *The Terminator* where once-beautiful cities and landscapes are ash heaps. But just as Arkansas has become a beloved rest spot for me, so beauty can follow and rise from the ashes.

Now I sat quietly, watching Natalie's shoulders shake as she sobbed, and I felt my own heart ache as she wrestled with my words. I held tender space with her in the final moments of our time that week as she began to realize that what she had been *told* was healthy sex was anything *but* healthy. Gently and carefully I went to one of the Scriptures I knew she was referring to—a passage that is utterly distorted by abusers—and explored it with her. As we closed the session, I saw deep pain etched in her face. She looked so small sitting on my couch.

Perhaps like Natalie you've just been confronted with the truth that what happened to you is not okay, that you are not at fault. Maybe you sense that your sexuality has been utterly destroyed by the mistreatment you've endured. It may need a complete revamp and healing. The road ahead may look rocky and steep, which is why I want to jump ahead in Natalie's story to tell you that she did survive and grow. She worked to set boundaries and listen to what her body, mind, and spirit needed. She challenged negative internal beliefs and paid attention to what delighted her. Perhaps most important, she evaluated her relationship and determined it was no longer safe to remain in it after her abuser steadfastly refused to change. She moved forward and found a healthy and supportive community.

That, in fact, is where the pathway to healing begins—by looking inside and outside ourselves to find support.

When teaching on domestic abuse and coercive control, I have the amazing privilege of facilitating grounding breaks when we're teaching hard topics, like sexual abuse and assault. And that's really the topic of this whole book. This is one of my favorite exercises to do with the students. It helps remind us of our strength as we root in to a God who deeply loves us and weeps with us. It also helps us release the energy in our bodies generated by hard and painful experiences.

This exercise uses the creativity of our God-given imaginations to bring truth to our minds and bodies. It is based on the imagery in Jeremiah 17:8: "They are like trees planted along a riverbank, with roots that reach deep into the water. Such trees are not bothered by the heat or worried by long months of drought. Their leaves stay green, and they never stop producing fruit" (NLT).

Sit or stand with your feet flat on the floor or lie on a comfortable surface on your back and bend your knees so your feet are flat on the surface of the bed or floor. If you don't have use of your feet, you can press your hands against a sturdy surface, like a table or wall.

Imagine you are a sturdy, steady oak tree planted by a river, and your roots reach deep into the ground to access nourishing water. Take some moments to visualize this. Imagine feeling immovable and safe no matter what comes your way.

Press your feet or hands into the floor or surface, noticing the resistance of the floor or surface. Picture roots pressing in deep and reaching the river. Notice the steadiness of your feet or hands. You may imagine sunny days with warmth cascading over you, as you remain deeply rooted as the river rolls quietly by. Spend some time just noticing how this makes you feel.

Next, you may imagine a stormy day with wind whipping you this way and that, the river rushing and roiling around you while your roots keep you steady and strong. Allow yourself to be mindful of any feelings that rise up in your body, but focus on the strong, steady feeling of being securely rooted.

Finally, you might imagine yourself in a drought, dry air pressing in around you. Now visualize your roots going in so deep that they reach the sustenance of the water, even if the water level is lower than normal. If you feel distress during this exercise, allow the feelings to arise but remain focused on the roots still holding you steady. Press into the surface a bit harder if needed.

End the visualization by imagining yourself back in the calm warmth, without drought or storm, rooted deep next to the river. Remember that while seasons shift and change, your rootedness does not.

———— SCANNING YOUR ENVIRONMENT ————

So many survivors struggle with hypervigilance—that state of always being watchful, waiting for the next thing. Many of the women I work with tell me, "I'm always waiting for the other shoe to drop, even when—maybe especially when—things are good." Brené Brown calls this "foreboding joy."[4] We fear that anything good we have will be taken away. Survivors are acutely aware of this because pleasant interactions with our abusers often turn into nightmares even before we've had the chance to experience the good.

This exercise helps you take the ordinary and consider it differently. Learning to see things with a new perspective can help ease you into more peace.

Get into a comfortable position. Scan your surroundings with a curious attitude. What catches your eye? Take a moment to focus on it. What sensations are you aware of in your body as you consider what you are seeing? Is the sensation pleasant or unpleasant? Without judgment, just notice and be curious. Is there something new about what you're noticing? Something you have never seen before?

If the feelings that came up were unpleasant, is there a way to behold the object in a more positive light? For example, if you notice unwashed plates and silverware in the sink, you might look at it more positively by remembering that you ate a late meal because your college-age daughter came home to visit and you spent time talking with her instead of doing the dishes. Are you able to shift your awareness to something pleasant?

When you're ready, continue to scan the area to notice something else and follow the process again. Carry on with this exercise as long as you like. Consider briefly journaling your experience when you're done.

2

RELATIONSHIPS START HERE

Healing the Connection to Self, God, and Other People

When we honestly ask ourselves which persons in our lives mean
the most to us, we often find that it is those who, instead of giving
much advice, solutions, or cures, have chosen rather to share
our pain and touch our wounds with a gentle and tender hand.

HENRI NOUWEN, *Out of Solitude: Three Meditations on the Christian Life*

I met Michelle, my best friend from high school, in tenth-grade chemistry. We connected over our shared love of professional football and our birth dates—we were born seven days apart, the two youngest students in our graduating class. She laughed at the annoyance I felt toward our chemistry teacher, snickering as I rolled my eyes whenever he would get up on his desk to make a point—something that he did fairly regularly and that most of our classmates thought was "cool." Frankly, I skipped chemistry more than I went to it. I'd pop in just long enough to turn in group work so Michelle wouldn't be penalized for missing homework.

In some ways, Michelle and I could not have been more different. I loved heavy metal; she was a New Kids on the Block superfan. I smoked and drank; she did neither. I'm pretty sure I wore black or tie-dye every single day while she gravitated toward a preppier style.

One of the major differences between us was the safety of our family relationships. I admired the close connection between Michelle and her mom. On the other hand, the bonds between my parents and me were very broken. My parents fought often and ugly, but they didn't seem to notice me all that much. I had no voice in my home, so I never learned how to advocate for myself or even express simple needs. For many other relationships, I ended up choosing some sketchy friends who took advantage of me when they could.

Despite our differences, Michelle and I had enough in common to form a deep friendship. We spent a lot of time together, and we both loved Jesus. Michelle and her mom—whom I call Mom2 because she was like my second mama—saw the good in me. Michelle was the one healthy, close friendship I had as a kid. In fact, Michelle and I are still friends to this day—more than thirty-five years later.

One day in our late twenties, I asked her and Mom2 why on earth I was even allowed to hang out with Michelle. Mom2 said, "We could always see who you really are. I knew Michelle wasn't going to do the stuff you were doing, and I knew eventually you'd stop." Michelle's friendship and her mom's positive regard for me were a healing balm I didn't even know I needed. They weren't afraid of my mess. I went back to this friendship over and over as I was learning how to have healthy relationships with myself and others.

Why does this matter? If we are going to pursue healthy sexuality, we need to begin by forming healthy, nonsexual relationships—first with ourselves and God, and then with others.

MY RELATIONSHIP WITH ME

I'll be honest. I'm still in an abusive relationship some days. This person talks to me in vile, evil language. This abuser sometimes tells me how awful I am. How ungodly I am. How I'm failing in this area or that area. It can be completely crushing.

The worst part—I know this abuser. She's me, berating me in my own shame-filled, critical voice.[1] She took up the mantle from the abusers in her life, believing and internalizing the curses they spoke, and made a vow of agreement that those condemning messages were true. This harsh self-talk wreaks havoc on my relationship with myself.

I know what she's been through and why some situations and feelings are still hard. Some days, though, it can be so difficult to give myself grace. That critical voice seems like it shouts at decibel levels equivalent to a rock concert.

I find this to be true of so many people. We are all so capable of listing, with excruciating detail, where we have fallen short or messed up or failed in some way. When I'm in session with a client and I can see how the crushing weight of shame is blinding them to the goodness God has given them, I invite them to do an exercise with me. I hand them a sheet of paper and ask them to write a list of good things about themselves. The scowl on their faces makes me really glad looks don't kill. Some go into fight mode and protest, "There might be a couple of good things, but don't you know how bad I am?" Others go into freeze mode and give me a blank stare while they silently retreat inside themselves. Some try to deflect or change the topic, diving into flee mode: "Man, it sure is hot today. I hate steamy weather."

However, when we take a few moments together to help them slow down and regulate their bodies, they often are surprised as they do the exercise.

There are good things there. This is true for all of us. We all have good qualities, no matter how much we struggle. Abuse and shame have conditioned us to look at the hard and bad, as well as to have a distorted perspective of ourselves because of what we've endured.

Of course, every human being is broken and falls short of what God made us to be. In those moments when my thoughts about myself seem stuck in negativity, I often remind myself of this verse: "Do you despise the riches of his kindness, restraint, and patience, not recognizing that God's kindness is intended to lead you to repentance?" (Romans 2:4, CSB). For context, in this passage the apostle Paul admonishes us not to think we can get away with judging others for what we ourselves do. But for me, it's also a reminder of God's

INVITATIONAL EXERCISES

As we work through the concepts in this book, it's important to engage in good self-care. Topics around abuse of any kind are activating and can be dysregulating, so we want to remain curious while giving ourselves grace. Both are key to healing.

These practices are an invitation to connect to your body. Like any invitation, it's one you can accept or decline at any point. You might try something and find it's great; but then when you try it again, it's not so great because it's a different day or you're in a different mood. That's completely okay.

There may be an exercise you aren't sure about or aren't comfortable with yet. That's also okay. You can decline that invitation. You are always in control, and you always have a choice. In fact, God Himself always lets us choose. He understands hard days and our limited capacity. He will not be disappointed if you decline an invitation to one of these practices.

If you discover that you are drawn to some of these exercises to calm or center yourself, I encourage you to include them on your own 911 card (see page 211). That way you can easily come back to them when you need them. Pick your top five and write them out on an index card or pop them into the notes app on your phone. Keep your list with you so that when you need it, you can refer to it and come back into yourself.

When you try the exercises in this book, pay attention to the way your body, mind, and spirit respond. I suggest the following guidelines and questions to my clients whenever they engage in a new practice.

Simple Ground Rules
1. Start with curiosity. Even if something is hard or feels scary or vulnerable, be curious about why you might feel that way. Don't try to solve anything. Just be curious about what you're experiencing.
2. Be aware of how the experience is feeling. Just notice.

Simple Questions to Consider
1. What feelings are you noticing?
2. Where in your body are you noticing the feeling?
3. What color and/or shape might you give the feeling you're experiencing?
4. What are you most curious about?
5. What do you need to be able to stay with the feeling?

Be aware that as you begin to check in with your body, it may tell you something you didn't expect. You may even have flashbacks or notice sensations and memories coming up unexpectedly. If that happens, you can either notice those things without judgment until they pass or transition into a grounding exercise, setting those memories or sensations aside until you can connect with your therapist about them.

Trauma shows up in our bodies. Learning how to listen is so vital to our healing. Body sensations help protect us by telling us important things. For example, if I touch a hot stove and feel pain in my hand, I now know it's a bad idea to touch it again or touch hot stoves in the future. I've talked about how disconnected I was from my body and how I missed important data to keep me safe and help me heal. I needed to learn how to connect up. Sometimes that starts with a simple check-in.

love and patience even in our dark places. Yes, His kindness and long-suffering lead us to repentance, but they also are evidence of His unfailing love. His best expression of that love, of course, is Jesus Himself.

THE MATTER OF LOVE

Did you know that Jesus *expects* us to love ourselves? He told His followers: "'You must love the LORD your God with all your heart, all your soul, all your mind, and all your strength.' The second is equally important: 'Love your neighbor *as yourself.*' No other commandment is greater than these" (Mark 12:30-31, NLT, emphasis added). We love our neighbors like we love *ourselves.*

Wait. What?

If you grew up in church, this may rattle you a bit. Some churches actively teach that *any* self-love is wickedness. In some cases, this emphasis grows out of a sincere desire to keep us from becoming wrapped up in ourselves alone. However, despite what may be a sincere desire, this teaching is out of balance. When an abuser uses Scripture to denigrate us—breaking down our sense of self—we may come to believe that we are just lower than the slimiest of slime. However, that's a major distortion of how God sees us.

We aren't supposed to hate ourselves. We are supposed to see ourselves rightly. We are image bearers of the Living God. We are precious to Him. We are His "workmanship" (Ephesians 2:10, CSB) and, when we follow Jesus, we are righteous because He is holy and lives in us. Yes, we also are sinners in need of a Savior, but we have incredible value, and we should see ourselves accurately. The Bible cautions us against pride, but we are not told we shouldn't love ourselves.

I have yet to see hellfire and brimstone shake people out of hard and murky places. What I have seen move people out of darkness is a right understanding of the deep harm they've experienced, coupled with enormous self-compassion. Don't hear this wrong: There are some things we have to turn away from because they're harmful and ungodly. In short, they're either sinful or they're survival techniques (such as coping skills learned in the throes of trauma that eventually become millstones dragging us down). Such things harm us (and sometimes others) and keep us from God's very best for us.

But abusing and berating ourselves isn't going to bring the change we seek—at least not for very long. Moreover, it's not how Jesus treated anyone who'd been traumatized. Read through the Gospels. He was so incredibly gentle and kind to those whom other people considered the worst sinners. And often the people who were despised by others but who experienced Jesus' love were the ones who changed. Consider the woman who wept before Jesus' feet as she poured expensive perfume on them at a fancy dinner. Jesus' fellow guests looked with contempt at this woman whom they considered immoral. What was Jesus' response? "I tell you, her sins—and they are many—have been forgiven, so she has shown me much love. But a person who is forgiven little shows only little love" (Luke 7:47, NLT).

Jesus is saying that the best place to be is in the middle—recognizing that if you follow Him, you are a sinner who also is being sanctified. Rather than condemning yourself or allowing others' opinions to discourage you, see yourself as Jesus does. Understanding how you got where you are—and the very real trauma that made you choose some unhelpful things because they were the only way you could survive—is giving yourself grace. Speaking for myself, I know that I could not have done certain things differently. I knew what I knew when I knew it. As a child, I was trying to survive serious neglect and abuse. I was trying to find love in places it didn't exist because I didn't honestly know what love was. And quite frankly, I was desperately looking for connection and belonging. I did my best. My guess is so did you.

In all honesty, some of those actions kept me alive. One of them is *fawning*. We twist ourselves into pretzels trying to keep another person happy, but we lose ourselves and our voice in the process. I was always watchful, trying to anticipate what my husband might want before he said it and if he asked for something I'd bend over backward to make sure he had it, no matter what it cost me. One night he was sitting down to watch a movie and wanted a big salad—which to him was a specific thing with specific ingredients. Anything less than that would have been unacceptable. I'd just finished a grueling twelve-hour workday and was exhausted, but that was not something I was permitted to share; he simply did not care. To point out that we didn't have any of the ingredients would have been far worse for me than going to the grocery store. Though we lived twenty minutes from the nearest one, I pulled myself together, headed out into the night, and picked up the ingredients for that salad. I didn't want to get mauled by the bear.

Some folks may call this "walking on eggshells" while trying not to upset our abusers. We stop calling out wrong and sometimes we become complicit in it (or we feel as if we've become complicit) because our survival depends on it. When we're finally free, it may take time to recognize that our response was a survival skill. Because we've often been told everything is our fault anyway, we just keep returning to that awful shame spiral. I hated that I didn't feel I could tell my husband no when something didn't make sense or was outside my value system. If I did dare say no, I had to be ready for whatever was coming. I never refused simply because I didn't want to do something—the cost would have been too high. This made for enormous tension and shame because I felt forced into places I didn't want to go. While the salad may seem like an innocuous example, this struggle extended to every relational area.

For me and so many of the clients and abuse survivors I serve,

OUR INTERNAL
PROTECTION SYSTEM

When we're traumatized, our nervous system automatically leads our body into a fight, flight, freeze, or fawn response.[2] I generally use the metaphor of a bear when explaining this to clients. If a bear comes into a counseling session, we're going to do one of four things to save ourselves from becoming lunch. We might fight—whether with loud words (screaming), posture, or physical forms of fighting—to try to stay alive. We might flee by running away and locking the bear in the office. We might freeze—literally shut down, either by dissociating (checking out) or by experiencing brain fog so that we have trouble thinking. (Interestingly, though we might assume freezing involves no activity, if we had a brain scan done, we'd see a whole lot happening that isn't obvious from the outside.) Finally, we might fawn over the bear, or as my therapist once put it: "In order to keep the bear from mauling us, we make it a steak to keep it happy."

breaking out of self-abuse means looking at things in balance. Some things happened to us that we could not control. And we acted in some unhealthy and unhelpful ways because of that. We can own what's ours without condemning ourselves. This sounds super simple—and conceptually it is—but it is absolutely not easy. The "accuser of our brothers and sisters" (Revelation 12:10, csb) loves to remind us of areas where we missed the mark. And on hard days when we're particularly aware of our shortcomings, we may agree with the enemy and completely forget that we are not condemned because all our debt was paid in Jesus' work on the cross (Romans 8:1). We may also forget that Jesus looks on us with compassion. He knows how hard things are on this earth, and He knows firsthand the sting of abuse.

One way to build self-compassion is by recognizing that it is often possible to hold two seemingly contradictory thoughts—what is called a dialectic—in balance. In fact, two seemingly opposite ideas can sometimes be synthesized in a way that increases our understanding. "I am doing the best I can in this moment, and I can do better" is my very favorite one. In my practice we tell clients, "It's okay not to be okay, and you don't have to stay there."

Being able to sit with the tension of these two truths is the pathway out of self-abuse. Yes, we have no control over some situations. But we also have control in other areas, as well as access to wisdom and healing. We can do things differently through God's incredible power in us (see Romans 8:11).

In the darker moments, the ones where I hear the enemy screaming at me about how awful I am—I have a choice to make. I can agree with my enemy and internalize his curse (make a vow, as we'll discuss in chapter 9) or take a deep breath and trust the Lord and His kindness. I can choose to see myself the way Jesus sees me—freely, fully, and forever forgiven. And if I blew it or reverted to a coping mechanism that no longer serves me or is misaligned with my overall values, I can turn around, go in a different direction, and trust that God's grace covers even that—whatever "that" is in a given moment. After all, we never catch Him by surprise. He knew what we would do before we did.

Again, this is a simple concept but it's not easy. Those feelings of shame are big and so real. In some ways, they're even comfortable. We know them because they may have been there as long as we can remember. They feel *true*. Some days we have to fight an all-out war to walk differently. Some days simply putting one foot in front of the other itself is our sole act of worship. Other days we may need our community to remind us of actual truth when we feel like we're spiraling into darkness at warp speed.

OUR RELATIONSHIP WITH GOD

Dan Allender says, "There is a power that uses sexual violation as its choice means to turn the human heart away from the Creator. This opposition to beauty and innocence is at the core of all sexual harm."[3] And abuse, when further coupled with Scripture (aka spiritual abuse), can absolutely upend our relationship with God. You were created to live in peace with yourself. God also intended for you to rest in Him. But if your father or your pastor abused you sexually or in any other way, how can you trust in the Good, Good Father or the Good Shepherd? Our faith can really be upended when those who are supposed to represent Him walk in wickedness and do unspeakable harm.

Before going further, I want to make an important note. In this book, I tell stories that point to some misguided teachings and actions my clients and I have seen in various church contexts. I have no issue with the church as a whole, but it's important to acknowledge missteps some churches make because many people are hurt there. That is the last thing most churches want to do, but churches can't reconsider things they don't think about. As you'll see from my discussion on engaging in healthy community, I think churches are important. I also think churches should seek to be healthy, safe places for all members.

My client Annamarie was unable to find safety in her church because her husband was an associate pastor there. Because he was seminary trained, she trusted his interpretation of Scripture. She started counseling with me because she was experiencing severe bodily pain, but there was no medical explanation. Her primary doctor thought maybe counseling could help resolve her suffering. As we worked together and I learned her story, it became apparent that she was in an abusive marriage. Her husband tracked her movements, telling her he did so to prevent even the "appearance of evil." She was never allowed to say no to sex because he said her body belonged to him once they married. She was not permitted to work and was expected to bear and raise the couple's children with no help from him. Over and over, he used Scripture to justify what essentially amounted to her captivity. As we worked together and she realized the traumatic effects on her body from the abuse, she became extremely angry with God. She wondered whether He even cared for women because she had so ascribed God's voice to her husband's. She also felt profoundly guilty for being angry at Him because she had been taught that she was never allowed to be angry, let alone be angry at God.

Annamarie's anger and confusion were so understandable. She

had been essentially groomed (systematically conditioned) to believe her husband. Because of his seminary education, she assumed his knowledge of God was superior to hers. She came to believe he spoke on behalf of God. As a result, her relationship with the Lord was severely harmed. She believed God did not love her and only loved her husband. We had a lot of work to do to help her separate God from her husband in her mind, heart, and body.

Another client, twenty-three-year-old Janna, came to see me because she was riddled with anxiety. As we explored her story, she dropped a bombshell in an early session.

"I don't even know how to talk about this," she said. She took a deep breath, and I noticed her body shaking. "I . . . I need to talk about youth group."

"Go ahead, I'm here," I told her.

"My youth pastor told me I was special. I was maybe thirteen. He told me that he could sense God's calling on my life . . . and he told me that he knew he was called to help me walk into that calling . . ."[4]

She paused. I knew where this was headed. I'd heard this type of story far too many times.

"He started out just rubbing my back, to get rid of the tension so I could hear God better. I thought it was weird, but he was so convincing that God wanted my body to relax. Then one day, he put his hand up my shirt . . ." She trailed off for a moment before continuing to share the details of how he sexually assaulted her.

Janna later revealed that part of her high anxiety was because she believed she had asked for it by wanting to be used by God. When this youth pastor told her that he saw such a calling on her life, she was eager to learn more. She trusted him as a leader, and he used that position of authority to harm her. She obsessed over whether she had been prideful in wanting to be used by God and whether God was angry at her for not having better boundaries. She blamed herself for what happened and saw herself as a disappointment to God.

Some church leaders aren't the initial perpetrator; they are a secondary perpetrator. Most Christian women go to their churches for help when they realize something is very off in their marriage. An uninformed or abusive church leader can cause deep harm by mishandling the situation. Many of my clients have been asked, "What did you do to make him mad? Are you being submissive enough? Are you having enough sex?" Even worse, some survivors have been told, "Perhaps you are just being called to suffer like Christ. Go home and submit more. Count each instance of abuse as something to rejoice in." When women experience that sort of minimization, mishandling, and spiritual bypassing, they often see it as God Himself admonishing them.

It's heartbreaking and absolutely nothing like our heavenly Father when those with power and who claim the name of Jesus do harm. I've often said that a good definition of spiritual abuse is taking someone's good and right devotion to God and weaponizing it against the victim for the perpetrator's gain. Such abuse can deeply damage women's faith, especially those who have always sought to be faithful Christians. They may begin to question the goodness of God and wonder why He didn't step in to stop the harm.

The first step to healing from spiritual abuse is to know that God *never* condones abuse. A simple search of Scripture to see how God views oppression and abuse is a good starting point. Spoiler alert: He is not a fan. In fact, He hates abuse and injustice and is always on the side of the oppressed. Some helpful Scriptures to get you started:

Psalm 9:9
Psalm 103:6
Proverbs 6:16-19
Isaiah 1:17
Malachi 3:5
Luke 4:18-19
1 Timothy 5:8

It may take a while for you to recognize how the abuse you suffered impacted your relationship with God. It's okay to take it slow and to feel all the things you need to feel. You may decide to step away from church for a while or permanently leave the church you attended if it harmed you or rationalized, excused, enabled, or even perpetuated the harm you experienced. You may struggle with Scripture and struggle to read or even hear the Bible. That happens for so many women. When you're ready, you might reengage with Scripture using a different translation than the one you normally use.

Regardless, a good therapist or trusted support group or friend can help you walk through all that you may feel. I had an incredible counselor who helped me walk through the aftermath of abuse and its impact on my faith. He held space with me while I wrestled through the experience and my theology. He helped me disentangle the inaccurate doctrine that had been used against me. He also worked through the hard questions with me. It took time, and I learned that God is totally fine with the amount of time it takes to rebuild trust. He's not mad at you, and He's not judging you as you wrestle through your faith in the aftermath of abuse. He Himself was abused, falsely accused, and physically assaulted. He knows what it's like to be us:

> It was necessary for him to be made in every respect like us, his brothers and sisters, so that he could be our merciful and faithful High Priest before God. Then he could offer a sacrifice that would take away the sins of the people. Since he himself has gone through suffering and testing, he is able to help us when we are being tested.
> HEBREWS 2:17-18, NLT

CREATED FOR COMMUNITY

Abusers isolate their victims, as we saw with both Janna and Annamarie. This allowed their abuse to continue unseen, whereas in a healthy community the coercive relational dynamic might have been noticed.

Even when you've come out of abuse, reentry to community can feel terrifying, especially if you think God is mad at you. Or if you're mad at Him. Yet relationships are vitally important. We are meant to live in community. It's clear in Scripture: "Let us think of ways to motivate one another to acts of love and good works. And let us *not neglect our meeting together*, as some people do, but encourage one another, especially now that the day of his return is drawing near" (Hebrews 10:24-25, NLT, emphasis added). So many people assume this verse means we are to go to church, and I agree that we can take that from this text. But why do we need to assemble together? Why not just avail ourselves of good teaching from a book, a podcast, a YouTube video, or some other online method? Because we were created *by* community (our Trinitarian God) to live *in* community. We have each been given different gifts (see 1 Corinthians 12), and together we make a single body of Christ. We are created *in* community *for* community.

Abuse distorts this very important design. First, as we've noted, abusers often isolate us from healthy community. Actually, they often isolate victims from *any* community. Once women leave an abusive situation, we often have no community. If our faith community was weaponized against us, it can make finding good, godly community terrifying.

Sometimes when abusers have so thoroughly distorted our self-perception, we believe that no one would want to be our friend anyway. This isn't true, but that belief makes taking a risk and seeking community incredibly hard. First, we need to combat the lies we've been fed even when they *feel* so true. How do we find friends who will support us and believe the best about us?

Part of healing is believing that you need community and then learning to put yourself out there. This can be dicey if you're not sure your "people picker" is in good working order. What if you gravitate toward unsafe people? What if you become involved in an abusive community?

Those are great questions and worthy of consideration. Sometimes it is better to go slow than fast. Do your own work in therapy to help you identify and build connections with healthy—not perfect—people. Search the Scriptures so you know what Jesus says about healthy relationships. But no matter what, you eventually will need to put yourself out there and give it a try.

There are some practical ways to enter into community again. First, reach out to those life-giving communities you were part of before abuse isolated you. Consider telling your story, at least in part, and letting them in on what happened. That can be super scary, but clients who have done this tell me that it was a healing experience. You don't have to tell them everything or overshare. Start small and gauge their reaction. If it's safe, go a little deeper. One client of mine was sure it would not go well, but was very surprised when her friends were understanding, empathetic, and willing to reengage the relationship. In fact, they had all seen how this person's spouse had isolated her over the years, but they hadn't known how to reach out to her.

In reality, when we've been mistreated, something in us fundamentally changes. Trauma leaves a mark. Sometimes those who haven't experienced what we have may not understand triggers or hard days. We can choose to invite them to understand. Many survivors don't want to be the educator on abuse trauma, but sometimes it's worth it. I've had women invite close family and friends to a session to help explain their trauma and then help them understand how to be supportive in ways the clients need. For example, they learn that trauma takes far longer to heal from than anyone wishes. They learn about triggers and how they can seem to come out of nowhere. Maybe even most important, they learn what words are helpful and not helpful when talking to their loved one.

Another way to enter back into community is through a support group. In-person groups are best, but online can be a good starting place. Gathering with other survivors can be so helpful in recovery and finding community. When done in a spirit of grace and humility, survivors groups can be powerful conduits of healing. One of the most joyous experiences in my life is serving at the Called to Peace Ministries women's retreat every year. So often women show up knowing no one and leave with a whole tribe—in some cases, they even meet people who live somewhat near them. These women connect with each other and know they share a common story—abuse. Over and over I hear, "She gets it. I don't have to hide this part of my story. I don't have to explain. She just knows because she's lived it too."

My only caution when beginning to engage with a group is to be mindful of bitterness. Some abuse survivor communities, specifically those online, tend to foster resentment. Abuse is deeply harmful and there is appropriate anger; however, I've seen some online groups encourage darkness and bitterness, especially toward church- or faith-related institutions.

In fact, church can also be a place to find community again. I know this claim can be really loaded for people when the church has been part of the abuse or at the very least turned a blind eye to their suffering. Finding a safe-enough church can be hard. How do you know what they really believe? Will they eventually treat you like your last church did? Becoming part of a church can feel like a massive risk. And what do you do with all the triggers that happen when you simply think about walking into one or if something hits a nerve from past abuse when you're there?

Again, I have no issue with the church as a whole, though it's true that some churches and organizations are not safe for survivors, either because they don't know better or because they are wicked (or some combination of both). There are also churches and organizations that are trying hard to make changes so they offer spiritual life and safety to everyone. There are good, safe-enough churches out there. By safe enough, I mean those that are trauma-informed with leaders who understand abuse and have decent policies in place to address it. They're still run by humans, which means they'll never be perfect, but they can be safe enough. It might take you some healing work to be able to set foot in another faith community, and that's okay. But don't discount it as an option for finding healthy community.

When it comes to opening yourself to community, be mindful, prayerful, and open. Notice your heart. If you find bitterness stirring, check in with yourself. If you notice yourself wallowing in sweeping sentiments like, *All places are terrible. There are no good churches. All men are wicked*, you are drinking poison. Though there is plenty of sin and wickedness in this world, there are many safe-enough churches and good-hearted people.

For the introverted among us, finding community can seem especially daunting. (For the record, extroverts who have experienced trauma find engaging with community tough, though we can generally talk to a brick wall when needed—at least I can.) Even if you're an introvert and derive energy from times alone, you still need trusted others in your life. You may not need a ton of trusted friends, but you do need a trusted inner circle. We are not meant to live this life alone, whether we derive energy from times of solitude or with other people.

Give yourself the time and grace you need to find a safe community. Janna was very resistant to seeking community at first, especially a church community—which was totally understandable. We had to address some of her trauma first. Then she was willing to try some meet-up groups that were focused on one of her interests. She found a great group that met to play board games monthly. She eventually decided she'd like to try church again too. She decided on a church in a different denomination from the one she had been abused in but whose doctrine she agreed with. It was brutally hard to walk through the doors the first Sunday. She had a panic attack and had to leave almost immediately. We processed her experience in our next session and considered what she might need to do the next time she tried to visit the church. She settled on some grounding skills she found helpful. She made it through the service the next time.

Janna ended up trying several churches across denominations before she found one that seemed like a good fit. They had a recovery ministry with a group for survivors of sexual abuse, which she started attending in addition to regular Sunday services. Over time, she began to build more connections. Being at a church that had a safe place for her to talk about her experiences without judgment, as well as finding community in shared interests outside of church, served as a healing balm. In those places, Janna found trusted others to be part of her life and in whose lives she could be part of too.

THE LIST

If you've been repeatedly told that your opinion doesn't count or that you don't really matter, it can be difficult to remember that God says, "You are precious in my sight and honored, and I love you" (Isaiah 43:4, CSB). That is one reason I encourage my clients to take a few minutes to itemize all the good things about themselves. It's a reminder of their innate value and the gifts God gave them.

So now I encourage you to give this a try. Take out a piece of paper and something to write with. Jot down as many items as you can think of; don't worry how big or small the list is. Do this by hand, not in an app or on a computer. There is something profoundly helpful about handwriting. It engages the brain in a much different and deeper way than typing. Research shows that the brain's motor and visual functions coordinate with other areas that support learning and memory creation.[5] To put it more simply—writing helps our thoughts stick to our memories better. And it forces us to slow down and be more present with what we're doing.

If you struggle to make a list, consider sending a text to people close to you who you know are honest and safe. Ask them what good things they see in you. I have clients do this when shame's voice is so loud they can't see for themselves. You may receive responses that may not feel true yet but that your friends see in you. If that is your experience, I invite you to consider that perhaps they can see more clearly than you can because they don't see you through your trauma.

BREATH PRAYER

Sara Beth narrowed her eyes and said, "I hate Scripture. I used to love it, but it was totally ruined for me. I wish I knew how to fix that, but every time I open up my Bible I want to just throw it across the room. It feels like a minefield for me."

That's a common sentiment I hear from survivors who experienced spiritual abuse as part of their harm. The good news is that God understands. He's grieved by what was done to you and the harm exacted through misuse of His Word. But there's more good news. There are ways to reengage with

Scripture gently and slowly. One way is by taking a small snippet in a translation that was not used to harm you and turning it into a breath prayer.

Breath prayers can be a great way to meditate on Scripture while also grounding yourself. Breath prayers help you slow down your physiology and your mind. Nearly any Scripture can be used as a breath prayer, but shorter ones tend to work better as you get acclimated to the process.

Take this invitation to select and try this exercise with passages that are meaningful to you. I know a Scripture can sometimes be triggering if it was used against you. If that's the case, feel free to skip this exercise, choose a different Scripture from the one in the example, or change the translation to one that feels better to you.

This exercise uses Isaiah 26:3 in the New Living Translation. As you take a breath in, read or recite the first line silently or out loud. On the exhale, read or recite the second line.

- Breathe in: You will keep in perfect peace all who trust in you,
- Breathe out: All whose thoughts are fixed on you.

Now, let's try a shorter one, still with an added prayer. We'll use John 11:35: "Jesus wept." Jesus showed his sorrow by weeping just before raising Lazarus from the dead. He already knew what He was planning to do: He'd told the disciples before they even headed to Bethany. But the pain and sorrow of those who loved Lazarus were not lost on Jesus. Even though He knew the miracle about to take place, He still wept with them.

- Breathe in: Jesus wept,
- Breathe out: And He weeps with me.

Psalm 27:13 (NLT) can be a great reminder of God's goodness here on earth. I love the phrase "the land of the living"— the land where we are in this body. To be living means we still breathe and have a heartbeat. We are still embodied.

- Breathe in: Yet I am confident I will see the LORD's goodness
- Breathe out: while I am here in the land of the living.

Practice these or other breath prayers for at least sixty seconds to start. Set a timer if needed to help you know there is a beginning and an end. Try to move toward being able to engage in breath prayers for about five minutes at a time.

YES, WE CAN BE FRIENDS

Seeking Out Healthy Relationships

Union with Christ is not me and Jesus; it's we and Jesus.
KYLE WORLEY, *Knowing Faith* podcast

It can be brutally hard to trust anyone after experiencing abuse. That's especially true if your abuser was a parent, caregiver, or someone else in a position of authority. Janna had difficulty trusting anyone who called themselves a Christian after being sexually assaulted by her youth pastor. She did get to the point that she knew she needed community, and she believed me when I told her that healing happens in community. But it was really scary for her to put herself out there. She longed for connection, however.

Like Janna, you may desire community but be unsure how to find healthy relationships. While it may seem as if some people are just naturally good at connecting with people and building friendships, it is possible for even the most introverted person to build community too. I encourage you to be aware of two steps you can take to connect with others in a healthy way: setting up boundaries and establishing internal safety.

KNOW YOUR BOUNDARIES

Boundaries get a lot of press, and rightly so. But what are they?

Consider the lines on a road. Each lane has one on the left and one on the right. When I first learned to drive, I was told to keep my vehicle between those lines. Can I choose to cross them? Yes, I sure can. I can absolutely take a hard right into a field and go off-road if I want. That may be unwise when I'm driving a Honda Civic. If I bottom out in a muddy spot, I could get stuck or tear up the transmission, making the car undrivable. Or worse yet, I could hit a tree and total my vehicle. However, there are times I could take that hard right, do a little off-roading, and *nothing bad would happen*. As my young adult son says, "I'm Gucci" (that means "I'm good").

But am I really good? There may have been no immediately obvious negative outcomes. Maybe there's a little dirt on the tires. But overall my car is fine. I'm fine. In God's economy, though, I'm really not great. Just because I didn't experience a negative impact in that moment doesn't mean doing donuts in the field was godly or wise. I've still put extra stress on the car, and I might not see that impact for a long time. There's also stress on my soul—a little desensitization has taken place. Regardless of immediate or even long-term impact, I haven't made the wisest choice. Living outside my values leaves a mark on my soul, even if I can't see it right away.

Boundaries are self-determined and generally based on our values. As Brené Brown says, "Setting boundaries is making clear what's okay and what's not okay, and why."[1] Just as those lines in the middle of the road clearly delineate where cars heading in opposite directions belong, Henry Cloud and John Townsend explain that "boundaries define us. They define *what is me* and *what is not me*."

> A boundary shows me where I end and someone else begins, leading me to a sense of ownership.
>
> Knowing what I am to own and take responsibility for gives me freedom. . . .

In addition to showing us what we are responsible for, boundaries help us to define what is *not* on our property and what we are *not* responsible for.[2]

In *Atlas of the Heart*, Brené Brown says that "boundaries are a prerequisite for compassion and empathy."[3] We can't really connect with someone unless we know where we begin and end—the "*what is me* and *what is not me*" that Cloud and Townsend are talking about.

Trauma therapist Victoria Ellis says that good boundaries "are loving to the other person, safe and healthy for me, clearly communicated, and with enforceable consequences."[4] In other words, rather than being selfish or restrictive, they provide clarity and freedom for us and other people. If you've never had boundaries before, setting them can feel a little daunting, and you might need a teammate to help you figure out what yours are—a trusted friend or a therapist can help you out here. And boundaries are going to be dependent on the type of relationship you have. The best starting place is to name your values. What is important to you? What are things you cannot tolerate in a relationship? (If you're reading this book—or if you're human—not tolerating abusive behavior should make your list for sure.)

STRIVE FOR SAFETY

I'd had a ridiculously rough day—the kind that was so dark I wondered if I'd ever see light again. It was the sort of day when I didn't feel like I could take a deep breath. I didn't feel safe in my own body. Nothing felt safe.

In that moment, when the darkness threatened to be all I could see, I took a step back. I could feel that my breath was shallow, and my heart was racing. I got still for a moment, closed my eyes, and checked in with my body. *What does it need?* I wondered. Then I personalized it: *What do you need?* I asked my body directly.

In order to regulate our nervous systems and heal, we need to feel safe. Over the years, I've learned skills to help me find that sense of safety in hard moments. On the day I am describing above, I realized I hadn't eaten in forty-eight hours. I hadn't been feeling well, and I was extremely busy. Food hadn't made the "to-do list." Food is vitally important to making sure our brains and bodies can function and stay within (or return to) our window of tolerance. I often teach the acronym HALT as a useful reminder of things that will dysregulate us quickly when not addressed: *Hungry, Angry, Lonely, Tired.* This isn't an exhaustive list, but it's the big four that we can be most aware of.

On this day, I was hungry and tired. I wouldn't be able to cope unless I addressed those needs. So when my body reminded me that I needed food and rest, I listened. I made what sounded good to me in that moment—a turkey and Swiss sandwich on sourdough with spinach, tomatoes, and my favorite brand of mayo. I paired it with a bowl of raspberries. As I ate, I focused on what was good about my meal—the flavors, the textures. Then I congratulated myself on having compassion on my body and on my struggling self. As I went to take a nap and address my other need—rest—I reminded myself, *You're safe. You've been through some tough stuff today. But you are safe. And look at you feeding yourself and caring for this body!* These acts, though they sound simple, were extremely important in the moment. I couldn't process a single blessed thing about the hardness of that day until I felt safe.

Because traumatic experiences damage a person's sense of safety,[5] we have to start there. We literally cannot fully heal until we establish safety. That means moving out of toxic relationships, systems, and situations and then learning to create safety inside ourselves.

Safety does not mean a lack of adversity. I don't think life is ever completely chill. It's life. What safety means for us is that we are in a place with enough stability and peace and a wide-enough window of tolerance to work through a given issue.

In an unsafe world, we must intentionally establish safety in ourselves and in our environment.[6] It doesn't have to be perfect (nothing in life is), but we do want it to be relatively steady. How long this

WINDOW WATCHING

When we experience a stressor, we have a certain capacity to handle it and keep our emotions in check. The emotional space we have to manage those emotions is called our window of tolerance. We function best when we stay inside that window. When we exceed our ability to manage our emotions due to too many stressors, we exceed—or go outside—our window of tolerance. The size of everyone's window is different, but we can learn to expand our window through mindfulness practice and learning to work through things that trigger us.

Triggers are anything that remind us of a traumatic experience. They might include a smell, song, or memory that reminds us of that horrendous experience. Triggers activate our minds and bodies, though I have found that the body reacts first in many people. Triggers may be expected or unexpected, and I've found that the unexpected ones tend to be the most unsettling.

takes really depends on a number of factors, including how long we endured trauma. For those who have been in a long-term abusive marriage and had childhood trauma, finding safety is going to take longer. And that's okay. Being gracious to yourself is key.

We all want to be healed right away—of course we do! We've spent so much time hurting that we just want to be healed. Though I firmly believe God can and does miraculously heal, I also know it's often more of a process than we'd like. It's often painfully slower than we want. Being able to radically accept that the process is taking what it takes is wisdom. Remember the old adage that the journey of a thousand mile starts with a single step. When you look back in a year, you won't be standing where you are today. Setting boundaries and striving for safety are key to building strong relationships with everyone—including the opposite sex.

A note about loneliness

It is painful to be lonely, especially when the people who should have been there for us betrayed us and harmed us in deep ways. This pain and isolation can lead survivors to enter into harmful relationships.

My client Charlotte groaned as she detailed abusive relationship after abusive relationship to me. She said, "I feel so dumb. Why can't I just get it together? How do I keep ending up here?" We'll talk more later about what happens when we don't know how to do the work of healing; however, part of what got Charlotte there was her attempts to manage feelings of loneliness.

While it is true that loneliness can lead to physical health issues and an increase in mortality,[7] we want to enter into relationships intentionally and healthfully. When feelings are so big and so painful, there are skills we can use to help us allow that feeling to pass so we can make wise choices. Many of those skills are built through the exercises in this book.

WHO IS MY BROTHER?

My heart fills with joy whenever I see women connecting with other women, either at the Called to Peace Ministries women's retreat or other forums where I speak. Many of them have just begun working on establishing boundaries and seeking internal safety in their relationships. Often, however, I find that women are much more cautious about striking up conversations with men. Though I understand, I believe that when women and men are discouraged from interacting, everyone suffers.

That's why while casually listening to the *Knowing Faith* podcast, I stopped washing dishes when I heard Jen Wilkin say, "God's Kingdom doesn't function as designed when we overlook this [brother-sister relationships] or diminish those in value."[8]

I nearly took a page from my Pentecostal sisters and did a victory lap in my kitchen.[9] Yes, yes, so much yes!

Before we can unpack healthy sexuality, we have to unpack healthy male-female relationships. This can be especially tricky simply because our society is vastly oversexualized. Yet intimate relationships are not just about sex. Healthy ones are about friendship first. If you don't know how to be a healthy friend, then a romantic relationship will be in trouble long before you get to physical sexual intimacy. We can imagine intimate relationships like a house. The foundation of any intimate relationship is friendship. Without that the whole house crumbles.[10]

Given the wider culture's obsession with sex, some people look to the church for guidance and information on what's okay and not okay in male-female relationships. Yet it seems as if the church often has nothing to offer but warning signs. Many teach that women and men cannot be friends, even though I think the Bible is clear that healthy male and female relationships are possible. The apostle Paul tells us how we should treat each other: "Love one another deeply as brothers and sisters. Take the lead in honoring one another" (Romans 12:10, CSB).

While some attitudes are changing and shifting, there are still a whole lot of thoughts on male-female relationships in the institution of the church. As just one example, I read a blog post in which I sensed the author trying hard to present a balanced look at male-female friendships, but he still concluded that women and men can't be friends. I'm picking on this article because, while I believe the author was trying to take a somewhat centrist position, he still comes to the faulty conclusion that so many in the church do—that friendships between women and men are dangerous.

One of the arguments the author makes against male-female friendships is that there might be "the sort of personal chemistry that often creates affairs."[11] That seems to imply that any "chemistry" must be sexual in nature. That blanket statement just doesn't ring true to me. I can have chemistry—an overall vibe and affinity—with someone and not end up having an affair. How well I get along with someone does not indicate how likely I am to begin an affair with them. I get along with lots of female and male friends. I've never had an affair with any of them.

In her book *Not "Just Friends,"* Shirley P. Glass details how affairs happen—and it's not because people of the opposite sex simply got along well and had a friendship. It's because other issues in their relationships and their souls were not being addressed. In short, they had unaddressed heart issues, not friendship issues.

The author of the blog article ultimately concludes that members of the opposite sex should relate as associates. He defines *associates* as people you see at events like church but with whom you don't share your heart, though you might need to share personal information as part of your common association.[12]

I disagree. First, if we distill friendship down to no other part of our selves than our sexual selves, then sure, there could be risk of infidelity. But we can't. My whole self is involved here—my *self* that has morals and emphatically does not believe infidelity is godly. My whole self pays attention to how I feel and takes anything to the Lord that is out of balance with His Word. Simply put, if I'm paying attention and living mindfully, then my risk of being unfaithful or immoral within friendship is really limited.

I've been friends with a certain man for more than a decade. When we met we were both divorced. We became friends, and never once did I ever consider him as a potential romantic partner. Why? It's not because he's not good-looking (and yes, we can recognize beauty and handsomeness without having sexual thoughts). It's not because he's unkind. In fact, he's incredibly caring, a deep thinker, and one of my favorite people to talk theology with. He's also a pastor—but was not nor has he ever been my pastor, so there is no power differential. So why did we never consider each other in a romantic way? Simply put, that is not the nature of our relationship. He's my brother, and I see him that way. I'm his sister, and he sees it that way. Our faith and our whole selves informed that for us. In fact, I remember talking to him as he was dating the woman who is now his wife. I rejoiced with him that he'd found such a wonderful woman and again as they got married and had a child together. I am friends with his wife, too, but he is my primary friend. He's not a mere associate to me, nor am I to him.

Some of my closest friends are guys. I have wonderful brothers in Christ who love and appreciate me. They know my heart and I know theirs. I know deep things about them and they know deep things about me. And never once have I ever considered them in a romantic way, especially my brothers who are married. And I'm not the only one who thinks like this! I have a multitude of friends, both male and female, who have somehow never fallen into infidelity by being friends with the opposite sex. At this point, you may be saying, "Well then, how do affairs happen? Huh, missy? Explain that, then."

I'm so glad you asked.

HOW AFFAIRS HAPPEN

Affairs are complicated. First of all, they're not just one-dimensional: I met you, we became friends, somehow we became more than friends, and we had an emotional affair or slept together. No one ever falls into infidelity or sexual sin by accident. Instead, they make a series of choices that lead there. Every. Single. Time.

As a therapist who is highly trained in couples therapy—this is quite literally a big part of my actual job—I have recognized time and again that the path to an affair is complex. First, married folks who end up meeting with me generally have unaddressed issues in their marriage. The majority of struggling couples wait years before getting therapy. Research is mixed, but a recent study notes couples wait, on average, 2.68 years after the "onset of problems."[13] I've had couples wait as long as twenty-five or thirty years to get help. As you can imagine, by the time couples sit down with me, their relationship is usually a total mess. Even couples who arrive within that 2.68-year window have significant challenges. Sometimes the couple have come to counseling because one party has been unfaithful. As we break down what happened in those situations, here are a few of the things I see:

- The unfaithful spouse met someone at their office/church/restaurant/work trip that soothed their loneliness or some need they hadn't addressed or expressed to their spouse. Instead of noticing it and taking it to God right then and there, the person used the quick hit of another person to feel better. That led to an affair. This is obviously sin that stems from *other* unaddressed stuff. In the majority of marriages that were nonabusive, this is how an affair began.

- Attachment insecurity issues are also an impetus for infidelity. Spouses have problems in the way they connect with their partners because of issues that began in childhood with their family of origin. When these deep wounds are ignored, insecure attachment issues can lead people to try to meet their needs in unhealthy ways, including infidelity.

- One spouse is sex addicted or sexually compulsive. Porn use (which also is adultery) can escalate to affairs or patronizing prostitutes or other sex workers. This has nothing to do with opposite-sex friendships and everything to do with trauma and in some cases entitlement. (And for the record—if you are in an abusive relationship, know that no amount of trauma in someone's history causes or justifies abuse. *Period.* There are millions of traumatized people who do not abuse anyone.)

- One spouse is an abuser and sees the opposite sex as objects. These abusers feel entitled. They may or may not struggle with sex addiction or other issues, but the root issue is their entitlement and pride. Again, this has nothing to do with opposite-sex friendship. (And I will say it again because it can't be said too much: A history of trauma does not justify abuse. Period. Full stop. Lots of people who have experienced trauma don't abuse others.)

- An abused spouse has an affair in an attempt—consciously or subconsciously—to get the abuser to leave. Such affairs are still wrong, but they didn't happen because one spouse was friends with someone of the opposite sex.

- An abuse victim has unresolved trauma that leads them into behaviors, like infidelity, that don't match their value system. This is called traumatic reenactment, and we'll look more closely at this in a later chapter.

Affairs are brutal, and betrayal trauma is a very real thing. Recently, I had a survivor share with me that she's certain the betrayal trauma she experienced was more harmful than if she'd been hit. She is not the first woman to share that perspective. I'm in no way minimizing betrayal trauma, nor am I excusing infidelity. What I am saying is that no affair happened simply because someone was friends with a member of the opposite sex. Other factors were in play.

I'm also not saying we should be foolish. There are times when a friendship with a member of the opposite sex may not be wise. We really need to resist the urge to be black and white, all or nothing here. Use discernment. Evaluate the relationship. And if you are coming out of an abusive relationship, do your work. Get therapy and heal. Realize that your safety button may be broken.

When we are wounded and swimming out in the ocean of life, just bleeding out into the water, what are we going to attract? Sharks. Then we get all confused about why they're chewing on our foot.

Additionally, we may be so desperate for love and care we could put ourselves in a situation where we are seeking it in a way that does not fit with our values or where we overly sexualize it because it's all we know. Be wise.

Learn what a healthy relationship is. Have healthy boundaries. Do your healing work.

When God talks about guarding our hearts, we are to be mindful and honest with ourselves and with God. What is happening? If you are in a friendship and you notice your feelings expanding beyond that, perhaps you need to take that to God and talk it out. It may be an issue to address in counseling. What is the state of your spousal or dating relationship if you're in one? Are you and this other person both single? Because if so, it's okay to date and to explore romantic relationships, and those feelings may be just fine. There are far more questions and considerations here than the gender of the two parties.

I'm not saying we can just ignore the role gender may play in our relationships, but I am saying that a healthy friendship between two people of the opposite sex is not wrong or unbiblical.

UNBIBLICAL THINKING HARMS WOMEN

Though these matters affect all of us, an unbiblical perspective on male-female relationships can prove especially harmful to women.

First, this sort of thinking perpetuates the notion that women are dangerous. This is something many women in our churches feel. I've had countless conversations about this with women over the years, both in women's ministry and as a counselor. I've also experienced it myself.

I distinctly remember a conversation I had years ago with a female church staff member while volunteering together at the church I attended at the time. In the course of the conversation she said that private interactions between women and men were forbidden. I was shocked. I asked her what would happen if I broke my leg and only a male staff or volunteer was around to help. She told me they'd not be allowed to assist me. They would wait until the paramedics arrived. I remember saying, "Even if they could get me to a hospital faster, they'd wait so as not to be alone with me?" And she said, "Yes. It's sinful if they help."

Read that again and consider the full implications. I'd be left to suffer because of my gender. I didn't ask whether it would be sinful for the team of first responders to treat me if they were all men. I was in my early twenties and lacked the backbone I currently possess. But honestly: Does that even reflect the heart of Jesus? This same Jesus who had so many women who followed Him? The same Jesus who had the woman caught in adultery brought before Him?

Do you really think Jesus would have told me, "I'm so sorry you had to suffer, daughter. I know Pastor Bob could have taken you to the hospital and your leg could have been cared for so much faster, but you are a female after all. We can't risk an affair."

And let's be honest, exactly who is thinking of infidelity when they are ill or have an injury! No man. No woman. No one. If a man was considering what sexual things he could potentially do to a hurting woman he's driving to the ER, there is a serious issue that needs to be called out. Any man like that should be disqualified from ministry.

How did we even get here: the place where well-meaning Christians are confused about whether women and men can be friends? I think it is related in part to purity culture.[14]

Purity culture was meant to combat the oversexualization I mentioned already. The problem is that it went too far and deeply distorted sexuality. Young men were taught that if they just waited, then their wives would satisfy their every sexual fantasy. Young women were taught that, if they didn't dress and act right, they were the problem causing boys to sin.

It is my professional opinion that purity culture coupled with the distortion of healthy male-female relationships actually fuels abuse culture in the church. Simply put, if a man is taught that a woman's sole purpose is to satisfy and serve him sexually, then he may see her as no different than a porn star or prostitute. She may be an object to him, not a living, breathing person made in the image and likeness of God.

But what do we see from Jesus? Rebecca McLaughlin does a fabulous job of showing His heart toward women, some of whom were His disciples.[15] He counted them as friends. They traveled with Him. And lest you say, "Well, He's Jesus. Of course it was safe," may I remind you that we are being changed from glory to glory to be like Him (2 Corinthians 3:18)? This is called sanctification. We are called to live like Christ (see Romans 12:2; 1 Corinthians 6:20; and 1 Peter 2:21). If we are living like Christ, our relationships—*all of them*—will look a whole lot like His. When we're allowing our hearts and minds to be transformed by Christ, we can be safe in relationships.

ABSTAINING FROM THE APPEARANCE OF EVIL

What about preventing the appearance of evil? Oh, this is a question I hear a lot. A whole lot. People typically point to this verse: "Abstain from all appearance of evil" (1 Thessalonians 5:22, KJV). It has been used to keep women and men from being around each other because if a man is talking to a woman, then it may *appear* that something suspicious is happening.

When I led a youth group about a billion years ago (at least it feels that long ago now), I loved those kids so much. I still do. They were incredible, and I wanted to see them walk in all God had for them.

After a youth group bonfire one night, two of the boys came up to me and said, "Hey, we want to learn to hear God's voice and we know you hear Him. Can you teach us?" Look, when teenage guys ask to learn to hear God's voice, the answer is yes. Unequivocally. It never occurred to me to say no because I was a woman. So after checking with their parents, I started meeting with these guys almost weekly to do a Bible study on hearing God's voice. We always met in a public place—never in my home—and spent a few hours studying God's Word. So I was taken aback when one of the older ladies in our church—who was not related to either of the boys—got upset. She was convinced this was against God's will because I was a divorced single woman teaching teen boys. My mere presence with them in public was considered by this person to be the "appearance of evil" because of my marital status and my gender.

Except there was nothing at all evil about it. That, however, didn't stop her from going to our church elders to express her concerns.

When I explained the Bible study to our elders, they essentially told me, "Stay in public; don't do anything wicked." No worries.

Public and not wicked—check and check. To be clear: I do understand that readers who were abused by church staff and leaders may be really worried here. Those who abuse children and teens have a serious heart issue, and it's evil. There should be checks and balances in place to protect our kids! That is why I was always aboveboard and transparent.

So what do we do with that verse from 1 Thessalonians? How do we know if something has the "appearance of evil"? Did you know that this verse can be translated, "Stay away from every kind of evil" (CSB, NLT)? Or "Abstain from every form of evil" (ESV, NKJV)? This wording makes a whole lot more sense to me. Of course we should abstain from every type of evil.

But healthy brother-sister relationships are not a form of evil to avoid. Sexual immorality is. So if you are in a healthy relationship with a Christian brother or sister, one with no sexual immorality or other sinful behavior (let's say bank robbing for fun), then there is no issue. None. Nada.

Consider how Paul, when visiting a city with no synagogue, went down to the riverbank, where he found only women (Acts 16:13). What did he do? He talked with them. You might be thinking, *Note the "we" language. Paul wasn't alone with a single woman; others were there.* Okay, fair enough. Still, Paul speaks highly of women like Lydia, who is never mentioned with a husband. She's described as a businesswoman with a church that met in her house. *Her house.* Just let that sink in. And if you want to cite the Billy Graham rule, remember that that rule was for Billy by Billy. It was his conviction. And it was right and good for him. It is not my conviction nor that of many others I know. And that's okay too!

Aimee Byrd correctly notes there is a difference between female-female relationships and female-male relationships.[16] Of course there is! I'm not going to sit on a couch and cuddle with a male friend, to be honest. But I will allow a male or female friend to hug me tight, to put their arm around me, and to comfort me when I'm sad. In fact, I recently asked a male friend if I could please have a big hug after a really hard day. I was grateful for his embrace and the needed co-regulation for my nervous system.

Also, what I will do with some male friends is not what I will do with all male friends. Those brothers with closer access to me are the ones who have proven they are protectors, not predators. We'll talk more about that later, but suffice it to say, at no point am I saying that there shouldn't be boundaries in opposite sex relationships.

What I am saying is that those boundaries need not lead to an all-or-nothing approach to male-female relationships. That's the path to poor theology. Honestly, having a skewed theology when it comes to opposite-sex friendships is so reductionistic. It communicates to women and men that we are run solely by our sexual desire, which minimizes who God created us to be. We were made as beings with sexuality, yes, but that's so far from who we are in our entirety. And as a single woman in the church, I find it beyond frustrating when I'm treated as dangerous simply due to my gender.

For example, at one church, I offered to help in the counseling space in which I'm licensed and specialized. My assistance was declined in favor of that from a married woman. While I don't know all the factors that went into their decision, at this particular church, it was clear to me that unmarried women had zero place in its walls. I watched many single women leave well before I did. Instead of treating us like sisters and letting us use our God-given gifts, we were marginalized. That was enough to make some of these women leave the faith altogether. Why stay when you're seen as either a wife or a liability? I wasn't a wife, so that left me to assume that I was a liability.

HEALTHY RELATIONSHIPS WITH THE OPPOSITE SEX

What do healthy friendships between opposite-sex people look like? How do we know if it's going in an unhealthy direction? I'm so glad you asked! Let's talk about that.

First, there should be no red flags. As I often tell my clients, those red flags don't mean it's a carnival. There should be nothing

YES, WE CAN BE FRIENDS

compromising in healthy relationships. Married male friends shouldn't be saying, "Boy, I wish you were my wife." That is a red flag. They don't say, "Don't tell my wife we talked . . ." Again, *red flag*. Good male friends are on the up-and-up, and there are no secrets between you. There is nothing I say to any of my male friends that I wouldn't also say to their wives. There is nothing they say to me that would be a problem if their wives knew about it.

Second, the relationship is honoring and has boundaries. There is no power imbalance, and boundaries are maintained. Your opposite-sex friend is not talking to you via FaceTime or in person while you are using the bathroom with the door open. You are not touching each other inappropriately. You aren't undressing in front of each other. You are using common sense.

Finally, you are mindful and paying attention to what is happening inside you. If you notice romantic or sexual feelings for a married friend arise, take them to Jesus ASAP. You may need some additional boundaries, up to and including ending the friendship, and you may need to talk it out in therapy. You may need to do all those things. Honestly, your primary boundary is the very simple "I don't have to act on my feelings, and I desire to be godly." Just because you feel something doesn't mean you have to act on it.

So how do we even deal with touch? How do we know what's healthy and appropriate when touch was so badly polluted by the abuse we suffered? We start, like so many other areas of healing, small. We have to get into our own bodies first.

LEARNING TO LISTEN TO AND FEEL SAFE IN YOUR BODY

Learning to listen to your body helps you identify areas that need attention and helps you connect to your physical self. This exercise is designed to help you do that. When I explained it to Selah, she looked over at me as if I had three heads. "What is my body trying to say?" she repeated, her tone incredulous.

I smiled. "Yep. I know this exercise sounds super weird, but are you willing to give it a try?" I always give my clients the option to say no. So many were not afforded the use of their voice while in the traumatic experience. I am determined they'll have it in my office.

Selah sighed. "Okay. Seems silly but I'll try." She settled in and began noticing her body. "My arms feel like they need attention."

"Okay, notice that."

Selah paused. "The sensation isn't unpleasant, but my arms feel tense."

"Just let yourself notice that. Does it stay the same or does it shift?"

Selah focused on her arms. "Huh," she said. "The tension seems to be melting away and it feels . . . good . . . to notice."

I smiled. "Go with that."

Selah continued noticing, eventually reporting that her arm tension had completely evaporated. "Okay, that's still weird, but it seems useful." We both laughed, and I noted how much I appreciated her honesty.

To try this exercise for yourself, get in a comfortable position. Your eyes may be open or closed, whatever is most comfortable to you. If you leave your eyes open, let them be in a soft gaze and looking down. Take some deep breaths and allow yourself to be aware of your body feeling supported by whatever you are sitting or lying on. Starting at the top of your head and working your way down, begin to notice your body. When you become aware of a sensation, an area of tension, an area that feels pleasant or restful, pause and notice it. Let your awareness be filled with curiosity and allow your attention to linger there. Be mindful of any sensations shifting just by allowing your attention to rest there. If nothing shifts, that is okay. We are just noticing and learning to listen to our bodies. Only notice two areas in any given session of this invitation.

BODY AFFIRMATIONS

For survivors of sexual trauma, kindness toward our bodies can be so hard. I personally had to wrestle with this a lot. The first time I tried this exercise, I dissolved into tears. It felt so impossible to me. Thankfully, I kept at it, and it's become easier. I still have days when this is tough, but I am so much kinder to myself as I wrestle with it. It's tough for many of my clients, too, regardless of body shape or size. But when they're able to access compassion especially for the more sensitive parts, it opens up so much healing.

This exercise helps us talk to our bodies (and ourselves) more kindly. You'll need a notebook or paper and something to write with. Starting with an attitude of curiosity and gratitude, begin to notice your body. Pick one part of your body and write an affirmation. For example, you might notice your foot and write, "Thank you for giving me a solid place to stand and for helping me walk forward." You may find it helpful to place your hand on the body part you're affirming. Some body parts may be harder than others, especially areas that have experienced direct harm. Be gentle and kind with yourself.

If you notice that this exercise is very hard for you, invite a friend, your support group, or your therapist to be present with you through this. This exercise is an important one, though. It may take some time to be able to affirm the more sensitive parts. It's okay. Take all the time you need.

4

ALL OF ME, FULLY PRESENT

Learning to Live Embodied

*While the abuser took control of our body to inflict harm, there is
much we have control over in our current body to restore health.*

DAN ALLENDER, *Healing the Wounded Heart*

Some days I'm in a war. It's bloody and ugly and horrible. There's no
way to sanitize this conflict. It's a battle with casualties. It's a physical
war against my body. She feels like an enemy some days.

My battle with this body began as a child. First, she was deeply
harmed by sexual abuse that lasted years. Then she was assessed in
every way imaginable. My parents, concerned about my size, signed
me up for a nationally known weight loss program before I even
entered puberty. In front of women three or four times my age, I'd be
weighed every week. Then came the pronouncement, which I took
as the judgment as to whether I was good or bad. For some reason
I could never lose weight like the middle-aged women in the room.
They would boast losses of ten pounds. I would sometimes lose two.
Other times my weight stayed the same. Sometimes I gained a pound
or two.

Week in and week out I kept food journals that the program leader would scrutinize. "Are you sure you wrote everything down? Don't forget—any bites, licks, and tastes—BLTs!" she told me. She spoke to me in a singsong voice—as if her words were the best thing on earth and I should rejoice in them. But as I stood there, my prepubescent twelve-year-old body cloaked in shame, there was no rejoicing.

On the rare occasions I lost more than a couple of pounds, the leader would cluck at me and say, "See! You just have to try harder!" For that day and moment I was okay. I was *acceptable*. I *belonged*. She didn't know how hard I was trying. The fastidious way I wrote *everything* down. Not missing a thing. Writing down extra *just in case* and then restricting food so I was sure I was right. I would never miss a BLT.

I continued recording my food intake in spurts until my thirties. I did lose weight on occasion, sometimes a lot of it, but if I messed up, the weight came rushing back—and brought friends in the form of more pounds. There is a popular meme out there that says something like "Skin cells die, hair follicles die, but fat cells must have accepted Jesus Christ as their Lord and Savior because they have eternal life." I feel that in my bones.

I was drafted into this war with my body. It happened so early in my life that I don't even remember getting my papers. It's literally as old as my memory. As so many trauma survivors do, I listened to those in control barking the orders. Eventually, I didn't need anyone to give me commands. I gave them to myself. And the voice in my head grew louder, *You're not doing enough. Eat less. Try harder.* No wonder I brought in the reinforcements and developed an eating disorder.

Sadly, this is the story of many sexual abuse survivors. Eating disorders are common among us for several reasons.[1] First, we're often told that food has moral value (there are "good" foods and "bad" foods). This gives food a false all-or-nothing paradigm and reinforces the black-and-white thinking that plagues trauma survivors. Survivors who already feel at fault due to the abuse they suffered often resort to trying to be "good" in other areas to fix what they feel is broken. Second, food is something we can control when everything else seems out of control—especially things related to our bodies. Third, women are often told that our worth and value lie in our body shape and size, as well as how appealing we are to the opposite sex. For some survivors, the subconscious hope is to waste away to nothingness so they won't be harmed again. Other survivors subconsciously gain weight so as not to be desirable. Food also has a dopamine effect—there is a certain pleasure when we eat foods we like that can give temporary relief to distress. Finally, there also can be a drive to self-punish for perceived wrongs that occurred as part of the sexual assault or sexual abuse. All eating disorders drive disconnection from our bodies, which may be a welcome respite in some ways for a sexual abuse survivor. While the connection between sexual abuse and disordered eating is not fully known, there is a link nonetheless.[2] It can complicate an already complex issue.

For me, no matter how little or how perfectly I ate, my body gained weight. Food then became a battleground in a million different ways. And that wasn't its only problem.

THE BATTLE GETS BLOODIER

Even apart from my weight, puberty and middle school were awful. Thanks to a raging case of untreated polycystic ovary syndrome (PCOS), I had periods that would rock my world. No amount of protection could contain the flow. As a teen, I wasn't allowed to use tampons (lest I somehow take my own virginity, which my mother stated would be the outcome), but two regular menstrual pads simply didn't do the job. I lost count of the number of times I stood up from my chair in class to see blood all over the seat. Middle schoolers aren't known for their kindness, so you can imagine how that went for me. I was overweight, dressed in polyester clothes because plus-sized fashion didn't exist then, and told in every possible way that my body was failing.

I tried every method I could think of to get my body under

control and make her obey and be skinny. Every diet. Every exercise plan. Every eating disorder. From starving myself to taking laxatives, nothing worked. My body had become my enemy. I just ignored her most of the time, but I would hate her whenever she acted up through illness or pain. And I loathed her even more because of the sexual assaults that occurred in high school and then the sexual abuse I endured for a decade in my marriage.

As if none of this were enough, I was told that my waistline indicated my level of godliness. If it had expanded, I clearly was far from God. If it had shrunk, God was pleased with me. This wasn't just limited to when I was a kid or young adult. When I was in my thirties, one pastor whom I considered a friend sent me an email telling me I wasn't fit for friendship because I couldn't manage my weight. By that point, I believed God hated my body too. And by proxy, He hated me.

After all, buried in my body was another, even darker secret: childhood sexual abuse by a neighbor. Together, all of these experiences worked to sever my mind from my body. I focused on achievement and learned to ignore my body as much as possible. At the time, I had no idea how significant trauma's effect on the body really is.

CASUALTIES OF WAR (The Cumulative Effects of Trauma)

This body-based war is common to those who have endured sexual abuse and other traumatic events in childhood. I was in my forties before I heard about and then researched *adverse childhood experiences*, a term that grew out of a landmark study conducted by Dr. Vincent Felitti and Dr. Robert Anda.[3] In the 1980s, Dr. Felitti, a specialist in internal and preventive medicine, ran an obesity clinic. He soon noticed that many of his patients would lose large amounts of weight, only to regain it. Eventually, he discovered that 55 percent of them had been sexually abused in childhood.[4] In the nineties, he teamed up with Dr. Anda, a researcher with the Centers for Disease Control (CDC), to examine the types of trauma and dysfunction that lead to poor health outcomes in adulthood. They discovered that people who'd been abused or neglected as children, or whose parents had been incarcerated or suffered from substance abuse disorder, mental illness, or domestic violence, had much poorer health outcomes. They called these negative circumstances adverse childhood experiences (ACEs).[5] The more of these situations a child or teen lived through, the higher their ACE score, and the more likely they were to be obese or suffer from heart disease, strokes, substance abuse, and/or mental illness. More recent evaluations of the ACE data revealed that autoimmune disorders were more likely as well.[6] Like Bessel van der Kolk says: The body does, in fact, keep the score.[7]

Where do I go?

I remember the day my innocence and my sexuality were shattered. I was nine.

I could hear the TV in my parents' bedroom, across the hall from mine. I mustered all my courage, breathed deeply, and took a step into their room.

My mother looked up. "What do you need?" Her tone wasn't welcoming, but it also wasn't angry.

"May I please come in?" I asked.

My parents looked at each other, and then my dad said, "You may."

I walked to their bed and crawled up next to them. After sitting quietly for a few minutes, I asked, "Mom, what is sex?"

My dad stared straight ahead. My mom looked at me and said matter-of-factly, "It's called making love, and it's what married people do."

That was it. I could tell by her tone that she was done with our conversation. We sat quietly for a few more minutes, sports of some kind playing on the television. I eventually got up and went back to my room.

When I asked that question, I was in my second year of being

BODY & SOUL, HEALED & WHOLE

molested by a female neighbor who was a couple of years older than me. My family had moved from Ohio to Florida when I was just eight. I'd been trying to get my bearings after relocating from family and all four seasons to a place where we knew no one and it was eternal summer.

This girl lived down the street. I don't recall how I met her, though I suspect it was playing outside after school. I was a latchkey kid who got myself up in the mornings and to and from school every day. I came home alone to a cool, dark house. I busied myself with homework, then play.

One day the girl asked me if I wanted to play house. I thought that sounded fun so I agreed. She asked me to be the mommy and told me she would be the daddy. At first it all seemed innocent enough. We got out my dolls and pretended to parent them. We used my vintage 1980s gold and brown kitchen playset to create "meals."

After a while she looked at me and said, "Mommies and daddies sleep together. We have to do that." I was confused. She told me we needed to take off all our clothes and get in bed together. It seemed like something we shouldn't be doing and I said so. She was insistent. She told me that to stay friends I had to play house "right." I was terrified to lose the only friend I had, so I obeyed.

After we crawled into my tiny twin bed naked, she touched my private areas and I froze. Deep inside I knew it was wrong, but parts of it also felt good. I was so confused. After she left, I hid in my closet. I felt like I was hiding from God, from myself, and from what had just happened.

My friend continued this pattern with me for the next three years. The night I bravely asked my parents about sex, I was hoping against all hope that I wasn't damaged before God. Their answer—and their lack of curiosity over why I'd asked the question—didn't help me. I felt dirty and ashamed and very mixed up. I just knew God couldn't love me and I'd need to try to make Him happy with me again.

Even when I was a child, my body was telling me she was not okay. We were not okay. She kept holding on to weight to try to protect me from the horrific circumstances we were enduring. In the ACE study, researchers noted that weight gain protected the participants from further sexual harm. It's not a conscious decision—neither I nor any other survivor I've ever met has ever said, "I think I'll do this so I feel safer." It's our bodies, created by a good God, who are doing all they can to help us manage horrific things that have happened to us. I've met other women whose bodies cry out in the forms of autoimmune issues, cancer, and more. Like me, they may blame their bodies rather than recognize how much they've carried. For many years, I misunderstood my body's cries. I saw her as my enemy. I thought she was keeping me from being truly lovable and from some of the physical activities others around me could do. No longer were my abusers the only ones inflicting harm on me; now I took charge of my own harm. I swallowed the evil done and said to me and then set about trying to force my body to get in line already and just do the "right thing."

I've watched similar battles in my clients too. Just like other women I know, I see these clients struggling with autoimmune diseases, hair loss, and obesity. I talk with countless women who vilify themselves because of their malady or maladies. (We rarely have just one.) *I must be broken or weak*, they tell themselves. They don't look at the abuse in which they live or lived as the culprit. But it is there, this silent destroyer that makes us think we—our bodies—are the ones responsible for the bad things happening to us. Even if the abuse didn't start in childhood, there is growing evidence of how long-term domestic abuse also impacts the body's health and well-being.[8]

WHAT DOES IT LOOK LIKE TO LIVE IN YOUR BODY?

The toll of sexual abuse is high, and I would not wish it on anyone. I ran into a friend recently who was out with his wife and three-year-old daughter. As I looked at her sweet and innocent countenance, I wanted better in this world for her. Better than a world in which one in five women is harmed sexually.[9] Dear God, may that little girl never, ever be the one in five.

Sadly some of us were *already* one in five at age three. And the war had already begun.

With trauma comes a death to a sense of self. According to a research article written by two philosophers, dissociation and other trauma responses can make it really tough to feel both "the subjective, lived body (*being* a body) and the objective, corporeal body (*having* a body)."[10] Traumatic dissociation messes up the relationship between those two aspects of ourselves and "gives rise to profound self-alienation" or a "death of the self."[11] I'd call it being disembodied: Our *subjective* sense of self and our *objective* physical self feel disconnected. After trauma, part of us feels dead, never to be regained. The researchers also noted: "Survivors tend toward experiencing the body as an object, reduced in vitality and responsiveness."[12] When our abuser treated us like an object, is it any wonder that we, too, fall prey to the belief that we are just objects?

While working through trauma isn't a cure-all, it will make it easier for your body to heal as your soul heals. Please hear me clearly: Healing trauma does not guarantee your body will magically be better, though that does happen sometimes. But anything you can do to give your body a break is good.

BEFRIENDING THE ENEMY

Working through trauma includes grappling with this reality: No matter how hard we might try, we cannot get away from our bodies. We are embodied. That means we each live in a body—an expression in tangible form, made in the image and likeness of our Creator God. When He first created humans, God called us "very good" (Genesis 1:31). As soon as Adam and Eve disobeyed God's one command, however, sin entered the world and what is good has had to reckon with sin's effects ever since. The first thing Adam and Eve noticed after eating the forbidden fruit was their *bodies*. Adam and

Eve were naked and ashamed, but they could not get away from their physical selves. Instead, they hastily tried to cover up. Tyler Staton, pastor of Bridgetown Church in Portland, Oregon, says it this way: "Women and men and religion and bodies have been intertwined forever."[13]

We live in these bodies, and our minds and souls are housed in them. Our faith cannot be divorced from them. In fact, disconnection from God is also disconnection from our bodies. After all, the Holy Spirit makes His dwelling place in them. And redemption starts in our bodies, which makes them vitally important to who we are.

When we've been abused, we enter into a very complicated relationship with our bodies. Abuse and its effects aren't merely bound together in our *minds*—our *bodies* are involved. We feel these things in our physical bodies. When a survivor leaves an abusive situation and relationship, they leave *in their body*. One physical foot in front of the other, out the door. They are not leaving with their mind alone. The physical body comes along.

That leads to a difficult truth: When we are abused sexually, shame and pleasure also are bound together in our bodies. I realize that acknowledging the way that shame and pleasure are bound in our bodies is a heavy statement because they feel so opposite and like they cannot be intertwined. Our bodies are designed to respond to touch—including sexual touch. Even in the most horrific situations, our bodies may respond with an orgasm. And that leads to a whole lot of confusion. *How can I experience an orgasm when I'm being harmed?* But we do because our body is doing what it was designed to (we will talk so much more about this in chapter 7). Even so, shame snakes its way in, convincing us that we are even more broken. We believe we are complicit in the abuse.

"Complicity is where you feel like you participated," says Dr. Dan Allender. "Where something in your body chose or felt the '*yes*.' It is not really complicit—but it *feels* that way when it happens."[14]

Even apart from abuse, the sexualization and pornification of our culture is all around us. Women are subject to vast overt and subtle sexual abuse and objectification. As women, our bodies get a whole lot of scrutiny. The ways we're portrayed in media, the ways social media perpetuates unrealistic standards, and the ways we're scrutinized by men and other women are pervasive and mind-numbing. We are told explicitly and implicitly what we should look like and how our bodies should function. If your body doesn't fit the prevailing ideal, then it is "bad."

A DEAL WITH THE DEVIL

You may have real hatred toward your body, and that has almost certainly been compounded if you've been sexually abused and feel like damaged goods.

I'd like you to pause and check in with your body. How do you feel about your desires of hunger or thirst? My guess is that most of the time you're gracious to yourself about them (though I know that if you struggle with disordered eating, this may not be an area of grace you can extend to yourself yet). But when it comes to your body, you may not be so gracious. Do you notice any animosity? If you notice hostility toward your body in this moment, will you continue to concede to evil in the hatred of your body?

I know that was a heavy question. First, let me say, *You are not at all responsible for the abuse you suffered. Ever.* What I am saying is that sometimes we buy the lie evil spews and hate our bodies as a result. Evil loves to destroy and will do whatever it takes to harm. I'll ask the question again so we can sit with it together. Imagine me there, holding this weight with you.

Will you continue to concede to—agree with—evil in the hatred of your body?

Evil wishes for us to live in less than fullness in God, and that includes in our bodies. Hatred toward our bodies is agreeing with Satan. Do we really want to stand in agreement with him? I sure don't. We didn't cause the abuse, and we can decide to disagree with evil, which pushes hatred of self. A therapist I know says it this way:

You didn't put the trash on your front porch, but you do have to be the one to clean it up.

My heart is breaking as I think about how we agree with evil and give ourselves over to hatred of our good bodies. I feel tears well up in my eyes as I imagine sitting on my couch with you as we wrestle against evil and take back our bodies and minds from it.

Please know, there is no judgment or shame here. If you are noticing you've aligned with the enemy on how you feel about your body, it's okay. You can shift from this place; you can renounce the vow you unwittingly made to accept his evil lies. This is about creating a shift—even if in the tiniest of spaces.

I began to experience this shift in my own body when I refused to keep listening to the enemy of my body *and* soul.

MAKING UP WITH MY BODY, MY FORMER ENEMY

When I was younger, being in my body often felt like being a prisoner of war. But my body, like yours, is not the enemy. Our bodies are actually our helpers. Scientists are still discovering the multitude of ways they serve us. For instance, our bodies were created with a proprioceptive system that is designed to tell us where we are in space; for example, how far we are from a wall or other objects—where we are in the physical world we inhabit. Unfortunately, abuse can sometimes compromise this system, and in my case, I realize that I don't always know where my body is relative to other objects. I was reminded of this one day a few years ago while vacationing away from the Texas summer. If you haven't lived in Texas in the midst of summer, I'll just let you know—it's like living on the surface of the sun.

I'd been camping in the Great Smoky Mountains. It's one of my favorite places, and it reflects my nickname "Wild Mountain River," given to me by a therapist friend. I love how he sees both the beauty and ferocity in me.

Though it had rained the previous two days, the weather was

warm and sunny the morning I headed out to the cold mountain creek running behind my cabin.

I'd brought trekking poles and water shoes with sturdy, grippy bottoms. I carefully approached the creek, which was gurgling over rocks and cascading down small waterfalls. Because of the recent mighty rains, the water was high and swirling about but still crystal-clear. I cautiously navigated down the bank to the edge of the water. I checked each step to make sure I was steady and then made my way into the creek. When I put my first foot in, I felt the shock of cold water and grinned with delight. It was all I had hoped for. Clear and cold, but not too cold. I decided to go to the middle of the creek. I was up to my calves in water. Happy as I could be. I played in the water for a bit, watching it swirl around and past me. Then I lifted my face, letting the sunlight filtered by trees hit my face. At last I decided to get out and dry off.

Carefully I made my way toward the bank. I couldn't quite see where I was putting my foot and thought I would land on flat ground. I didn't. Instead, a slick rock moved when I applied my weight to it. Down I went. I can't even imagine what I must have looked like, falling forward into the cold water. Thankfully, my trekking poles did their job, and I didn't fall too hard. My left arm and left shin caught rocks, but not too badly. I was soaked in cold creek water from the chest down. I slowly stood back up and checked out my body. No blood. Definitely some light road rash from the rocks, but nothing terrible. I breathed a sigh of relief, climbed out of the creek, and then headed back to my cabin to change.

Once inside, my left elbow started to throb and my shoulder began to hurt. I panicked. *Oh, no!* I thought. And then the voices from the past poured over me. *Stupid, fat girl. What were you thinking? You know better. You can't be normal. You can't do what other people do.* I caught my breath.

Tears welled up in my eyes. I prayed to God, asking Him to forgive my carelessness. I *must* have done something wrong since I fell. Creek water still dripped down my legs as I froze under the weight

LET'S HAVE A WORD

Sensuality

The delight I felt next to the creek while listening to the rushing water and watching glints of sunlight on the rocks is an example of a sensual experience. Though *sensuality* is another word often hijacked in our oversexualized age, at its core it refers to the enjoyment we feel when our senses are engaged in a positive way. Its synonyms include "pleasurable" and "delightful."

Food can be a sensual experience when we allow good tastes to permeate our awareness. We can delight and find pleasure in a good meal. We might relax when we enter a home filled with the fragrance of a lavender candle. When we snuggle up in a warm, fuzzy blanket, its touch can be a lush (yet another synonym for *sensual*) experience. Yes, there are sexual connotations to this word as well, but we want to see it in its fullness here. Allowing the fullness of sensual experiences of all types, including the nonsexual areas of our life, can bring us great joy.

Mindful Moment

Take a moment to think of your favorite place and consider it with all your senses. Notice what you see in this location and what makes it stand out to you. What do you notice in your body as you do this? Is there a smell, temperature, or taste in this setting? Let your whole body experience remembering this place. Take a couple of moments to journal about it.

of enormous accusations and fear. I felt the pull to concede to evil about my body.

This time, though, something new took place. I recognized what was happening and questioned these thoughts. "Wait. Why am I repenting? I didn't take any undue risks. I was careful. I was appropriately attired. I wasn't sinning. I fell in a creek. Which is an accident. I didn't do anything wrong. *Whose voice is this really?*"

I took a deep breath. Then another. I repeated to myself, "This wasn't sinful. I fell in a creek. Because I was careful and prepared, I didn't face-plant on a rock. Just because I slipped doesn't mean I don't get to enjoy the fun I had before I fell. *And this accusation is not my voice.*"

I stopped dead. *"THIS ACCUSATION IS NOT MY VOICE."* I said it again, out loud this time, and with some gusto. *"THIS ACCUSATION IS NOT. MY. VOICE."*

That was one of the first moments that I realized I was making the shift from seeing my body not as my foe but as my friend. I was beginning to break the vow of self-contempt I had made with those who had abused me. I was (and am) being set free from captivity.

RELEASING CONTEMPT

Recently I had to have an echocardiogram of my heart. I wasn't worried about it going in, but then I ended up with my shirt off in front of a male technician. I can now handle most situations, but on this day a particular aspect of this exam triggered a body memory of the sexual abuse I'd endured in marriage. The tech did nothing wrong or inappropriate, but my body told me, *This feels familiar, and it's not good.*

I started to shake uncontrollably, and my mind filled with images I'd much rather forget. As I sat in my truck afterward, trying to put the pieces back together, I lamented that my body still holds so much. Despite excellent therapy and a great deal of healing, now and again something most definitely surprises me.

I immediately went to self-loathing. *How could I be feeling this way? How could this still sneak up on me?* This time it took support from my therapist to help me unwind and regain equilibrium after this bout with self-contempt.

My clients experience this too. Often, I hear stories about a flashback or body memory that snuck up and derailed what was otherwise a good day.

What does "holding ourselves in contempt" mean and how does it mess with our embodiment? Contempt means "to despise." It's seeing ourselves with hatred. Drs. John and Julie Gottman refer to contempt as sulfuric acid to a relationship.[15] It is the one thing that will ruin a relationship faster than anything else—and it is always abusive. If we direct contempt at ourselves, how can we possibly be in a healthy relationship with self? How can we be connected to our bodies?

We can't. We cannot be fully embodied when we hold ourselves in contempt.

I think Satan likes to use self-contempt because it keeps us so stuck. It's a battle I fight with and for my clients. I don't think I've sat across from a survivor of abuse who didn't struggle with contempt.

Vanquishing self-contempt is hard but very worth it. Once we're free from it, we gain a whole different relationship with our self and our bodies. We experience ourselves—and the goodness God put inside us—differently, and I have found that this is key to healing.

Take Lara, for example. "How did you feel biking down the Virginia Creeper?" I asked her one day. The Virginia Creeper Trail is a scenic, thirty-five-mile former railbed that cuts through the Virginia and North Carolina mountains.

Lara looked at me and smiled. "Free. I didn't have a care in the world. My body felt good. My mind felt good. I didn't hate myself for those hours rolling down that mountain. I couldn't believe what my body and I could do."

My client's smile looked like a ray of sunshine. She truly *felt* different. The room *felt* different as we talked. Not only was the sunlight streaming in from the window, but it also *felt* like it was emanating out of my client. For the first time, she had experienced herself without contempt and hatred. The lies that often swirled in her head about her worth, value, and ability had been quieted by a bike trip down a mountain. Her body and mind worked together in concert. She was fully embodied—and it was a beautiful sight to behold. We took the rest of the session to rejoice in that healing and apply it to other spaces in her life.

You may not be able to hurtle down a mountain on a bike, but my guess is there are things you can do to help you feel embodied; in other words, to feel connected to your body rather than disconnected from her as if she were your enemy. I love this definition of being embodied: "It means that connecting to the sensual side of living through touch, movement, and sensation can help you strengthen the mind-body bond. In turn, you can become more engaged, present, and an active participant in your life."[16]

Did you catch the word *sensual* in that definition? Being embodied is being fully connected to yourself and the world around you. Even as we begin to accept that our very good bodies are functioning as intended, we may struggle to accept healthy touch—either from ourselves or others. Maybe we eschew it completely or maybe we seek it out in unhealthy places.

As we come back into our bodies, we can notice how they respond in various situations, including those involving touch. We also have more control over what we allow or don't allow when we've befriended our physical selves and no longer see them as our enemies. This is part of God bringing beauty from ashes.

EMBODIED MOVEMENT

If you're like me and most of my clients, learning to become embodied requires some practical steps. Trauma survivors—especially those who have experienced sexual trauma—can struggle terribly with being embodied. Here are a few exercises that can help you get started. As with any exercise, do what feels good to you. This is an invitation to your body to something potentially new. New things can be tough sometimes, and that's okay. These are just meant to help you connect to your body. If you're struggling, getting some support from a therapist or a group that practices being embodied could be really helpful.

In this first exercise, you simply want to begin feeling comfortable moving your body. Feel free to start small, just one or two minutes. It can be any type of movement that feels good to your body—stretching, walking, etc. Be creative. I often walk because my body can tolerate it. Keep your mind gently focused on the act of movement and how it feels to your body. If your mind wanders, gently and without judgment bring it back. The "without judgment" part is super important here. As we already talked about, we can line up with contempt and evil if we're not careful, but taking a nonjudgmental and curious perspective prevents us from aligning with the enemy.

This exercise can be triggering if you aren't used to being in your body. You don't have to be afraid of triggers, though they are decidedly no fun at all. Mindful movement will help you just be present with and in your body. Your actual physical body and your felt sense of your body can match up, even if it's just for a few minutes.

CHECKING IN

Learning how to connect to our bodies again—or maybe even connect for the first time—is a learned skill. A long time ago, I was in a group learning these skills. The leader told us to become aware of the bottoms of our feet. We'd already been noticing the rest of our bodies. But for the life of me, when we got to the feet I could not do it. I panicked and actually had a panic attack. *Have I somehow lost my feet?* I know, not the most rational thought; but I was not the most rational person in that moment! I opened my eyes and looked down. Yes, I still had feet. It took me weeks of practicing to learn to come into awareness of a body part that was very clearly there. But once I got it, I got it. Now, even as I'm writing this, I'm aware of the bottoms of my feet just by thinking about them.

So let's learn to check in with our bodies.

Sit or lie in a comfortable position. Take a few moments to slow your breath, breathing in through your nose and out through your mouth. Try to let your exhale breath be longer than your inhale. Then check in with yourself and ask, "How is my body doing today?" Just notice, without judgment, whatever comes up. Allow your awareness to mingle with curiosity. Then, ask yourself, "What sensations am I aware of in this moment?" If you're able to continue in curiosity, consider what your body might be trying to say through those sensations. Afterward, consider briefly journaling your experience.

Important note: As I mentioned earlier, if you're just learning to notice and check in with your body, you may have sensations or memories come up that you aren't expecting or that are emotionally activating. If that happens for you, you can either surf the experience—meaning noticing it without judgment until it passes—or you can transition to a more grounding exercise (see page 19) and table those memories or sensations until you can connect with your therapist about them. It's not unusual for our bodies to get really excited and do a lot of talking when we start listening to them!

COMING HOME TO YOU

Learning to Inhabit Your Body

We need to teach how to touch with true care. Care for
our own bodies and for the bodies of others, because
those bodies were created by a good and caring God.

LORE FERGUSON WILBERT, *Handle with Care*

"Give your skin a little love. It's our first boundary."

I heard the facilitator's words and watched as she gently stroked
one arm, then the other. She was leading us in a grounding mindfulness exercise during our training in trauma care. I still felt so weird
doing this practice, even though I'd been working for a year to begin
getting comfortable touching my own body. I took a deep breath,
closed my eyes, and gently massaged one arm and then the next. I felt
my fingertips glide over my skin. It felt nice, weird, and dangerous all
at the same time. I reminded myself it was compassionate and gentle.
This practice was meant to enable me to give myself love in a physical
and tangible way, honoring my body for the work it was doing in the
class. I breathed deeply and focused on the sensations. I relaxed into
my own caring touch. Instinctively, I placed my palms on my cheeks
and breathed into the kindness of being held.

I'd first been encouraged to touch myself in this way the previous year during earlier trauma-care training. After a lunch break,

the facilitator invited us into a grounding mindfulness exercise. As I stood there, I dutifully followed his instructions on movement. Then he invited us to gently touch our own arms and faces. I panicked, my heart racing. "What do you mean? No. *Absolutely not.*" I shocked myself with my vehement resistance. This practice felt radically unsafe. I was unsteady on my feet.

Then he modeled gently stroking his own arms and face. My heart raced. I felt stiff and scared to move. My palms were sweating. Finally, shaking like a leaf in a strong wind, I gently touched my right arm with my left fingertips. I felt nausea well up. I stopped and had to sit down, with the room spinning around me. What was happening?

My experience of being so totally undone and confused by touch—even self-touch—isn't unique to me. So many survivors I've worked with look at me like I have six heads when I suggest it in a session. Touch of any kind has become radically unsafe. To consider touching one's own body with kindness—let alone letting anyone else touch their body with kindness—seems impossible and sometimes even *wrong*. Like *sinfully wrong*. And I'm not talking about sexual self-touch (though we will later in this book).

Touch, however, is critically important to our health. It is vital before we're even born. One study found that babies as young as eight weeks of gestation use touch to self-soothe![1] You've likely heard about studies that detail how depriving babies of touch can quite literally kill them.[2] Why do we think this would change as adults? In fact, research shows that this need for tactile connection continues throughout our lives. A 2001 study, for instance, shows that touch in older adults can also improve their well-being.[3] Neurochemicals like oxytocin (which I've heard referred to as the "cuddle chemical") help us feel bonded to one another and can even prevent depression when we lose a partner.[4] Touch is one of the ways oxytocin is released in our bodies.[5]

Marriage counselor Gary Chapman even identified touch as a love language: one of the five primary ways that people feel loved by others.[6] Even if your main love language isn't touch, it is still necessary for life. A friend of mine says we all have "skin hunger," and the first time I heard her say that, it resonated. We do have skin hunger—a need to be touched in safe ways. Our bodies long for healthy and safe touch. Going without healthy touch leaves us missing something important.

While speaking at a conference about healthy touch, I listened as the women shared their stories. One said she had never been hugged by her father. She'd grown up in a conservative religious structure that kept rigid lines in place, so men simply were not allowed to touch anyone other than their wives. She longed for hugs from her dad though. She said she believed he must love her because he supported her in other ways, but physical affection was decidedly absent. Her husband was abusive, and her paradigm for touch by a man was unkind and harmful.

Another woman piped up and said she had yet to meet a safe man. Her husband had deeply harmed her both sexually and physically. Her conservative upbringing also taught her that women and men could not be in relationship unless it was a marriage. She, like so many other women I've worked with, had no concept of a healthy brother-sister relationship. So when she ended up married to a wicked man, she could look to no other paradigm for an example of a healthy marital relationship. "What is kind, healthy touch anyway?" she lamented. When her church learned about his abuse, the leaders asked her what she had done to make her spouse mad. Had she not been submissive?

Her pastor advised that she have more sex with her husband. Because she was not permitted to say such things, she didn't tell him that her husband demanded sex whenever he wanted it and she always assented, even if it was demeaning and even if she was hurt. She left the conversation with her pastor defeated, feeling like she had to try even harder. Given the abuse and neglect she'd suffered, is it any wonder that she was confused and conflicted about touch?

Touch feels like a minefield for so many victims. What is safe? How can we consider it without something horrible blowing up? Is it even worth trying to figure out? It is worth it—and we'll figure it out together.

MINDFUL INVITATION

Re-regulating in a Peaceful Place

Talking about touch can bring up a lot of feelings and fears if you've been physically harmed. Sometimes having a peaceful place in mind can help manage such distressing feelings. Take a moment now, if you feel comfortable doing so, and breathe deeply. Think of something or somewhere pleasant. It can be a real place you've visited or one that you just imagine. There are only a couple of rules here—no people or pets allowed. While we love our sweet pets, they can occasionally be distressing. And people can be, well, "people-y" in not great ways even if they're awesome. This is meant to be a place of respite for you. If you're comfortable with Jesus or God being in this place with you, He is the exception to the rule.

Allow that place to come into focus and notice what you can there. Be sure to look for the details. Take your time. You are not in a rush. Notice any sights and sensations. Really allow them to come into focus for you. Spend a few moments there. Then notice whether there are any smells or tastes in this place. What do you sense? Can you bring those details into clearer focus? As you breathe into this peaceful place, notice what your body is doing. Are you still or moving? What are your hands and feet doing? Notice how the movement or stillness feels in your body. Allow your body to relax as you envision being in this peaceful place. Take some deep breaths, if you feel comfortable doing so, and spend as much time in this peaceful place as you desire. If it's helpful, you can name this place to help you remember it. Know you can return to it at any point.

KINDNESS VERSUS UTILITY

In her book *Handle with Care*, Lore Ferguson Wilbert says, "We need to teach how to touch with true *care*. Care for our own bodies and for the bodies of others, because those bodies were created by a good and caring God."[7] How do we learn healthy touch when touch has become sexualized, dangerous, and confusing? The good news is that we can learn safe touch and unravel the harm done to us. We can defuse the mines that seem triggered by touch.

When I read Wilbert's book, I was struck by her account of gently washing her face and extending herself compassion through self-touch.[8] While doing some story work with my amazing story coach,[9] I realized I had never touched myself that way. It helped explain why I was so undone and disoriented the first time a seminar facilitator invited me to touch my arms and face. It stunned me to realize how utilitarian I was in my self-touch. Of course I shower and wash my body. I engage in a skin-care routine. But those were not acts of kindness. Instead, they were acts of utility. Be clean, but who cares if you're kind to this body?

Turns out it really does matter, and learning kind self-touch is part of healing from abuse. When we were abused, neural pathways within our brain became sensitized. They learned that touch was not a safe experience. When touch by others has been a minefield, safely and kindly touching ourselves builds new neural pathways in our brains. Without this new experience, our bodies will remain resistant to all touch. Engaging in compassionate self-touch—as simple as gently stroking our arms—teaches our brains and bodies that touch can be safe.

When first invited to touch my arms and face, I started small. I placed my hands on my cheeks and just noticed how it felt. I'd love to say it felt awesome, but what I actually noticed was how awkward—even silly—I felt. I wanted to roll my eyes and just stop. But I also knew I needed to try it. So I refocused my mind on what I observed. I paid attention to the warmth of my hands. I noticed the coolness of my cheeks. I noticed that when I placed my hands on my cheeks, I automatically took a big, deep breath. I remember thinking, *That's interesting.* Then I noticed that my breathing had slowed down and other parts of my body relaxed into my hands touching my cheeks. Something felt *comforting* about this posture. It felt gentle. It felt safe, and it felt good.

I've since had clients practice self-touch. I guide them in session to do things like gently stroke their arms or hold their faces.

Sometimes I encourage them to gently place a hand on their chest and notice their breath. They take the time to feel how their hand feels against their chest and notice whether it's warm or cool. They notice how their skin responds—both the skin on their hands and the skin on their chest, even through clothes.

They also notice what emotions arise. Most feel awkward at first. It does feel a little silly, but it's so doggone helpful when they get used to it! Sometimes those first touches feel dangerous, though they are not. As the women learn to persevere through the hard moments, they notice feelings like self-compassion or grief. When bodies have been abused, touch, especially near sexual areas like breasts, can cause grief to well up. While grief may be uncomfortable, it's also healing. It's often the first indicator that what happened to someone was not okay, but it is okay to feel the sadness of that.

I was with a client recently who was processing some deep childhood sexual trauma. She was working hard to let herself walk through the pain of it and feel it and process the harm done to her. At one point I noticed her place her hand on her left shoulder. I softly asked, "Can you tell me about your left shoulder?" She shook a little as she talked. "This is where I feel shame starting to rise up in my body. I'm telling my body it's okay, and I'm safe to talk now. I'm giving my body compassion so she can keep doing the work."

I tried hard not to tear up as I observed this woman's deep compassion for herself as she gave her body the gentle touch it needed in that moment so we could keep processing. It was a simple but powerful use of self-touch in her healing process that day.

Now that we've had the opportunity to practice self-touch and get more used to that concept, let's consider touch from others. This can be really fear-inducing for a trauma survivor. Even something as simple as hugs can be triggering to someone whose body has learned to be on high alert. Alternatively, we can let people too close to us because our warning system is offline due to not being allowed to have physical boundaries with our abuser(s). But as we've noted, healthy touch from another human is vital to our well-being.

LET'S HAVE A WORD

Alluring

If I asked you to think of something you found particularly attractive or enticing, what would come to your mind? Though the term *alluring* has often been sexualized in our society, there are numerous appealing things in this world. A bright, well-laid-out clothing boutique is enticing and will draw you in. An artfully plated meal might be almost too pretty to eat. During a women's retreat for domestic abuse survivors, I led a discussion on wonderful words like *alluring* that too often we think of only in sexual contexts. Later that evening, I smiled as I began receiving numerous texts with pictures of attendees and their dinners that they had labeled *sensual* or *alluring*. It was a great joy because these women were applying these words in full appreciation of God's incredible goodness. It was, for some of them, the first and tiniest step of freedom in gaining an expanded view of the world. I know it may not seem like much, but some days the tiniest of movements is what's needed to start to shift the whole ship.

By now you may know that, for me, one of the most alluring sights is a hiking trail leading to a waterfall or clear, cold creek. The thick canopy of trees, the soft dirt trail, and the sound of moving water draw me in. I feel excited and expectant at the trailhead, and the experience orients me to my Creator who made these good things.

Mindful Moment

What do you find alluring? What draws you in? Try to focus on the positive things. What do you notice in your body as you bring this alluring image to mind? Take a few moments to journal about it.

LEARNING TO ACCEPT TOUCH FROM OTHERS

I cried out as my chiropractor tried to adjust my lower back and hips. I felt a searing, white-hot pain. I whimpered through the adjustment, praying I could keep myself on the table. He was a kind man and was not trying to hurt me. Unfortunately, my body registered any touch in that area as dangerous and sent pain signals to my brain to try to protect me.

Shame welled up in my body, a hot, tingly feeling that crept up my neck and wrapped around my face. My skin flushed, and my eyes burned with tears. At first I was angry at my body for protesting over treatment I knew would help her function better. Then I remembered that she was just trying to protect me, and memories of harm were still locked up in her. From working with my clients and talking to countless women at retreats, I knew I wasn't alone in this experience.

"I don't know why hugs hurt me," Sheila lamented. "They're supposed to be pleasant. Maybe I'm just not a hugger?" She had left an abusive relationship, but her body wasn't sure it was free. Her nervous system was stuck in the fight/flight/freeze response, and her body knew only how to register pain to try to keep her safe.

If you relate to the experiences of me and Sheila, you'll want to begin the process of helping your body digest what happened to it during abuse and learn a different way forward to allow you to accept healthy touch from another person.

The path to healing starts with compassion for yourself. I have yet to meet anyone who has beaten themselves into submission. Understanding that your body is doing what it can to protect you—even when it no longer needs the same protection—is the starting point to help it learn to process touch differently. Also, patience is essential. The way forward is rarely as fast as we want it to be. And really, isn't that often how healing is? Never as fast as we want it to be.

Beyond practicing gentle self-touch, one tool I've seen clients use to reorient themselves to healthy touch is massage therapy. A skilled, trauma-informed massage therapist who is able to truly hear what level of pressure you need is ideal. Some of my clients need light pressure, which often doesn't feel gentle to the trauma survivor at first. The massage therapist also needs to be open to any places the survivor is or is not comfortable with touch and go slowly. For example, a survivor may be totally fine with a neck and shoulder massage but not yet ready for hip or leg massage. A good massage therapist will honor that.

Trauma touch therapy can be a helpful type of massage for those who've been abused.[10] Massage therapists trained in this modality use somatic experiencing, which helps clients release the bodily sensations connected to trauma and then move back into their bodies. It's often most effective when done in conjunction with excellent counseling because things may come up during the massage that need to be processed. An amazing trauma touch massage therapist I know keeps a notebook and pen close by her so that clients can jot down what bubbles up and take it to their therapists.

I have seen trauma touch therapy help unlock many of my clients' bodies, which helps further their healing journey. It's a burgeoning field, so if you have a massage therapist you really like you might suggest they get trained in this method!

If you aren't ready for a full-on massage, manicures and pedicures can begin orienting you to touch. Some people love these and some do not. You might have to try it if you haven't (or if it's been a while) and see how you feel about it. Most manicures and pedicures come with a brief massage component, so you can see how your body responds to touch. Like anything else, if it doesn't go as planned the first time, don't give up. Sometimes you may have to try things multiple times; process them with counseling, a support group, or friends; perhaps try a different salon or space.

COMPASSIONATE TOUCH

Start by taking a deep breath and getting comfortable. You can be in any position that feels good to your body. Take a few moments, with your eyes open or closed, to just settle in where you are. If it feels safe and comfortable to you, gently place your palms on your cheeks. Notice the warmth or coolness of your hands on your face. Notice how your body responds to the touch. If you feel contempt rising up, notice it without judging it. Try to refocus your mind and body on pleasant sensations if you're able to notice them. Perfection is not required here; gentleness toward self is key.

As you're comfortable, try touching other parts of your body with compassion. Can you say a kind thing about each body part? If you struggle, that's okay. Just keep trying to find one kind thing. Get help from a therapist, support group, or friend as needed.

HAVENING

Where do you begin if the idea of self-touch feels totally foreign to you? A good place might be to try the practice of havening,[11] which I often lead clients in my private practice through. Havening is a way to self-soothe and incorporate gentle self-touch. When touch has become harmful, this is a way to experience it as safe and to calm your nervous system.

Start by rubbing your palms together for as long as you'd like. I encourage clients to start by doing it for one minute. If you aren't used to practicing mindfulness skills, a minute may feel like four hundred years and that's okay. Set a timer if that helps it feel more contained.

Then try giving yourself a hug and rubbing your arms. Practice that for one minute. Breathe normally and just focus on the touch. If you notice your mind wandering or shame popping up, be gracious to yourself. Gently, and without judgment, turn your thoughts back to what you're doing and the present moment.

Finally, taking your fingertips, start at your hairline (or where it would be if you don't have one) and stroke down your face. Practice this for one minute. Again, feel free to set a timer if this helps it feel more contained as you learn the practice. If you find this practice helpful, you can gradually increase the time. I usually encourage clients to work toward ten minutes per day of overall mindfulness practice because there is good evidence that it helps reduce anxiety and depression.

As you practice havening, you may notice emotions arise and that's okay. Just notice them and let them come. If it's distressing, practice another grounding skill that is a resource for you.

WHY TOUCHY-FEELY CAN BE A GOOD THING

Touching and Its Role in Your Body

With the coming of Jesus to earth, God's characteristics were expressed concretely in the body of Jesus. He touched and was touched.

LORE FERGUSON WILBERT, *Handle with Care*

I'm fortunate to have good brothers and sisters who give me the safe touch we all need. One close brother in Christ often puts a hand on my shoulder, squeezes my shoulder or arm, or puts his arm around me as we talk. I feel known by and cared for by this person. He is in no way inappropriate, and I'm friends with his wife. He's just a kind friend, and touch is one way that he shows his care and warmth.

I noticed this sense of being known with my very best female friend as well. One day when I was having an incredibly hard day, she graciously put her arms around me and held me. I put my head on her shoulder. When she had a dark moment while sitting with me in church, I took her hand. After years of healthy, nonsexual touch for the both of us, we have a close, beautiful friendship. The ways that our brains and bodies work together have created a very precious and life-giving connection for us.

If the only touch you've been exposed to has been sexual and harmful, I realize that just the mention of intimate touch may send you spinning. But there is such a thing as *healthy nonsexual intimate touch*. As someone in recovery from sexual harm, this is something I think so much about. Nonsexual intimate touch includes receiving long hugs, holding or squeezing hands, or touching an arm during a conversation. When we relegate physical touch to guarded side hugs or sexual touch only, we miss out on so much.

That's why, after practicing embodiment and safe self-touch, another way to move forward from trauma is to begin allowing friends to touch you and allowing yourself to touch them. As already mentioned, even if touch isn't your primary love language, you need it as a human being. You can go slow and tell your friends what you're trying to do. Many clients have told me this feels awkward, but when they do it, they report that it ended up being life-giving and connecting. It helps them build deeper relationships. If you're neurodiverse and have sensory issues, giving and accepting hugs may be more of a challenge. You are still human and still need touch, but the setting and sensory input should be tailored to your unique needs. A therapist skilled in working with neurodiverse people could be a real asset as you explore healthy touch after abuse.

The bottom line: I believe intimate touch is vitally important no matter who you are.

Once at a women's retreat, I explained that hugs should last about twenty seconds to get the oxytocin flowing.[1] Then I warned them all to get ready for the awkward hugs! While many of the women laughed, I lost count of how many purposely found me for long, awkward hugs afterward. They needed the comfort and closeness (not to mention the oxytocin release) that such hugs can bring. As an abuse survivor where touch wasn't safe, you may have learned to live without it. If you need an actual invitation to bring more safe touch into your life, please accept this as my invitation to you to explore this sort of connection.

One caveat I'll give about seeking healthy, nonsexual, intimate touch: Know who you're touching. This relates to the opposite sex in particular, but it really does apply to anyone you allow to touch you. The men I touch and allow to touch me are good friends who have proven themselves as trustworthy. They are truly brothers—not predators trying to act like brothers. If you aren't sure you can yet discern which men are safe, then start moving toward touch in safe female relationships. I can't stress enough that, as a survivor early in the healing process, it can be easy to get sucked in by someone who seems safe but isn't. On the other hand, it's also easy to reject touch entirely. We're looking for that healed middle path—healthy non-sexual intimate touch from safe people.

In chapter 4, we talked about learning to be embodied. This also helps us know when touch is healthy and when it's not. I love a good hug most of the time—but there are times when I avoid them. I've learned to listen better to my body. She knows what's up faster than my brain can process input and give me a cognitive thought. For example, when an acquaintance hugged me longer than I was comfortable with, my body reacted immediately. This person had not yet earned trust commensurate with a long hug so nothing about it felt good. My body stiffened and my heart rate accelerated. I heard my body and listened.

You may wonder whether I confronted this person. No, I didn't. The hug wasn't malicious; it was just out of place for the type and nature of the relationship. I did, however, make myself unavailable for further hugging by stepping back from this person. Having boundaries does not always mean verbally expressing them. It may mean adjusting physical proximity. If the distance between us had not been respected, however, I would have spoken up. Knowing your boundaries and being able to hold them is vital to healthy touch.

HOW INTENSELY SHOULD YOU HOLD A BOUNDARY?

Because of their need for self-protection, survivors commonly hold tighter boundaries than necessary in certain situations. If the intensity with which we hold boundaries ranges from one to ten, with ten being strongest, the women I work with often go right to a ten, even when such intensity might not be needed. For that reason, as my clients are practicing receiving safe touch from others, I teach them a skill designed to help them determine how intensely to hold their boundaries around touch. The questions below are adapted from Marsha Linehan's *DBT Skills Training Manual*.[2]

1. What capability do you and the other person have to meet the need? For instance, if you know you can offer a friendly greeting to an acquaintance at church but recognize that they are likely to overstep what's appropriate, the intensity of your boundary is likely to increase.

2. Next, what are your priorities? What are you trying to accomplish? A little distance? A complete severing of the relationship? As you can imagine, as you move toward cutting off a relationship, you're going to increase the intensity of your boundaries.

3. Are you setting a boundary because it's needed or because you're fearful (or is it needed *because* you're fearful since the other individual is not safe)? This is a time to ask some honest questions. Is setting the boundary necessary to care for yourself? If this is the case, your intensity in holding the line should increase. Is setting the boundary appropriate and godly? If you aren't sure, you may want to talk it out with a therapist, friend, or support group. Sometimes we need a little support as we learn how to relate to others after we've been abused.

Linehan terms the next aspect your "rights." In our context, we are going to look at it from the perspective of God's Word.

4. Is the person required to adhere to a boundary—such as not touching you in a way that feels unsafe—because doing so would be God honoring? If so, then your intensity level in limiting contact should increase.

As an aside, remember that you get to decide what is done with and to your body. It's *never* God honoring for someone to violate a boundary there. Ever. Do you have the authority to ask for what you need? When it comes to your body, yes, you most definitely do. If you are not comfortable with touch in a certain way, then you absolutely have authority over your own body. If you're married, I understand the sticky wicket presented by 1 Corinthians 7:3-5 (NLT):

> The husband should fulfill his wife's sexual needs, and the wife should fulfill her husband's needs. The wife gives authority over her body to her husband, and the husband gives authority over his body to his wife.
>
> Do not deprive each other of sexual relations, unless you both agree to refrain from sexual intimacy for a limited time so you can give yourselves more completely to prayer. Afterward, you should come together again so that Satan won't be able to tempt you because of your lack of self-control.

What I'll say is this: In a respectful, kind, nonabusive marriage, you will not be forced to do something you aren't comfortable with. Note, too, that husbands are also told they don't have authority over their own bodies, but rather their wives do. This means you can tell your husband you don't want his body on your body. And if you're in a relationship that is demeaning or unsafe, I encourage you to reach out to an organization like Called to Peace Ministries for help exploring whether the relationship is abusive.

5. Next you want to consider your goals, both short-term (immediate) and long-term. What do you want to be able to do? If you want to be able to feel comfortable with touch in the long term, then your boundaries may be more intensely set in the

BODY & SOUL, HEALED & WHOLE

short term as you learn to navigate healthy touch. Boundaries are not a wall; instead, they are more like a fence where you can open and close the gate or move the limits as needed. You may start with a more stringent boundary that you loosen as you learn the person is safe. As I mentioned previously, the men I allow to touch me appropriately are the ones who have proven themselves over and over as safe.

6. Linehan calls another consideration give-and-take, but I'm going to call it mutuality. After all, the Bible talks about mutuality in relationships. Women are made in the image and likeness of God, just as men are. According to the book of Genesis, people were told to have dominion over all the earth—but they were never told to have dominion over each other. Appropriate mutuality regarding honor and touch is important. First Timothy 5:2 says men are to treat "older women as mothers, and younger women as sisters, with absolute purity." If your boundaries regarding touch are crossed by someone, appropriate mutuality is lacking, so your intensity in holding that boundary should increase.

7. Err on the side of caution as you learn whether or not touch is okay with each person. It's okay to take your time. There is no rush as you learn. In some cases, if you've become overly touchy without being sure someone is safe, you might need to take a step back as you reevaluate.

   Good brothers will be gracious as you learn and grow, and they will understand that your needs might differ at various times. My client Lucy learned this as she explored healthy, nonsexual intimate touch with a male friend. One day her body was on fire after therapy where she'd engaged in hard and deep work. She saw her close friend John afterward. When he went to hug her, she instinctively recoiled from him. He was confused since she was usually eager to hug him.

"Therapy was rough today," Lucy said. "I feel a lot in my body right now, and a hug doesn't feel good in this moment." John—being a good brother—honored that statement without shaming her or pushing the boundary. As they hung out and talked, her body calmed and moved back into rest. Once she told him she could handle a hug, he gave her a long twenty-second embrace with her full consent and comfort. John could have been offended when Lucy first refused a hug. After all, she generally welcomed them and didn't she already know he was safe? Instead, John honored her and didn't take her boundary personally.

8. Finally, consider the timing. If you are struggling with touch in a given moment, hold a firmer boundary. For example, my client Adeline is neurodiverse. In situations where there is a lot of stimulation, like at a concert, physical touch is not welcome because all the stimulation combined basically short-circuits her brain. She keeps a firm boundary of no touch—no matter who you are—in those spaces. So hugging her in the middle of a rock concert would be a hard no—the timing would not be right. Afterward, when she is back at home in a more peaceful environment, touch may be welcome.

I know boundary setting can be confusing, especially if this is all new to you. Some people struggle to increase intensity while others need to dial back from a 10. That's okay. True friends who are safe will understand as you wrestle with your limits. If this is really hard and you need support, a DBT (dialectical behavior therapy) skills group (particularly the interpersonal effectiveness module) can be so helpful. A therapist or good friend who has healthy boundaries or is farther along the recovery road can help too.

This might seem like a lot. Just remember to take your time. The goal is progress, not perfection. One step at a time is just fine.

HOW TO EXPRESS YOUR NEEDS

If you're coming out of an abusive situation, you may not have been allowed to express any need or boundary. You may even have come to believe you aren't allowed to have needs. If that was your situation, it can be useful to have statements in mind to help you whenever you need to ask for what you need or say no to something.

Something you might not know about therapists is that we have to participate as a client and work on our own stuff whenever we learn new skills. I love this because I absolutely believe I can't take anyone where I'm not willing to go myself. After one training practice session, I was thoroughly dysregulated—meaning I had all the feels. I needed help getting back into my body, and physical co-regulation was the ticket to me getting there. Thankfully, I was able to ask a friend over lunch, "Hey, that last session was rough. May I please have a hug?" This particular friend isn't really a hugger, but he'll hug me if I ask. He graciously gave me a big hug, which helped me get back into my body. He also thanked me for asking for what I needed in that moment. I'll add the caveat that not all people will be comfortable with a hug when they're dysregulated. You know your body, but this is an example for me where I needed some physical touch to help me settle.

If having some ready responses could be helpful for you, here are some I've come up with. Feel free to modify them to match your needs and then consider trying them out. Practice helps build the muscle we need to say these things.

1. "Would you be willing to give me a hug right now? I could really use one."
2. "I'm not feeling huggy or touchy right now. I can let you know if that changes."
3. "Right now I need some space and don't want to be touched."
4. "It would feel really good if you could stand close to me."

A final reminder: You are allowed to ask for what you need and say no to something that's not okay for you in a given moment.

Remember: *Consent is an enthusiastic yes or it's a no. There is no in-between.*

As an abuse victim, you were not allowed to use your voice. Part of your healing and recovery is learning to use the beautiful voice God gave you. This might be super hard and take some work. Find safe people and practice with them. You might start with just your therapist, but ideally you'll work toward building a community that will be in this work with you—just like you'll be in their work with them.

Again, even if your love language isn't physical touch, you need it! In fact, touch can help you regulate your emotions.

PHYSICAL TOUCH AND CO-REGULATION

Robin, a sweet, soft-spoken client, sat across from me on my couch. I asked a question about the holidays, and as she told me a story of what happened, her countenance changed. Her body tightened, and tears began to flow. She was in deep distress, and her body shook as she sobbed. I asked her permission to come over and sit beside her, to which she agreed. Then I asked her gently if I could touch her arm. She agreed. As I sat beside her with my hand on her arm, I took unhurried, deliberate breaths, slowing my own body's physiology. Over time, her body began to quiet too. She melted into the couch. I stayed close to her as we worked through the trauma she'd experienced.

What happened? How did her body shift simply from my presence and touch? The simple answer is co-regulation. Her nervous system was able to sync with mine and slow down. Co-regulation begins with attunement, which is defined as "to bring into harmony; to make aware or responsive."[3] It begins in childhood with our caregivers.[4] When we attune to another human, we are being responsive to them as we bring ourselves into harmony. Psychiatrist Curt Thompson says, "We all are born into the world looking for someone looking for us."[5] We need healthy, secure attachment. We may or may not have gotten that as a child, but we surely did not get that in our abusive situations. We can, however, form secure attachment with friends.

While physical touch isn't always part of co-regulation, it can be and sometimes is necessary. Dr. Thompson also says, "Healing shame requires our being vulnerable with other people in embodied actions. There is no other way."[6] This means being in our bodies with other people.

We have nerve cells in our brains called mirror neurons that quite literally do what they're called. Mirror neurons fire when we observe another human doing something—like attuning to us calmly and with empathy and compassion.[7] Our brains and body physiology line up. While mirror neurons and co-regulation can happen via video (like during a Zoom session), they seem to work best when we're actually in the same physical location with someone else.

That is why when we're upset and a good friend who is calm and physically present hugs or sits close to us, our bodies can begin to regulate with theirs. They might put a hand on our arm, wrap an arm around us, or sit next to us with our sides touching. There are many ways someone can help us physically co-regulate.

I know the power of co-regulation from personal experience. Once when I was about to teach on this topic at a women's retreat, I had a panic attack that just about took me out. Several of my friends saw I was not doing okay, and they came to support me. As we gathered in the hallway, one friend sat down with me on a bench outside the room where I'd soon be speaking. We sat body to body, our shoulders down to our ankles touching. She slowed her breathing and was just present with me. Another friend prayed aloud for me as she laid hands on me. Slowly, my body returned to a calm, non-panicky baseline. What I remember most was that I felt *loved. Deeply loved.*

That is the power of safe touch. When we learn to feel loved and cared for, to have healthy, nonsexual intimate touch, we can move toward healthy sexual intimate touch.

Even so, we're not quite ready to go there. First we need to talk about arousal structures and templates.

This exercise involves allowing a friend you trust to touch you. If you don't have a friend that you trust yet but have an older kiddo (about eight and up), you can try this with them.

Sit face-to-face with the other person. Place your palms against their palms (like you're about to play patty-cake). Notice what shifts or changes in your body. Ask them to notice what shifts or changes in their body. If you think it's silly, what do you notice about laughing together while you're still touching? Do other emotions come up? What happens if you try synchronizing your breathing together? Just notice the process and be curious. If you like, you can journal about it afterward.

WHAT TURNS YOU ON

Understanding Your Arousal Structures

As we begin this journey, ask yourself, Where is it that I come from? And where is it that I am going? *May your heart be curious as you study the great tragedy and beauty that your story reveals.*

JAY STRINGER, *Unwanted*

My client Esther sat forward on my couch. Her body was tense as she told me how mad and frustrated she was at herself. We were processing some recent challenges, and she wasn't sure where they were coming from. She was confused as to why she struggled during winter every single year. She was plagued by anxiety, but she couldn't put her finger on the cause. "I'm starting to feel like I'm crazy!" she told me. I assured her she wasn't crazy.

As we worked together to figure out the source of her current stress, I asked how old she felt. She told me she felt young—maybe seven. I asked her to float back in her mind to that time period and tell me what she noticed. Her face suddenly contorted in pain and sorrow as the tears began to fall. Her breath quickened, and she covered her face with her hands.

She said, "I can smell the cinnamon rolls my mom was baking."

I helped her breathe into the moment and access the memories safely. She went on to describe the fear and shame she had experienced whenever her father yelled and called her stupid and lazy for forgetting to feed the dogs or pick up her toys. She said she never felt his approval and always felt so small and scared when he walked into the room. Due to his business in landscape architecture, he was only really home in the winter. As her mind took her back to that time, her body was vividly feeling all those seven-year-old sensations in the present moment. I gently helped her work through and process that memory, helping her body metabolize the trauma she had experienced.

I imagine that if we could have done a brain scan as we talked, we'd have seen Esther's brain light up like a Christmas tree. If we could have tracked her vital signs, we'd have measured increased blood pressure, heart rate, respiration, and maybe even sweat. We'd have seen a high level of arousal that, in this situation, we'd call dysregulation.

Arousal is a state of excitation. Our brain is activated by stimuli, and we feel and act because of it.[1] Arousal has a role to play in many aspects of life, not just sexual function.[2] Arousal helps us wake up. It stimulates our autonomic nervous system—the part of our bodies that controls everything that is done automatically. Arousal—positive or negative—also has an impact on our emotions. When stimulus comes in and we make meaning of it, our emotions are activated.

Dan Allender calls the mosaic of things that bring us pleasure our arousal structure.[3] Odds are there are a ton of things that bring you pleasure—a great meal, your child's laughter, a beautiful location, a sunrise or sunset. As we've seen, we can get aroused by lots of things that are neither sexual nor negative.

Sometimes, though, arousal *is* sexual. Sally told me about a chill girl's night with a few women in their thirties. They had gathered around a fire on a fall evening after a good dinner. A few of them held glasses of wine as they transitioned to a dessert of dark chocolate s'mores. They were talking about things women talk about when in a close group of safe women. In this case the conversation led to sex.

LET'S HAVE A WORD

Arousal

Have you ever been in a football stadium during the final minute of a tied game between rivals? When the teams huddled on the sidelines during a time-out, the air around you was likely charged with the sounds of cheers and whistles. You may have caught yourself smiling at someone nearby who was wearing a similar jersey to yours and giving a thumbs-down to the people a few rows over whose hats identified them as fans of the other team. As the players broke and ran back on the field, you and all the other fans in that stadium were experiencing arousal—a state of physiological or psychological excitation and activation.

We can get aroused by many things that are neither sexual nor negative. An exciting sports contest is just one example. But if you're a trauma survivor, you are likely more familiar with negative factors that lead to intense emotional reactions. We often call these triggers. When someone says they're "triggered" by something—a thought, smell, sight, or sound—the emotions or body sensations commensurate with a traumatic experience come rushing back. Triggers are arousing; they awaken the body, mind, and senses, generally in negative ways.

Clinician Deb Dana, who is an authority on complex trauma, talks about *glimmers*. These are the opposite of triggers. While they also activate our minds and bodies, these positive sensations and experiences bring a sense of safety and well-being.[4] They also cause excitation, but we perceive them as pleasant. In fact, glimmers are regulating. They help us feel *on-kilter* (not a word, but we're gonna use it!).

Glimmers can be internal or external. When I'm doing a resource spot for clients—identifying a pleasant place they can notice when things are hard—we look for peaceful places on or in their bodies, even if it's very small.

I'll say, "Let's check in with your body. Start at the top of your head and work your way down. What feels at peace? Maybe even feels good? Bring your awareness there." We'll spend some time noticing that pleasantness. These feelings are internal glimmers.

External glimmers may be an epic sunrise or sunset or a cold mountain stream on a hot day. For example, when I was writing this chapter, I was facing a gorgeous lake and could watch the sunlight reflect off the water. Occasional boats meandered by, causing the lake to ripple. I could hear a small waterfall nearby and the birds calling out to each other. These glimmers were incredibly regulating to my nervous system.

One of the ladies took a sip of her beverage and said, "I don't
know what's going on with me! This fire is turning me on!"

Some of the ladies laughed, a couple of them nervously. One of
them said, "I don't get it. I mean, fires can be romantic . . . but turning you on? That sounds weird."

Actually, it's not at all strange. Each person has an arousal
template—a unique collection of thoughts, images, sensory details,
etc., that stimulates their sexual interest. It helps explain why nonsexual things can sometimes trigger sexual thoughts.

As we dive into the concept of arousal, as well as arousal templates
and structure, it's important to maintain a curious posture toward
ourselves. These can be hard and triggering topics, but ones we need
to talk about. When I work with survivors, I often hear them vilify
their experiences and speak with self-contempt. But we can't change
what we aren't curious about, and I've yet to meet anyone who beat
themselves into healing or being healthier. What isn't addressed can
breed shame, and shame thrives in darkness. I hope you'll use the
skills I've woven throughout this book to help you hold your story
with curiosity.

AROUSAL AND AROUSAL STRUCTURES

Sexual arousal in particular involves a complex interplay between
your body and brain. The mix of physical sensations, emotions, and
thoughts involved in arousal vary significantly from person to person
and even from one moment to the next. When something triggers
your sexual interest, whether it's a touch, a thought, or a sight, your

body responds by releasing hormones and increasing blood flow to certain areas. This can lead to an increased heart rate, increased breath rate, and increased blood flow to the genitals. Alongside these physical changes, your brain sends signals of pleasure and desire, which are reflected in our emotions.

But how do we know what stimulus leads to sexual arousal? What, specifically, turns us on?

As we talk more about healthy sexual activity, we need to understand what Dr. Patrick Carnes calls an *arousal template*—"the total constellation of thoughts, images, behaviors, sounds, smells, sights, fantasies, and objects that arouse us sexually."[5] Our arousal templates and structures are formed in a variety of places, not just the bedroom. They are shaped by our faith, family, friends, the media we consume, and more. These factors register at a subconscious level, according to Dr. Alexandra Katehakis.[6] They aren't something we generally choose. I have never met or read about anyone who said, "I think I'd like to be aroused by a picturesque sunset."

To put it another way, our arousal structures and templates are the mosaic or compilation of things that give us pleasure sexually in some way. They're a subconscious weaving together that has been influenced by a host of different stimuli across a large number of seemingly diverse areas. Arousal templates also begin to form early on in our lives—from the moment we enter the world—and shift and change across our lifespan. Some preferences may remain relatively static, like generally being attracted to men with red hair over dark hair. Other things, like being drawn to men who take charge in a group, may develop later on. Our arousal templates, however, aren't static, and things that were never intended to become sexualized can end up in the arousal template.[7]

Okay, you might be thinking, *could you give me an example in easy English?* Over time a woman may have experienced delight at a sunset (nonsexual), which brought her pleasure. Let's say the smell of spring (nonsexual) also is pleasurable to her. She may also have experienced joy when with an intimate partner who cares deeply for her (heading toward sexual). Perhaps this delight came with gentle, caring, and kind touches that culminated in physical pleasure like an orgasm (sexual). Let's say that, after they watched a gorgeous sunset over the ocean, the woman and her husband return to their secluded cottage where the scent of spring blossoms wafts in through an open window. If he begins touching her in a pleasurable way, she will likely experience sexual arousal. If this happens enough (and it probably wouldn't have to happen a lot), sunsets and spring scents will connect with sexual arousal, and she will likely experience arousal when those sensory experiences happen together—just like Sally's friend noticed that she was "turned on" (sexually aroused) by standing by the campfire.

Other factors play into sexual arousal as well—such as what we believe about sex, where we are in our menstrual cycle (due to the hormones in our bodies), and the physical and emotional characteristics in our intimate partners that we're attracted to. This is an oversimplification of a very complex process, but I'm hoping you get the idea. Because neurons that fire together wire together, when we experience pleasurable experiences like a sunset and spring scents, they might lead to sexual thoughts because those items have become part of our arousal template.

WHEN TRAUMA TARNISHES YOUR TEMPLATE

Our example's arousal template was built around memorable sensory delights and the love of a caring husband. Too often, however, the arousal templates of the women I see are fused to violence or other stimulus by repeated exposure to pornography or violence or other harm done in the bedroom. By the time I see them, sex is often the last thing they're ready to discuss, both because it feels utterly terrifying and because they are still in the immediate aftermath of dealing with abuse. They may have already been harshly judged for the abuse they suffered ("What did you do to make him mad?" is something too many of them hear), and they fear I will judge them too. Sex is neither good nor safe to them. It's the stuff of living nightmares.

But it's a topic that we need to discuss. And when the women are brave enough to go there in my office, I see healing take place. Together we begin to pick up the pieces so they can move toward a sexuality that is far more beautiful than they dare to dream. We begin by looking at the ways their arousal template has become distorted.

Completion and mastery

Like many of my clients, Annie is a trauma survivor who experienced sexual assault as a college student. Annie is a force. She doesn't always see it, but as I've watched her heal over the years, I've seen her presence and personal agency grow. She's smart, witty, and a ball of energy. She often whirls into my office like a Texas tornado, ready to get down to the business of healing. On this day, however, she came in timid and looking defeated. She slumped on the couch and promptly pulled a big pillow into her lap. I spent a moment studying her face and body language. Something big was up.

I slowed my breathing and slowed myself down to match her. "Annie, I'm so glad you're here. What's happening in your body right now?"

She teared up and took a big breath. "Everything feels heavy. I'm a mess. I don't even know how to say this."

I gave her the gentle space I knew she needed in that moment. As her face dampened with falling tears, she hid her face behind the pillow and haltingly said, "I've been going home with random men. When I go out, I have no intention of doing that, but then I just do. I'm not sleeping with them, but I'm spending the night at their houses. I'm such a stupid sinner. What is wrong with me? I'm asking to be raped. *Again.*"

"Oh, Annie. You are not just a stupid sinner. You're trying to work through the trauma that resulted when you were raped. Let's talk about the concept of completion and mastery," I said kindly.

She peeked out from behind the pillow with a glimmer of hope and a good bit of skepticism.

What was I talking about? When we experience trauma and then try to process it, sometimes we make unconscious attempts to return to the previous trauma to "get it right this time"—to do what we wish we could have done the first time, to master our trauma.[8] In Annie's case, she had been raped by a boyfriend. When she went on what she thought was a normal date to dinner at his house—as she'd done a dozen times before—she had no way of knowing that he had other, wicked plans. Despite her saying no to him repeatedly when he began forcefully removing her clothes, he did not listen to her.

Now Annie was attempting to heal the trauma by going home with men and not sleeping with them. She was trying to master the situation she'd been harmed in. As you can imagine, going home with men you don't know is not a safe choice, and she was fortunate that she had not been harmed further. But her approach would never actually solve her issue because she couldn't go back to the same situation and have real mastery over it.

Traumatic reenactment

What people call "immorality" in sexual abuse survivors is almost always traumatic reenactment, where a survivor of trauma "re-create[s] and repetitively relive[s] the trauma in their present lives."[9] Someone who was sexually abused in childhood or in their marriage is likely to end up in future relationships with sexual abuse. Some well-meaning but I believe misguided folks surmise that the traumatized person must be addicted to trauma and therefore is continually seeking it out. That's not something I generally see in practice, though the brain may be conditioned to feel as if chaos is normal. Reenactments also can be triggered by strong emotions that feel too familiar to the trauma. For example, a survivor may fear abandonment and so pull away from a relationship before that can happen. Of course, this results in further abandonment, which reinforces the belief that abandonment is imminent, leading to more traumatic reenactment. It ends up being a vicious cycle.

Another reason survivors often continue to engage in unhealthy patterns is homeostasis. In other words, our internal systems of being want to stay static. Some survivors, therefore, return to familiar situations, even when they are harmful. If you have experienced sexual harm, it may feel oddly comfortable to you because it's what you know.[10] There is likely a good bit of cognitive dissonance (more on that in a bit), but our draw toward the familiar is so high that it can pull us back in. Not only that, but survivors may not realize that something is not normal. If you've experienced only harm in sexual relationships, how on earth would you have any idea what is healthy? Even when you do recognize that you've been harmed, your brain has been wired to accept it because of the way neural pathways are created.

Sorting through sexual harm and its effects on the arousal structures can be complicated. That's one reason I sometimes go with clients on a hike for a walk-and-talk session. These sessions are a little less formal than those in my office, but they're done very purposefully. We walk side by side or in single file. If single file, I walk in front of or behind my client, depending on their preference. Because walking is a form of bilateral stimulation that engages both sides of the brain, I find it's a great way for clients to process hard things without having to look directly at me as they share something.

One afternoon I was with my client Raina on one of these sessions. I was walking behind her when she suddenly stopped in the middle of the trail and whipped around. She looked up at the tree canopy and let out a loud and desperate groan. "I thought what my ex-husband was asking me to do was normal. I thought I'd said my yes to everything at the altar. When I asked my dad about it, he told me men have needs, and it was my duty as a wife to meet them. So even though nothing felt good and he hurt me and asked so many awful things of me, I just did what I thought all women do. It got worse and worse and I was able to escape, but now I keep finding men who are domineering and it's their way or the highway. I feel irreparably broken." Raina sat down in the dirt and wept.

I got down there with her and held space as Raina grieved and wrestled with her experience. She shared that her mother had once confided in her that her dad was addicted to pornography. Then her mother told her it must have been her own fault because she wasn't available enough sexually. Raina said she grew up thinking she must provide complete satisfaction for her husband in the bedroom or she'd have a porn-addicted husband too. She reenacted her mother's trauma, then her own.

Slowly, she and I processed the trauma, sitting on the ground together as sunlight filtered through the trees and wind fluttered the leaves. I find that some of the best healing happens in the dirt—in the dirt on the trail, and in the dirt of our own hearts.

How a survivor might enter into trauma reenactment is as individual as the survivor herself. If you're reading this and thinking, *Oh no. This sounds a lot like me*, please don't lose heart. Traumatic reenactment is such a normal reaction among the women I work with. So often I hear, "How did I end up in another terrible relationship with another abuser?" I'm so glad you're here. This doesn't have to be your forever story. Just by reading this book, you're taking an active part in the process of healing and changing.

Trauma bonding

We are created for community and connection with others. However, a trauma bond is formed when we become attached to our abusers.[11] This can happen in childhood during abuse or as an adult in an abusive relationship. Until she recognized that her first husband was an abuser, whenever Raina felt uneasy about what he asked her to do in their bedroom, she immediately reminded herself how well he provided for them financially. She also felt it was her duty as a wife to please him in all respects. She had seen her mother do that with her father, so it was what she knew, and she felt beholden to her husband because he held all the cards in their relationship. Trauma bonding is a survival mechanism wherein the abuse victim takes care of the abuser. The victim may ignore abusive behavior and focus on

CONNECTING WITH CREATION

As you now know, it's not unusual for me to do sessions in the woods with clients. Sometimes it's far easier for a client to regulate her nervous system in the woods than in my office. In fact, research supports this. Twenty minutes in nature can reduce our levels of cortisol, our stress hormone.[12]

This has been true in my own experience as well. In 2022, I had the worst physical year of my life, nearly dying from the confluence of several medical issues. It felt like I was warring against my body in so many ways, while she was begging me to truly hear her. Finally, I began regaining some physical strength. On my way to a retreat in 2023, I decided to attempt to hike my favorite mountain. Many years prior, it had been not only my first hiking summit, but because the Appalachian Trail crosses it, it was also my first time touching those white blazes (markers) on the trail.

So coming back as I healed seemed fitting. I vowed to listen to my body and not fight against her. If she was able to climb it all, great. If not, also great. That day, my body got me to the summit where I was treated to sweeping, 360-degree views of the Blue Ridge Mountains. The weather was near perfect, and because it was a weekday, only a couple of other people were up there.

Tears slid down my face as I beheld God's creation. I lay in the grass, feeling the mountain summit beneath me, looking up at the sky as my headphones played Lori Estelle's "You Restore." The lyrics quote Psalm 23 about God making us lie down in green pastures. As this part played, I noticed that I felt at peace and fully present in my body.

Connecting to creation makes a difference.

the times of rest and ease or moments of kindness. After describing how their husbands have wounded them through words or actions, clients often tell me, "But he's not like that every moment; there are times when things are okay or even good."

Exposure

Neural pathways are built based on what we're exposed to. The more something is presented to us, and the more legitimized it is, the more normal it becomes to us. This is a concept called habituation.[13] Mere exposure to sexualized ads, pornography, violence, and the like makes it appear more normal to our senses. Before we know it, something has been woven into our way of seeing the world that would not otherwise have been.

Another way we may experience exposure is from our very own brain. When we tell ourselves in the thick of an abusive situation that everything is fine, okay, and normal, we may inadvertently be habituating ourselves to harm. So many survivors do exactly this when held captive in an abusive marriage. If they've been told that they must submit no matter the cost and that the husband has the final say because of his headship, they may believe that this is just the way things are, that this is what normal and godly looks like. In my practice, I've noticed that when women finally realize that is not accurate, they see they have been drinking poison for a long time. No wonder change is difficult!

Exposure also comes from the sheer number of messages Christian women receive about what healthy sex and sexuality look like. Often what they've heard is nothing like what the Bible says. Thanks to purity culture telling evangelical women that they are solely responsible for men's lust issues, they often come to me with significant distortions about sexuality.

As a teen who grew up in what was ostensibly supposed to be a grace-based denomination, I heard plenty about what women could and could not wear. My clothes were critiqued at youth events. Youth leaders sent letters home with me and the other girls about what the dress code was for any event. There was never any mention of what boys were and were not to wear. I distinctly recall feeling that if a boy lusted after me, it was wholly my fault. As mentioned earlier in this chapter, arousal templates are influenced by a myriad of factors—including our faith tradition.

VIOLENCE AND AROUSAL

How do completion and mastery, traumatic reenactment, trauma bonding, and exposure show up in the arousal template? Remember that pleasure and pain can register in the same parts of the brain.[14] That is why the adage that there is a fine line between pain and pleasure is true.[15] I often work with teens who self-harm. As we talk about the process they engage in, very often they will tell me the pain actually feels *good*. That's because it gives a dopamine hit to their brain.[16] We also see this with tattoos. Have you ever heard someone say tattoos are addictive or arousing? This is because neurochemicals are released when one is applied, so despite the pain, getting one may feel like a pleasurable experience in some way. It stands to reason that when we combine pain with sexual pleasure, violence may be woven into our arousal structure. Neurons that fire together wire together.

If someone is tied up and painfully hit during sexual activity that results in an orgasm, the same parts of the brain are lighting up in response to the violence and sexual release. If this happens often enough, the arousal template may be adjusted to include pain. Like your social media algorithm, your arousal template adjusts to show you more of what it thinks you want. That means even when the abuse ends, survivors may find they are aroused only if violence is included. I also think it's important to note again here that our bodies can respond with feelings of pleasure even in horrific situations. This can be extremely tough for survivors who don't know what is happening. They may feel as if they must have wanted the abuse because their body responded with pleasure and they're aroused by violence. We can see attempts at completion and mastery here, as well as the result of exposure.

For clients like Annie and Raina, confronting the darker elements that have been woven into their arousal templates is difficult work. Yet acknowledging where we are with self-compassion and curiosity is the first step to healing. As Kristen Neff says, "The only way to eventually free ourselves from debilitating pain . . . is to *be* with it as it is. *The only way out is through*."[17]

FINDING THE INTERNAL GLIMMER
(INTERNAL RESOURCE SPOTS)

This is a great exercise to help you learn to notice the God-given resources in your own body. I've done this with survivors in big groups, and it's so fun to process their experiences at the end. They're often as different as individual snowflakes because they're as unique as the person doing the exercise.

Sit or lie in a comfortable position. Take as many moments as you need to let your breath become steady and even. Then starting at the top of your head or the bottoms of your feet, just begin noticing what you feel in your body. Look for areas that feel good or at peace. It can be the smallest area—like your pinkie toe or your eyelashes. It doesn't matter the size or location. When you notice it, focus your attention there and notice the feeling of peace or goodness. Linger there as long as you like. Consider journaling about your experience afterward. Were you surprised by what you noticed or where you noticed it?

CONNECTION TO CREATION
MINDFULNESS

I'd love to help you find a way to connect with nature like I do with my clients. I want you to have the benefit of the healing God provides us there.[18]

We are God's creation, and we are connected to other aspects of God's creation. For example, we are connected to the earth by gravity. If we didn't have that we'd go flying off into space. We're connected to air by the breath in our lungs that brings us life. We're connected to our children through biology. We're connected to our friends through relationships that take place in the very real material world. We're connected to the body of Christ through the indwelling of the Holy Spirit in our actual living and breathing bodies. This exercise helps us take time to notice our connectedness to creation.

You can do this exercise inside or outside, according to your preference. Lie down on a comfortable surface. Notice the surface and how it feels under you. Notice how gravity keeps you connected to that surface. Think a positive phrase like, *God keeps me connected to the earth, and He is always here for me.* Try to notice your breath in your lungs as you breathe in. Notice the gift of air. As you breathe, notice your body slowing down, supported by the surface beneath you. Notice your breath expand a bit and your body soften into the surface you are lying on. Stay in this place as long as you like. When complete, perhaps journal about the experience.

Come back to the exercises any time you need to.

8

DISENTANGLING

Building Healthy Arousal Structures

*May your heart be curious as you study the great
tragedy and beauty that your story reveals.*

JAY STRINGER, *Unwanted*

My client Ellie opened her husband's underwear drawer to put his clean clothes away and stumbled across a stack of pornographic DVDs. As she instinctively picked one up and read the title, her body recoiled. She dropped the disc back in the drawer, slammed it shut, and sank down on their bed. She was stunned. She had no idea her husband watched porn. She was confused and felt ill.

When he arrived home, she confronted him. He told her he used the films to enhance his sexual ability. She didn't believe him at first, but he was so convincing. When he told her they should watch them together, she refused. He claimed that viewing them would put her at ease and teach her a few things. He insisted that he was leading her as her husband and that all sexual things were permitted once a couple was married—nothing was off-limits. She'd married him as a virgin, and she wanted to be submissive to his decisions. Not only that, but she wasn't aware of any instructional books for Christians on sexual intercourse, so she reluctantly agreed.

The first time they watched one of the videos, Ellie felt repulsed but also strangely drawn to what she was seeing. Her husband seemed to be very pleased with her too. As time progressed, the content of what her husband wanted to watch with her became darker and darker. She began to feel scared and ashamed of what he asked of her after they'd watched a video, but she also felt helpless to make it stop. After all, she had agreed to make this part of their sex life.

Other areas of their relationship were scary too. He controlled everything, from their finances to where she was permitted to go and with whom she could spend time. He flew into a rage if he even suspected she might disagree or—heaven forbid—disobey him. Eventually, after reading a series of books and online articles, Ellie realized she was in an abusive relationship and sought help from her church. They provided access to counseling and protection when her husband threatened to harm her. She left her abusive marriage, worked hard at healing, and eventually remarried a lovely man. But something inside her still felt stuck, so she came to see me.

As we continued to work through her trauma, she eventually trusted me enough to tell me the story of being drawn into pornography by her ex-husband. Her body, covered by the weighted blanket in my office, shook as she covered her face with her hands and said, "I don't know how to say this. I can't think of sex without thinking of pornography and sometimes . . . a lot of times . . . I go looking for what I used to watch with my ex. *What is wrong with me?* Why do I feel like I need to do that in order to even engage in sex? I can never, ever tell my current husband, even though it's getting in the way of our relationship. I know good Christian girls don't do this."

There is nothing at all wrong with Ellie—or with you if this story feels familiar. Ellie's story is stunningly common for women who were forced to use pornography by their abusers. As with other forms of violence, pornography use and pornographic images can become fused to the arousal template. Remember, neurons that fire together wire together. It is really important for us to directly combat toxic shame here.

In addition to scenarios of sexual activity, pornography includes another hallmark: violence. Porn often depicts domestic violence against women,[1] including marital rape.[2] In fact, porn consumption is a huge problem among young people. It quite literally sets the stage for later domestic abuse due to its devaluation of sex and women, as well as its total distortion of healthy sexuality.[3] Porn dehumanizes women[4] and normalizes male aggression in sex.

Pornography use by those in the church is prevalent—more prevalent than I think folks would like to admit or talk about.[5] One reason that the fallout from pornography is so insidious is that, even if we are repulsed by the content, our bodies may experience arousal after viewing it. That is a total mind-bender for most people.[6] One reason I often point this out to my clients is that, after suffering so much, they are likely to be confused and ashamed about its impact in their own lives.

BDSM (a sexual practice that often involves bondage and the giving and receiving of pain) is often included in pornography, and some people say it can be a healthy part of a consensual adult sexual relationship. I wholeheartedly disagree. Any time one person dominates another for their personal gratification, it is a problem. Sex should be a beautiful, pleasurable experience for both parties with no one being demeaned.

I've worked with some survivors who have engaged in BDSM, and their arousal templates include violence. This is a super tough topic for many women, especially Christians. In such situations, activities that have been fused to their arousal templates do not align with their values system. This creates great distress for them. Other abuse survivors, on the other hand, may think, *Well, now I'm in the dominant position.* That perspective sure sounds like either attempted completion and mastery or trauma reenactment. The arousal templates of those who feel drawn to BDSM have been fused to violence and may need some gentle adjusting.

I don't come to my concerns over porn and BDSM lightly. They come from many years of working with women who have been sexually harmed, teaching domestic abuse advocacy, and being one of the authors and teachers of a course on intimate partner sexual violence. I hear stories daily that are horrific.

I'm not a prude when it comes to sexual activity, and I firmly believe it should be amazing and fun for both parties. But I also am not a fan of women being told something is healthy when it is not. Domination of another, humiliation of another, and harm to another do not fit within God's paradigm for healthy sex—whether you are the harmer or the harmed.

As much as I despise pornography and BDSM, assuming that their use by trauma survivors is purely a matter of sinfulness leads to missing a valuable opportunity to help them heal. "You're sinning" and "You need to stop it" aren't super helpful. Even if both of those things are true, a better approach is, "Tell me how you got here." Ellie, for example, was a traumatized woman who had been through unspeakable things. Her efforts to seek out pornography after the abuse had a lot to do with what had happened to her—not to wickedness within her heart. The complex interplay of abuse, traumatic reenactment, trauma bonding, and exposure had fused pornography to her arousal template. She needed help to disentangle what was happening inside her.

Before we continue, please be aware that I'm not saying people aren't sinners in need of a Savior. Far from it. What I am saying is that trauma responses are far more complex than "sinner" or "not sinner." When we shame people instead of seeking to understand the root cause of their behavior or attitude, then we are acting in collusion with the abusers in their lives. The women I work with wouldn't say that they think all is well and their arousal templates are great. They're feeling shame, they have no idea who to talk to, and they castigate themselves because of their perceived sinfulness.

It's heartbreaking to see, and I believe the church can do so much better here. My mind goes back to the story of the woman at the well in John 4. Jesus never shames her. The same is true for the woman caught in the act of adultery in John 8. Jesus never minimizes sin, but He also never minimizes trauma. We'd do well to ask questions and offer help rather than to condemn.

FANTASY AND AROUSAL TEMPLATES

I had just spoken at a conference on healthy sexuality after abuse. Following my talk, where I'd explained arousal structures and how violence can get woven into them, a woman came up to me. After thanking me for the presentation, her eyes studied the floor as if she were afraid it would come to life and bite her. The she said, "I need to know what to do with fantasies. Does that arousal stuff you talked about extend to that too? Because the stuff in my head . . ." She trailed off and looked like she wanted to run away or melt into the scary carpet.

I gently said, "Can you look at my face?" I wanted her to see the immense compassion I was feeling for her in that moment. Shame dies when you put things in the light and your pain is beheld by a compassionate witness. Once she looked up, I told her, "Yes, our fantasies absolutely are affected. I'm so glad you asked about fantasy life because so many people don't, and it's important."

Of course, we fantasize about lots of things—not all of them are sexual. You may daydream about a lake house, an upcoming vacation, or what you'd do if you won the lottery. Rarely do we vilify ourselves for that kind of fantasy.

We may also fantasize about the type of person we hope to date and eventually marry. We may fantasize about the type of home we'll inhabit with that potential person. Maybe we'll just go #vanlife and be mobile, having romantic adventures in beautiful places. (This is an example of an arousal template that includes sexual arousal in a vacation setting.)

We may also fantasize about sexual activity with a partner or (if we're single) with someone we're not married to. What we like or

LET'S HAVE A WORD

Desire

Desire is another word that can get hijacked by sexualization. Desire means to hope for or long for. For women who have been harmed sexually, it can be tantamount to a swear word. So often women are reticent to talk about desire at all, maybe because we've been told we aren't allowed to want anything except what our abuser says we want.

I was often told in my abusive marriage that I didn't really *want* to hang out with friends. I was told I *shouldn't* desire relationships outside of mine with him. That invariably led to an accusation of sexual infidelity with whichever friend I hoped to spend time with. Bear in mind, these were all female friends, and I am not someone who would be unfaithful anyway. But I was told that my hopes or longings really weren't what I said they were. And that spread to the bedroom. If I said I didn't like something or it made me feel uncomfortable, I was told that I *must* be mistaken.

Once out of that relationship, it took me a long time to figure out who I was and what my *actual* desires were—and then a *really* long time to even sense a desire for another relationship. It took me even longer to figure out what to do with sexual desire as a single woman. Once out of an abusive relationship, desire can feel dangerous. Most women desired a healthy relationship to start and it was a desire left unmet by the abusive relationship. There is real fear that desire, if allowed to reemerge, will be unmet.

Mindful Moment

Consider something you desire or long for. Let's keep it out of the sexual and relational realm for now. Maybe you're really craving a milkshake or sushi. What do you notice? What kinds of thoughts do you have about this desire? It's important to be nonjudgmental here. Just notice, to the best of your ability, what this desire evokes in you. Notice what you feel in your body as you consider this desire. Journal about this experience.

would like may all play through our mental movie. If we've been harmed sexually and violence has become part of our arousal template, then that will show up in the fantasy.

It can be jarring when survivors realize that their violent fantasies are arousing. As you can imagine, this often brings significant shame for the Christian. She just thinks she's broken and a totally depraved sinner. What is she actually? A traumatized woman who has had her arousal template polluted by the evil done to her.

By the way, while we don't need to beat ourselves up over such fantasies, we don't have to allow mental movies like these just to play out either. In the moment, we can practice taking our thoughts captive (2 Corinthians 10:5)—we notice it, we recognize that it does not align with our values, and we give it over to God. Then we consciously turn our attention elsewhere. As we shore up our identity in Christ, we can move in a different direction. As Jay Stringer writes, "The gospel tells us that our belovedness will never change according to our wanderings. But our belovedness is intended to change our wanderings."[7] I'd say that includes our mental wanderings.

CONTEMPT AND AROUSAL STRUCTURES

In abuse, violence toward *self* often becomes the norm. Survivors vilify themselves all the time: "I should have known. It's my fault I missed the red flags." That pervasive violence also gets meted out toward their sexual selves. This self-contempt, too, can get fused to their arousal structures, making traumatic reenactment even more likely. When I was learning narrative focused trauma care, I was struck by this quote from Dan Allender, which I summarize here:

> Holding yourself in contempt can help you feel a sense of power—therefore becoming part of your arousal structure. Your own violence against yourself can help you relieve shame. When you relieve shame, it can become part of your arousal structure. Sometimes we use shame to overcome other shame—we overeat or overspend or overwork to combat deeper shame—the harm that happened when we were sexually abused.[8]

In other words, we may turn to areas of addiction or compulsion—sexual or nonsexual—to overcome shame. If we are drawn to sexual activities or fantasies that don't align with our beliefs, we may shut down sexually altogether and turn to other behaviors to manage that shame. This isn't a conscious decision. It plays out from the subconscious. We often are able to see the connection as we walk through the therapeutic healing process, but it can be a mystery at first.

We are, invariably, sexual beings. It's wired into us, just like so many other things. But it feels unholy at times—tainted and sometimes dirty. As Allender states, "We live in a world where sexual desire seems anything but holy. Instead, it is bound to self-absorbed indulgence, transgression, and violence."[9] And that sure sounds like how abusers have used sex against us. This isn't at all how God meant it to be. He intended for us to enjoy sex and its ability to deepen connection in a marriage relationship.

As trauma practitioner Rachael Clinton Chen puts it, "Sexual harm is an efficient way for evil to wreak havoc."[10]

So I say, "Let's fix that mess."

MAPPING YOUR AROUSAL TEMPLATE

When helping my clients understand their own arousal template, I often draw on TUBES. That is the acronym I use for *Thoughts*, *Urges*, *Behaviors*, *Emotions*, and *Sensations*. I'm not sure where it originated, but I heard it from another therapist years ago and have used it ever since. In fact, we have laminated copies in all our offices for use with clients. Here's a quick rundown:

Thoughts: what we think about, whether in the form of words or pictures, or both

Urges: what we want to do behaviorally

Behavior: what we actually do

Emotions: how we feel

Sensations: what we feel in our bodies

By this point, you may be well aware of what your arousal template is, or you may have no clue. The following journaling prompts can help you explore your template. If this is dysregulating for you, I recommend that you consider these questions with a trusted friend, a support group, or a well-trained trauma therapist.[11] This exercise is not meant to be shaming at all. God already knows what's there, so you can't catch Him by surprise. You can't change what you don't know. When you are aware of what is woven into your arousal template, you can consider where you might want to do some work to shift it.

This chapter opened with a quote on being curious. Please be gentle and gracious as you walk through this section and explore your arousal template. Have a curious posture as you answer the questions related to each category.

Thoughts: What comes to mind when you think about sexual activity? This might be the general content of your fantasies. Are there objects that elicit arousal for you? This could be types of clothing, cars, sex toys, etc.

Urges: What sexual urges/desires do you have? As mentioned earlier, desire can feel dangerous, but it's important to consider and understand them. Think broadly here; there may be things not overtly sexual here that play a role in your arousal. That's totally fine! Remember, we are being curious.

Behaviors: What sexual behaviors do you actually engage in? There may be none, or there may be some like engaging in self-stimulation (we'll talk about that more in another chapter), watching pornography, or reading erotic fiction.

Emotions: What emotions trigger sexual thoughts or fantasies? What emotions do you notice during sexual thoughts, urges, or behaviors?

Sensations: What do you notice in your body when you are sexually aroused? This could be anything from your heart rate increasing to sensations in your genital areas. What sounds, scents/smells, visual cues, touch, or tastes elicit sexual arousal?

Take a look at your answers to each of these. What do you notice? What, if anything, surprises you?

As you're looking over your answers and getting a better feel for your arousal template, you might be noticing that the way your body responds doesn't match your values system. This is called arousal nonconcordance.[12] This term applies when our psychological feelings about desire don't line up with our body's actual physical response. To put it bluntly, a woman who is being raped may not psychologically desire her attacker, but if her body is being stimulated sexually, she may have an orgasm because her body is responding to the physical stimulus. That absolutely does not mean she desired the rape in any way at all. It just means her body did what it was designed to do and physically responded.

Again, I want to help you guard against any shame you may feel about this. Someone might tell you that if you really valued health and wellness, your body wouldn't respond as it does. Scientifically that's just not true.

When our arousal templates become fused to things that don't line up with our values system, like pornography, we will experience incongruence. Survivors are often told, both explicitly and implicitly, that they're the problem, leading them to believe they're broken. Shame gets heaped on them.

That's why learning what our arousal templates include and understanding the concept of arousal nonconcordance can be so helpful. They allow us to begin making adjustments to heal our arousal templates and bring them in line with our values. We'll explore the actual healing process in chapter 10.

WHO'S REALLY TALKING HERE?

Recognizing and Breaking Vows and Curses

We must bless what God blesses and curse what he curses. Finally, we must bless what our body experienced in the suffering of arousal and curse only what God curses: the shame and contempt of evil.

DAN ALLENDER, *Healing the Wounded Heart*

When I was about thirteen, I went with my youth group to yet another Christian event. We'd heard a good-enough concert and now we were being preached at. I'd love to say "preached *to*," but that wasn't the tone from the leaders onstage.

After telling a joke or two, a preppily dressed youth pastor began giving a message. I froze when he said, "Anyone who has sex before marriage is cursed. Damaged goods." I looked at the floor. I hadn't had sex, per se, but I'd done sexual things. I mean, some I never asked for, but that didn't matter. I knew I was damaged goods. I listened as he spoke more words over us all, trying to make sure we were sufficiently scared. It worked. I was definitely scared.

After the youth pastor finished speaking, some bodybuilders came onstage. They broke chains with their bare hands. We were told we could break chains, too, if we accepted Christ in our hearts. I'd already accepted Christ at four years old, but maybe that hadn't been enough. Maybe I hadn't really meant it. Maybe I needed to do it again. So, when they gave the altar call, I went up and swore I was surrendering my life this time. Of course I'd sworn that at the last three youth events where I'd been told I was damaged goods because of my sexual history. At other youth events, we were encouraged to rededicate our lives if we had backslidden. I was sure I had. So I'd go repent then too.

In all this talk about sex, no one ever talked about rape. Molestation. Abusive relationships. (Teen dating violence is something people should be quite concerned about—one in ten teen relationships is violent.[1]) The very real and normal desires of teens with hormones surging through their bodies also was never mentioned. Every teaching I heard was "wait until marriage, or you are wicked and a disappointment to God." In talking to my clients, I've come to believe that my experience was fairly normal. Over and over in sessions, I hear them echo that same message back to me.

So many times as a young woman I'd remind myself I was damaged goods. The words spoken over me by well-meaning but very much not trauma-informed pastors became words I agreed with and spoke over myself. When I say we need to break curses and vows, these are the sorts of statements I'm talking about. In this chapter, we'll consider how they are connected to the distorted sense of sexuality among those who've been abused.

CURSES

The term *curses* can seem a little woo-woo, but let me explain how very important it is to understand. Curses come first and are spoken over you by others, just like the declarations those pastors spoke over me. I don't think they were consciously cursing everyone listening—especially those already harmed or who'd be harmed in the future—but nonetheless that is what they were doing.

Curses are also spoken over us by our abusers. I was told no one would ever want me, I'd never find another person who'd want to be with me, I was ungodly, I was unlovable, I was lazy, and the list went on. Some things were implicitly spoken over me through gaslighting or actions. For example, my abuser would say things like, "It's hard to be around you" or "I do everything around here." These are direct or explicit, but the unspoken words were *You are too much* and *You are lazy.* When I heard these explicit and implicit curses in an abusive environment, they wore me down.

Whenever we say, "You are _____," we are speaking words of identity over others. Sometimes they can bring life. "You are kind and caring" is a life-giving statement. Of course, not all life-giving words are as positive as "You are amazing," because at times we all need to hear something about ourselves that we cannot see. In fact, "You aren't acting out of your true identity as God's child" are words of life as well as healthy correction.

Connection always should precede correction. This is why social media arguments or debates from a stranger or even an acquaintance may offend or bother you, but they will rarely change your mind. Unless you know someone in 3D (as in, they are part of your real life), their tweets or posts typically won't make much of an impact unless God reinforces their message in another way.

Connection is also key to the power of curses. As with correction, we won't listen to a demeaning statement made by someone who isn't in relationship with us. But when someone in our lives—particularly a person with power—speaks a curse over us, the words land and wound. After all, part of their power over us is that abusers know our weaknesses, often better than we know them ourselves. They are masterful observers—sort of like lions watching a herd of antelope to find the weakest and most vulnerable animals so they can pounce.

Anna Mary, who often went by AM, grew up in a very abusive family. After a particularly bad beating, she tried to get help in elementary school from a trusted teacher. Unfortunately, the school called her family instead of child protective services, and that night her parents abused her in ways that ensured she'd never speak up again. Over and over when she was young, her mother would tell her things like, "You're nothing. You're worthless. You are so stupid."

Despite AM's good grades and obvious smarts, her mother never seemed to have a nice thing to say. If she came home with a 97 on a test, her mother would ask why she hadn't gotten 100.

When AM met her husband, he seemed like her knight in shining armor. He was confident and took care of every physical need. But if she did something he didn't like, he'd call her stupid or tell her she was just a worthless housewife. So she tried harder to be what he wanted. He also told her that she had to please him in the bedroom whenever he asked. If she could get nothing else right, he reasoned, she needed to at least do that. She didn't think much of it. After all, he was so good to her that she never wanted to upset him. He had a good job, and she was able to stay home to raise their children. But all the while, she was drinking in those curses.

Once her kids entered high school, AM started her own medical transcriptionist service. But as the years went by, her body began to fail. She developed a serious autoimmune condition that left her unable to function some days. Even then, though, her husband expected her to perform sexually for him. When serious signs of depression emerged, her medical doctor became concerned about her mental health. She was referred to me.

While it didn't take me long to recognize she was in an abusive relationship, it took more than a year for her to see it and to take steps to leave. While her health issues didn't completely resolve after she left, they did get better. What lingered even longer was what she believed about herself. She was convinced she was dumb. Conversely, I saw a woman who had started her own successful business and created a schedule that worked around her health issues. She had raised amazing kids who were successful adults, and she had good relationships with all of them. Overall, she was thriving.

Curses are fueled by the kingdom of darkness. Whether or not the curse speaker realizes it, they are being used as a tool of Satan to harm you. I'd be remiss if I didn't point out that this is, quite frankly, a form of spiritual war. Ephesians 6:12 (KJV) says, "We wrestle not against flesh and blood, but against principalities, against powers, against the rulers of the darkness of this world, against spiritual wickedness in high places." Dan Allender says it this way: "A curse opens something in the spiritual, unseen realm against the one who is cursed and the one who curses."[2]

Throughout her life, AM had had many curses spoken over her by people she trusted and was close to. Those curses seeped in through her pores and wedged deep into her soul, and those powerful voices were persuasive. How could they not be? The curses started with her caregivers, the very people she depended on for life.

Then, AM made vows based on the curses spoken over her.

VOWS

Curses are filled with contempt. By the time I met her, AM was weighed down by the disdain and lack of respect she felt from her husband. The curses spoken over her became vows, which form when we agree with and internalize the curses directed at us. As Dan Allender says, "Contempt over time becomes a judgment that moves us to align our heart with darkness through a curse."[3]

Without realizing it, we align our hearts with the kingdom of darkness. If this has been your experience, it does not mean you're responsible for your abuse—you aren't. You do, however, need to know what and who you're agreeing with.

Vows are akin to drinking poison. The toxin then permeates your body, mind, and soul. You believe those venomous statements are true. In some ways vows provide a sense of safety. Dan Allender says they're "an anesthetic that lessens the searing pain"[4] of the curse. So we drink deeply at that well, hoping for some sort of rest. Rest, however, never comes. At some point, your abuser no longer even has to speak the curses over you (though they usually still do). You speak them over yourself, even once you're free of the abuse. This is one reason for some traumatic reenactments. You believe this is who you are, and so you live that way. In essence, you become your own abuser. You don't realize this is what you're doing, however.

AM and I worked to identify and dismantle her vows. She'd agreed with the curses that declared she was worthless and stupid. She'd swallowed them and lived as if they were true. They kept her trapped because she functioned now as her own abuser, repeating those phrases over and over to herself. She'd stub her toe and say, "Geez, AM. Get it together. If you weren't so dumb, you'd have been more careful." If she missed a turn in a city she wasn't familiar with, she'd say, "Obviously, AM, you're stupid. No wonder no one wants you." I started picking up her comments in counseling and pointing them out. She had no idea initially how often she spoke these things over herself.

One day she described how a client called her after she'd inadvertently sent him the wrong invoice. "He was nice enough about it," AM said, "but I wanted to die. It just goes to show how dense I really am."

Then I asked her the same question I'd asked myself back when I'd fallen in the creek: "Whose voice is that?"

She paused. "Mine," she said.

I also paused, giving her time to think. "Is it really? Is that your voice? Where did you first hear those words?"

She paused again. Then her eyes widened. "I heard them from my mother. Then my ex." Her eyes got even wider and her mouth fell open. "Holy mackerel. That is not my own voice. But dang, it *feels* so true!"

WORDS MATTER AND SO DO THEIR ORIGINS

I've said it numerous times—words matter. From how we define things to how we speak over ourselves, our words have power. It makes sense, really. We are made in the image and likeness of God, the God who spoke the world into existence (see Genesis 1). Jesus Himself is the Word made flesh.

Of course, after the Fall, the words people spoke to one another were no longer exclusively life-giving. The New Testament writers have a lot to say about that: "With the tongue we bless our Lord and Father, and with it we curse people who are made in God's likeness. Blessing and cursing come out of the same mouth. My brothers and sisters, these things should not be this way" (James 3:9-10, CSB). Who, having been made in the likeness of God, is being cursed with vows uttered as part of abuse? We are.

Trauma trashes our sense of self.[5] Our abusers have rewritten it by proclaiming who they say we are and are not. The sense of self spoken over us by our abusers doesn't look at all like what God says about us, but the complex dynamics that cause traumatic responses make these curses *feel* true. We start speaking these words over ourselves and they continue to *feel* true.

In modern psychological vernacular, we call this *self-talk* or *negative cognitions*, and research shows that negative cognitions actually make post-traumatic stress disorder (PTSD) symptoms worse.[6] Additionally, self-talk[7] affects how our brains function, which makes sense. Think about it this way: Curses spoken over us are oppressive, which just sucks the life out of us. After all, they keep us in constant fight/flight/freeze/fawn mode as we try to avoid danger. It's why we can't thrive in an abusive situation. But life-giving words spoken over us make us feel lighter and more at peace. Our brains and bodies have more capacity to function the way God intended.

So as you can see, the words we take in—first from our abusers and later from what we say to ourselves—matter a whole lot. Changing that inner dialogue is our ticket out of the captivity of living with the vows we've unwittingly made.

BREAKING VOWS AND CURSES

Thankfully, the curses spoken over us and the vows we've made with them can be broken. It's a process, and it takes a bit of time to *feel* differently—but we can begin living differently. That process begins with securing our identity and knowing what vows we made to begin with. Then we can begin the process of breaking those vows.

Securing our identity

I know my junk—things about me that I feel would make me unlovable if others knew them. And to some that junk *would* make me unlovable. Thankfully, one person does know everything about me and loves me regardless—Jesus. Not only that, He speaks life over me in a way that seems too good to be true.

Breaking the vows we've made, then, starts with securing our identity, which is "a consistent sense of personal existence . . . a secure internal base."[8] The surest foundation for our identity rests in what God says. And interestingly, a sense of self rooted in what Christ says about us helps us accept and manage our emotions without being overwhelmed by them. In short, it helps us deal with our feels in healthy ways. This is important when working to process the impact trauma has had on our lives.[9]

One way to build a stronger identity is to remind ourselves of the way God sees us. Who does He say we are? In His eyes, once we choose to follow Him, we are

a royal priesthood (1 Peter 2:9)
daughters of the King (Psalm 149:2)
co-heirs with Christ (Romans 8:17)
sealed for the day of redemption (Ephesians 4:30)
saints (1 Corinthians 1:2; Ephesians 1:1)

The One who created us speaks these truths over us, regardless of how we *feel* in a given moment. And of course He knows so much better than anyone else who we really are.

These statements of our identity aren't meant to be trite. As I've mentioned before, I am not a take-two-verses-and-call-me-in-the-morning girlie. These truths declare *war*—war against the kingdom of darkness that would dare try to lie to a daughter of the King.

We fight against the thoughts and beliefs that don't line up with who God says we are:

> For the weapons of our warfare are not of the flesh, but divinely powerful for the destruction of fortresses. We are destroying arguments and all arrogance raised against the knowledge of God, and we are taking every thought captive to the obedience of Christ, and we are ready to punish all disobedience, whenever your obedience is complete.
>
> 2 CORINTHIANS 10:4-6, NASB

These verses are battle language. And I love it.

Like any other trauma survivor, sometimes I still get caught in the negative cognitions that feel so very real because I do know my imperfections. I drank in the curses spoken over me and made vows that I've lived under far longer than I'd like to admit. However, my imperfections are not my identity. It's so easy to forget that. At times, I feel like my attempts to shift this thinking are going to pull me apart. If I had a nickel for the number of times I've thought, *Who am I to even write this book when some days this battle is still so fierce for me?* I'd be sitting on a beach in a tropical location drinking an icy drink out of a pineapple with a paper umbrella stuck in it.

I am so aware I'm at war whenever I try to shift those negative cognitions toward something far truer. That's why I keep a list of who I am in Christ close at hand, and I try hard (though imperfectly) to read over them when I feel especially shaky. My go-to list was originally compiled by Neil Anderson[10] and is broken into three sections: I am accepted, secure, and significant. Our abusers attacked us in all three of those areas, and the crafty ones twist Scriptures to pour poison into our identities.

One such distortion is being told you have a "Jezebel spirit" when you speak up or disagree with an abuser who tolerates nothing less than blind compliance. Jezebel was a wicked queen, but her sin wasn't speaking her mind. Rather it was failing to obey God and murdering people. Another example is wives being told that they are to submit to their husbands regardless of what is asked. Some people fail to read the verses around that one—the ones that dictate how husbands are to treat their wives (see Ephesians 5:25-28). They also fail to note that *submission* in the original language is not *subjugation*. God never called us to be blind doormats to our spouses.

Looking at the truth over and over and over can help us internalize the truth about who God really says we are.

We begin putting our foot on the neck of evil when we start to declare, "That is not what God says. This is not my voice, nor is it God's. This is the voice of the abuser and the voice of the accuser, and I'm not walking as if this is truth anymore."

Knowing the vows

In order to break vows, we have to know what they are. Often I'll have clients write down what they believe about themselves. If they have difficulty doing this, I share a list of negative cognitions many people struggle with to get them started. I always warn them it's not uncommon to check off all that are on the list! Once they've identified these negative identity statements, we make note whenever I hear them using it in a session. It's an effective way to help them recognize the lies they've been buying hook, line, and sinker.

Here are some ways to identify any vows you've made:

- Look for places where you say, "I'm just _____" (something negative like worthless, damaged, stupid, a fraud).

- Ask yourself, "When did I start believing this? Who did I hear this from first?"

- You may have to sit with it a bit to figure it out. Remember, we're so used to this being our normal it can be tough to find the origin at first. Your brain will say "of course this is true" and flood you with all kinds of "data."

Community can help too. I once taught on this concept at a conference. During a time of prayer, one of the women broke down and shared her belief that she was a terrible mother, housekeeper, friend, and wife. She went on and on. Another lady came near to pray for her and quietly asked, "Whose voice is this, really?" The sweet sister sat for a moment and said, "It's my husband's." She sat in stunned silence as the tears fell down her face. She looked over at me, eyes wide, then looked at the sister praying with her. "Oh my goodness. It's not my voice. It's my husband's." I watched in awe and joy as her body visibly relaxed as the weight of the lies was lifted.

This story also proves how much abuse messes with our identity. Once we know what curse we have agreed with, we can start breaking it.

Actively breaking vows

Anna Mary and I did the exercise I just described, listing a number of vows she'd unwittingly made. I then gave her a list that summarized who she is in Christ. Her homework was to notice when she was agreeing with a vow. She would then take out the list of who she is in Christ and speak those words over herself instead. She was instructed not to judge herself as she did this exercise but just to acknowledge the truth of who God says she is. Even though those statements didn't feel true in the moment, she was able to intellectually believe them because God doesn't lie. She kept this up for a few weeks, and we then processed her experience in subsequent sessions.

One day, several weeks after we started this intentional practice, we checked in. AM was brighter and more bubbly. She said, "I can't believe it!"

I smiled. "Tell me more."

AM excitedly said, "I still hear the vows in my head, but it's so much faster that I go, *Oh, that's a vow. Let's see . . .* and I look at the list on my phone of who I am in Christ, pick one, and say it slowly and with intention. I don't tell myself it's a stupid exercise anymore.

I just do it. I figure, what have I got to lose? And the weirdest thing is happening. The truth stuff feels more normal. More true. It's really weird. But cool. But also weird."

We laughed together.

Sometimes victory isn't a big leap; sometimes it's small, intentional steps. And yes, sometimes healing feels weird and other times it feels like the truth isn't true.

SPEAK IT UNTIL YOU BECOME IT

The group was staring at my co-leader and me like we had just used a foreign language. In some ways, we had. We were explaining what it means to "act opposite." Every feeling comes with an urge to take an action of some kind—even taking no action is a decision and basically an action. The opposite action is a concept where you notice what your urges are and act contrary to them. You do so with your whole self. You decide you are all in—every bit of you—to take the opposite action.

Emma is a great example of how opposite action can play out. We were working together to help her break the vow she'd made that she had no agency, no personal choice. Her ex-husband had led her to believe she had no power. He routinely refused to let her have any say in their lives. She was not even permitted to choose what she made them for dinner. Through decades of abuse, she believed the curse that she was weak and powerless. Since freeing herself, she was learning who she really was and what she really liked. She'd gotten a sales job and was excelling in so many ways—except in staff meetings. She worked largely with men who had decades of sales experience, and she noticed that she was extremely intimidated by them.

She described going into the sales meetings and shrinking back, feeling unable to speak up. We looked at her list of negative cognitions and considered how her sense of being powerless was playing out in her workplace. We explored the urge that arose whenever she had that powerless feeling. She told me it was to shrink and avoid speaking up, so she would be quiet and was always the last to share her numbers. She did so timidly, looking down as she talked.

Then we discussed what an opposite action might look like. If she chose to believe who she truly is in Christ instead of the vow she'd made with her abuser, how would she act? She thought for a few minutes and said, "I would walk in like I owned the place. Then when they asked for updates, I'd jump right in rather than go last. I'd look folks in the face instead of looking down. Acting as if I have power."

This wasn't an act of fantasy. Emma was a great saleswoman, and her numbers showed it. Moreover, she was as worthy as every other salesperson in that room. We had a factual basis for the opposite action. We practiced during our sessions for several weeks. When she was ready to give it a try during a sales meeting, she told me she envisioned it going well right before walking into the conference room. She took a deep breath and imagined her coworkers as an account she wanted to win. She absolutely slayed it in the meeting. Afterward her boss came up to her and said, "Emma! It's about time you showed up! I've been waiting for you to reveal who you are! Your numbers do that so clearly, but I've never really seen you show up here. So glad you decided to really join us today!"

Though it took a long time to feel like *her*, she continued practicing the opposite action in various situations. Some, like that meeting, went great. Other situations were harder or didn't go as she'd hoped. But with each one, she was gaining her voice and walking in her personal power. The opposite action helped Emma experience herself differently.

This is not "fake it till you make it." Far from it. This is choosing to act as who you truly are and then taking appropriate relational risks to walk that out. Opposite action is rooted in truth. I'm five foot two. If I tried the opposite action of stepping onto the court during an NBA game and dunking the ball, I'd be very unsuccessful unless there were a ladder or a trampoline. What would likely end up happening is that I would be arrested.

For those of us who have experienced sexual abuse, the opposite action in the area of our sexuality might entail acting as though we are worthy of love, respect, and care—because we are, even if we don't feel it at first. It might look like learning to speak up with our safe spouse to say, "I don't like this" or "That doesn't feel good to me; can we try something else?" instead of staying quiet and giving in to their desires.

EXPERIENCING OURSELVES DIFFERENTLY

A big part of healing is experiencing ourselves differently. Opposite action is one way to do that. Another way is in community.

For the longest time, I thought I was a big burden. The biggest burden of all the burdens to ever burden anyone. Sadly, it was just one of several vows I'd made after others had spoken that curse over me. I was staunchly committed—like many trauma survivors—to do it all myself. Any time we ask for anything from our abusers we are belittled, made fun of, or forced to "pay" in some way. We are often told we're too much or a burden. And we often drink those words in until they become our own.

Healing, however, happens in community. We were never meant to do this life alone. My therapist assured me that I was not a burden and encouraged me to challenge that vow. So the challenge I came up with was to ask someone for help on a home project where I really did need assistance. Asking for help was terrifying. What if I was met with the same response abusers had given me? My therapist reminded me that my community of friends was solid, filled with great women and men.

So I asked.

I remember feeling like I'd barf as I sent the text. "Hi . . . I need some help with getting a shelf installed. I tried, but I couldn't do it alone. Would you mind helping me out?"

I waited for the response, expecting it to be, "Sorry, I'm busy."

My friend texted back, "Absolutely! What time are you off work tomorrow?"

When my friend showed up to help the next day, I timidly thanked her.

She looked at me and asked, "Why are you being weird?"

I took a deep breath. "I don't want you to think I'm a burden."

She laughed. "Tabitha, you are not a burden. You are loved." And she hugged me tight.

Relationships are give and take; we are so often told in the church that we are just supposed to give. That's not true. The same is true in sexual relationships. We can experience ourselves differently sexually. We don't have to say yes just because our spouse asks. We don't have to say yes to anything if it demeans our personhood.

We also can experience ourselves as worthy of love and having a voice. I practice those truths a lot with my community. I practice using my voice with people who are safe and who love me well. I even practice talking openly about sex and sexual healing with those folks. That's where this book came from: a generous and kind community who gave me the chance to try talking about things I knew needed to be considered but were so hard for me to discuss because of my own history of harm.

SPEAKING WORDS OF LIFE

Bottom-up therapies

Some of this isn't cognitive. We can't think ourselves to healing—if we could, this book wouldn't even be necessary. Trauma isn't stored in our thinking brains. It's stored in our bodies and the parts of our brains connected to feeling. Sometimes God uses therapies like Eye Movement Desensitization and Reprocessing (EMDR), Brainspotting, Somatic Experiencing, Internal Family Systems, and more full-body therapies to help heal us. Finding an experienced therapist who knows what they're doing can be used by God. For more on how to find such a therapist, see page 217.

Centering, contemplative, and deliverance prayer

I know this might sound overly mystical to some readers, but this type of prayer has been a game changer for some of my clients. Centering yourself and focusing on Jesus and the prayer is key. Then, you can actively call out the curses and vows and break them in the name of Jesus. These are deep, honest, contemplative prayers that invite Jesus in as you cast down strongholds. You don't need anyone else to pray such a prayer with you.

Blessing

A final way of breaking curses and vows is to bless our goodness. It can feel really difficult to bless our bodies if we feel it betrayed us by having an orgasm as we were being sexually abused or betrayed us in other ways, like through illness. I think Dan Allender says it best in *Healing the Wounded Heart*:

> We must open our heart to what seems impossible and inconceivable: the delight of God. We must bless what God blesses and curse what he curses. Healing requires entering our stolen story to grow faith by remembering the past and learning to grieve. In turn we regain hope by receiving kindness that disrupts the reenactments that kill our dreams. Finally, we must bless what our body experienced in the suffering of arousal and curse only what God curses: the shame and contempt of evil.[11]

There is grief in blessing here, but orienting ourselves kindly toward the little girl or woman who had so much stolen from her and so much harm done is vital. We can bless the love she craved when she was groomed and harmed. We can acknowledge the love she gave to her spouse, though he required the unspeakable from her. We can bless the woman who gave all she could to her relationship, only to be told it was never enough. We can bless how her body responded even though the touch was violent or unwanted.

I had to learn how to bless my younger self who had been so harmed, and I was able to do that in a story work group, which is designed to help participants reexamine their families of origin stories to identify any internalized patterns or messages from that time that may still be holding them back. It's a great way to identify any curses and vows from childhood.

My story work facilitator looked at me kindly. I always felt so seen by her—both my adult self and the smaller, younger self who had been so horribly abused.

After I'd shared a story of how I'd been sexually abused, she looked at me compassionately. "Can you bless that little girl?" she asked softly without a hint of contempt or judgment. She was inviting me to see my younger self in the story I'd shared and bless that younger version of myself.

"I . . . I don't know," I stammered. Tears slid down my face.

"Mmmm." She closed her eyes and placed her hand on her chest. I felt so near to her even though we were talking through a screen. Good story work always feels so close.

"She was so *good*. So *good*," she said. "Do you feel close to her right now?"

I did. I felt very near to the little girl who'd trusted the person her parents left her with while they went out. She was just trying to obey and she had no idea what was being asked. She was only six.

"Mmmm," she said again. "She was so *good*. Trying to do the right thing. Can you bless her?"

"I think so." I took a deep breath.

I imagined my adult self coming close to my little self and looking into those wide hazel eyes that were curious. The twinkle they had when she was excited or full of joy. I sat down on the floor beside my little self.

"We didn't deserve this, you know," I told her. She nodded and looked up at me in my mind's eye. "You trusted and obeyed because you were taught to do that. You always wanted to serve and follow God. So you trusted what people told you. You are so *good*. You are so, so *good*. I can bless your goodness. I can bless our goodness. What happened should never have happened. But you are not wicked. And I bless our goodness. I bless the goodness of our body."

This was a powerful moment in my healing. My ability to bless the little girl who had been so harmed by someone who should have been trustworthy was key in learning compassion for what happened to me. It was key to allowing myself to feel grief so I could experience healing and, later, joy.

As Allender says, "The work of redemption is to replace curses with blessing, death with life, and ambivalence with joy."[12] Blessing the self who was harmed and blessing her goodness breaks those curses. This doesn't mean we're perfect or don't need to allow God to sanctify us. What it means is we can see clearly and can call good what God also calls good. We choose to believe who we are in Christ. We no longer see ourselves as damaged goods, but as sweet girls and women who have survived harm that came from trying to do and give all.

This is real work and it's not easy work, but it's definitely healing work. You will likely use all these methods and more to break the vows you made with the kingdom of darkness. You don't have to go it alone, either. A good therapist, support group, or friend can help you with this work. Healing happens in community.

LECTIO DIVINA

As you begin engaging with contemplative prayer, you might use the ancient spiritual practice of *lectio divina* ("divine reading") as your rhythm.

1. Select a Scripture to read. Let's take Galatians 5:1 for our example: "It was for freedom that Christ set us free; therefore keep standing firm and do not be subject again to a yoke of slavery" (NASB).

2. Reflect on the Scripture. Read it again slowly and really soak it in. What do you sense God saying to you?

3. Respond to what you are reading and experiencing in prayer. Be super real:

God, I know Your Word is true, but it sure doesn't feel like it. Some days I feel trapped in these beliefs. But I know You mean this. You really did come to set me free. Not only from sin and death, but also from abuse and the harm done to me. While I may not see all the healing this side of heaven, I know You are Healer. In Jesus' name, I break the vow I've made that I'm trapped. I'm not trapped. I may not be able to feel free yet, but that doesn't make it less true. Help me to believe it and feel it and walk in it.

This is just an example—you pray how you're led and what you feel.

4. Finally, end with rest. Read the passage again slowly and rest in God's presence. Bask in His love as best you can.

DECLARATION OF WAR

I want to end this chapter with a reminder that this is war. And I want to end with a declaration. Feel free to speak this out loud over yourself if it's helpful to you. You may also be helped by writing your own declaration of war and speaking those words aloud. Whatever you do, speak life over yourself. Those words matter.

I stand against the tyranny of curses spoken over me from the lips of abusers.

I declare war on the insidious lies that have plagued my mind and soul. I will no longer make or keep vows with the kingdom of darkness or manipulative whispers and actions of those who sought to diminish my worth and distort my reality.

To the lie that I am unworthy of love and belonging, I wield the sword of truth and self-compassion and declare my inherent value as a daughter of the King of kings.

To the lie that I am defined by the scars of my past, I proclaim my past does not dictate my future. My scars are a testament to resilience, not my defeat.

To the lie that I am powerless, I remember that the very power that raised Christ from the dead lives in me.

To the lie that I am alone in my suffering, I remember the fellowship of suffering that is in Christ. In Him I have a Great High Priest who intercedes for me and understands the depths of my pain even I cannot fathom.

Let it be known, to every falsehood that has taken root within me, I shall wage war with unwavering resolve, armed with the truth of who I am in Christ Jesus.

May the echoes of my battle cry resonate far and wide, inspiring fellow survivors to join me in the great cloud of witnesses as we cast down lies and rewrite the abusers' narratives of our lives. Victory is ours, for Christ has already won, and truth has set us free.

HEALTHY SEX AMIDST SORROW

Putting Sexual Intimacy in Its Appropriate Context

*I'm afraid I'll be shattered if I face these things. I feel I'll be
broken beyond repair. There will be a million pieces and
I'll never be able to put them back together again. . . .*

*"You aren't meant to put them back together. You already
were shattered by the things that happened, and the
millions of shards of glass have been slicing you apart from
the inside. They have to get cleaned out. The wounds will
be treated and what will remain is a beautiful mosaic."*

TABITHA WESTBROOK, a 2022 journaled prayer and sensed response from God

When I was eighteen, I had an affinity for any artwork featuring
celestial bodies. Suns, moons, and stars drew me in every time. One
piece at a small home furnishings store near my apartment particularly caught my eye. For years, I pined over a black, wrought-iron
coffee table with a mosaic top fashioned from broken tiles in blues,
purples, yellows, golds, and whites, picturing a constellation of stars
with moons and suns sprinkled in. I found it incredible that someone
could take a pile of broken pieces and turn it into a beautiful, whimsi-
cal piece of art you could put in your home.

That reminds me of God's promise to exchange beauty for our
ashes (Isaiah 61:3). Think of it: Those fragmented pieces caused by
our sexual trauma (and any other trauma) can be exchanged for a
beautiful mosaic that looks nothing like the harm done to us.

Please note that healing does not mean we act as if nothing bad happened. Something very bad did happen to us. We don't minimize that. In fact, no matter how much healing you've done, you may be knocked over at times by a fresh wave of grief. That is normal.

Mosaic artists have to look over a sea of broken bits. They look at color, texture, shape. While others might see a worthless pile of fractured pieces, they know what *could* be with the right order and the artist's touch. Slowly, they take each shard and begin to create something beautiful. God does the same with our broken parts, the ones shattered by our abusers. He is the divine artist, and we are His workmanship (Ephesians 2:10).

I've loved hearing Beth Moore say several times over the years: Jesus "knows it's scary to be us."[1] The even better news? He stays close beside us after we've been broken. Consider how frequently this theme shows up in Scripture. "He will never leave you nor forsake you" (Deuteronomy 31:6, 8). The psalmist says God "knows how weak we are; he remembers we are only dust" (Psalm 103:14, NLT). He is at our side when we "walk through the darkest valley" (Psalm 23:4) and when we go "through deep waters . . . rivers of difficulty . . . [and] the fire of oppression" (Isaiah 43:2, NLT). He's our great High Priest (Hebrews 4:14, NLT), and He prays for us when we don't even know how with "groanings too deep for words" (Romans 8:26, NASB). As comforting as those passages are, you'll notice that not one of them says that He will necessarily remove us from difficult places. That applies to the healing of our sexuality too.

THE HARD WORK OF HEALING AND RECOVERY

What this means is that healing and recovery won't always be easy. In fact, suffering is part of this life (see 1 Peter 4:12; John 16:33), and that includes the hard work of healing. This is a concept most folks don't really think about. Most women I work with say, "I just want to heal!" And that is factually true! They do want to heal! They want

I am not asking you
to give up your grip
on the shards you clasp
so close to you

but to wonder
what it would be like
for those jagged edges
to meet each other
in some new pattern
that you have never imagined,
that you have never dared
to dream.

—From "Blessing for a Broken Vessel" by Jan Richardson[2]

to embrace a healthy sexuality—one that honors God and enables them to enjoy the good gift He designed their bodies, minds, and souls to receive. But before we consider what God's plan for sexuality is and how to embrace it, we need to acknowledge the factors that can make this journey feel so slow.

Quite simply, getting on the road to recovery requires a great deal of work. Our brain's neural pathways are conditioned to see the world the way it used to be or has always been, so it requires work to change how we see something and view it in a healthier way. Changing our arousal template and structure is difficult. Breaking vows takes deliberate, strenuous effort. This labor is well worth it in the long run, but it is most assuredly work.

Not a one-and-done

"Why do I have to do all the work when he did all the harm?" Allie shouted one day during a session before crumpling into a puddle of tears. We were meeting via Zoom, and in the little square box, I watched her flop her face down into her arms on her desk as she cried. She was lamenting that even two years out of her abusive relationship, she was dealing with waves of grief and the aftermath of trauma.

This meltdown hadn't come out of nowhere. She had been profoundly triggered by a show she'd watched on a streaming service that alluded to sexual assault. Her body had tensed up and then her mind was inundated by images of the harm she'd endured. She described shaking and crying and not being able to find the remote to turn it off because she was so rattled. She was exceedingly frustrated by her body and mind's reaction to the input. After wailing for a few minutes, she began to settle a bit and said, "I just wish all the work wasn't on me. I wish I didn't have to work so hard for healing when he just gets to skate through life like none of this ever happened. I can *never* forget it happened."

What Allie was experiencing is what so many survivors confront: the seemingly never-ending work of recovery while their abusers go on as if nothing has happened. It's frustrating, heart-wrenching, and so unfair.

Working through abuse and living within a biblical sexual ethic is not a one-time process. There are layers to recovery, some of which need to be revisited across our lifetime. I think of it like peeling an onion. We deal with one layer today and then, when God deems it's time, we may revisit things from a different perspective. For some, it feels like going around the same mountain repeatedly, but I think of it more like following a switchback. A switchback is a way to get up a steep mountain by using a back-and-forth, zigzag path so you only have to scale one level at a time. You're still on the mountain, but you're steadily climbing. Healing is like that—we are climbing out of the dark valley of the shadow of death to the high places with the Good Shepherd.

I'll level with you: Sometimes, in some ways, I think healing brings more pain. It's a better pain than what we experience when we haven't begun to heal, but it's pain nonetheless. Perhaps it comes from facing the stark reality of brokenness and suffering in this place and the very real "not yet" of being here while we await eternity. It stems from the deep wells of grief over what happened, what didn't happen because of what happened, what else happened because of what happened. . . . Yet I'd rather have real than what I had unhealed. But real is hard. And the more I sit in this liminal space—where the now and the not yet meet in shimmering waves, where the veil feels so, so thin—I recognize that the call to a posture of tenderness toward this weary and scarred heart is vital.

Not only was Allie bothered by the fact that her abuser seemed to get off scot-free, but she was also frustrated that she couldn't follow a clearly delineated series of steps to recovery. She was beginning to recognize that recovering a healthy sexuality wasn't as simple as checking off a series of action steps. Unfortunately—and fortunately—it's more complicated than that.

It's *unfortunate* in that the complexity and all the moving parts make it more of a challenge to heal. Our sexuality is part of our identity, but it is not our whole identity. That makes unweaving the toxic elements more challenging. We might ask ourselves, *Is this for now? Do I need to give attention here? Or is this other aspect more important in this moment?*

It's *fortunate* in that we are not one-dimensional. We can begin to heal in one area while still working toward healing in another. We aren't limited to all-or-nothing progress—and that's a gift to someone who's been abused. As survivors, we've been forced into black-and-white thinking, but as we heal, we get to be the multifaceted, so-much-more-than-we've-experienced people we were created to be. It's a breath of fresh air to realize that we don't have to "arrive" somewhere—parts of ourselves can arrive while others are still on the journey.

It's so common to want a checklist you can just follow to move forward. But you are unique. As I often say during domestic abuse advocacy training, "You are the only you that you have." The journey to recovering (or discovering, if you never had one) a healthier sense of your sexual self will be as unique as you are.

In an earlier chapter, I mentioned that a therapist I know compares trauma recovery to trash someone else threw on your front porch but that you have to clean up. After hearing so many stories of the trauma responses that result from harm, I've added this: We also sometimes add another bag ourselves. Then something leaks, then we find rats. And even after the cleanup is finished, there may be porch boards to replace and stains that are permanent.

I mention this because you may be wondering whether the work of healing is worth it, and I can assure you that it is. Even if you have to clean off the porch, and even if some marks and scars remain, you will end up with a clean porch—one that will be less likely to have trash tossed on it in the future. And there won't be rats.

The problematic ways we talk about sex

As I've said throughout this book, the words we use about sex matter. In our hypersexed society, so many terms get overly sexualized. In addition, sex is often just a way for some marketers to attract eyeballs. From advertisements to entertainment, the adage "sex sells" is evidenced everywhere. More than once while watching a movie, I've said, "Well, that whole sex scene was quite literally unneeded to further the plot." Not only that, but mere exposure to sexualized ads, soft pornography, and violence makes it seem more normal to our senses.

It's understandable that the church has long tried to push back on the unmooring of sexuality from God's design for it. Yet the words used to try to describe a godly sexual ethic have also been polarizing. Take the word *purity*, for example. Depending on when you grew up, purity culture may have been a major part of your youth. According to The Gospel Coalition, purity culture is

> the term often used for the evangelical movement that
> attempts to promote a biblical view of purity (1 Thess.
> 4:3-8) by discouraging dating and promoting virginity

before marriage, often through the use of tools such as purity pledges, symbols such as purity rings, and events such as purity balls.[3]

Though boys were sometimes asked to sign purity pledges or wear purity rings, the bulk of purity culture messaging was directed toward girls. As I said earlier, purity culture started as a way to protect young people, but in some instances it became a way to enslave and enable abuse. Moreover, *purity* in the sense of purity culture simply meant not having sex before marriage. That's it. Such a narrow view overlooked so much more about sex and sexuality. A healthy sexuality goes beyond whether or not we have intercourse outside or inside marriage.

So if we solely use the word *purity* to describe a healthy sexuality, we are treading on dangerous ground. Yet we cannot discuss sexuality without considering an aspect of purity, which is being "free from moral fault or guilt."[4]

Another word used by some people within the church when talking about healthy sexuality is *chastity*. Merriam-Webster defines *chaste* as being "innocent of unlawful sexual intercourse; celibate; pure in thought and act."[5] It is a less commonly used word than *purity* and has old-fashioned connotations, perhaps because of its association with chastity belts, which were garments that allegedly had a lock and key to keep women from having intercourse. Based on a quick read of available internet info, it doesn't appear chastity belts were a real thing,[6] but I suspect some modern Christians think they might be a good idea. As a teen, I heard some churchgoing adults discuss them as something that should be "brought back." Again, assuming that chastity relates simply to avoiding sexual intercourse diminishes the true idea of healthy sexuality. But as with purity, I think part of the definition for *chastity* is useful as we continue our exploration of healthy sexuality—the idea of "being pure in thought or act."

WORDS STILL MATTER: What Is a Biblical Sexual Ethic Anyway?

I know you're here because you want to understand healthy sexuality after abuse. As I've said from the start, how we talk about stuff and the words we use matter deeply.

A biblical sexual ethic honors God's boundaries and rhythms for our sexual lives. It aligns with His plan for sex, recognizing that He is good and has our good at heart. He's not a cosmic buzzkill who doesn't want us to have fun. He created sexual activity and intimacy to be pleasurable. That's why orgasms feel good physically. It's why cuddling releases oxytocin so that we feel close to our intimate partner.

And God wants women specifically to find pleasure in sexual activity. Why do I say that? The sole purpose of the clitoris is to feel really good when stimulated.[7] If God didn't intend for us to enjoy sexual activity, there would be no nerve endings there. The simple fact is that, in God's economy, women are allowed to both desire and enjoy sex with their husbands. Sexual activity and intimacy are for procreation, yes. They are for emotional and physical closeness. They are *also* for physical pleasure and enjoyment. All of that is biblical.

A biblical sexual ethic neither condones nor prohibits areas not addressed in Scripture. Instead, it provides a framework by which we can learn to critically evaluate our choices. It's a way of looking at God's design and then deciding how to think and act based on Scripture and, if the Bible isn't explicit, prayerfully seeking to discern the Holy Spirit's leading in our lives.

This approach isn't black-and-white, all-or-nothing. It is nuanced with shades of gray and isn't enhanced when we make up arbitrary rules. For many of us, those arbitrary rules got us into trouble.[8] We may have kissed dating goodbye or used a courting system or bowed to a tyrant because we were told that was godly. But Scripture doesn't prescribe any of those things.

That's not to say we should follow our whims. A biblical sexual ethic also is boundaried. It fits within God's healthy and good limits for it. Our sexual activity and expression are submitted to God as Lord and Creator—just like every other area of our lives should be. Because God intended safety, both for ourselves and others, to be woven into our sexuality, we are better able to protect all image bearers of the Living God when we follow His design.

I think the book *She Deserves Better* says it so well: "The way we express our sexuality should honor, respect, and dignify ourselves and the people around us. It isn't just about whether you've done the deed but is more about living to honor God with your body."[9]

> It means that even though, frankly, you likely wouldn't have long-term repercussions if you *did* have sex and used protection, *you still choose not to out of reverence for God and out of respect for the image of God in others and yourself.* It's not about being afraid of causing irreparable, permanent damage to your purity; it's about choosing to live differently simply because it's the right (and the wise!) thing to do.[10]

We don't follow a biblical sexual ethic so we can be pleasing to God. As Christ followers, we already are pleasing to Him. We are already loved by Him. We choose this ethic simply because we desire to submit all things—including sex—to Him.

What does it look like to live this way—to honor God, myself, and others with my body? I'm so glad you asked.

WALKING OUT A BIBLICAL SEXUAL ETHIC
Back to boundaries and safety

I used the illustration of off-roading when introducing boundaries in chapter 3. We choose not to drive our vehicle off the pavement, not only because it could ruin our transmission or tear up our car, but out of respect for the rules of the road. Likewise, we hold boundaries around sex because it honors God, ourselves, and our partners to stay between the lines established by the One who created us.

Boundaries around our sexual activity should be loving to the other person, honoring them as an image bearer of the Living God. They are a fellow human being who deserves more than just being consumed by our lust or to meet our needs. Your own safety and health are also vital. You need to be both emotionally and physically safe and healthy in all sexual activity. You are also an image bearer of the Living God, and as such, are worthy of far more than being used to satisfy someone's lust.

For us single ladies, that means our boundaries honor us as image bearers of the Living God. We are loving to ourselves, not allowing ourselves to be consumed by the lust of another. When we need to, we wrestle with the desire we feel and continually submit it to God. If we desire a partner, we are absolutely free to pray for and seek that. There is nothing at all wrong with dating. We should, however, have a plan for what physical touch we are okay with in that arena. And no matter how strong our desire for companionship and a partner is, we do not ignore red flags. As I mentioned earlier, those red flags do not mean it's a carnival.

An intimate partner is just that—a *partner*. Intimacy between a woman and man is meant to be a partnership between two image bearers of the Living God in which mutual connection and satisfaction take place. As partners, they're both on equal footing and have a say. It's not just her needs and wants; his matter too. And they aren't just using (consuming) each other.

This doesn't negate your own sexual desires. But you can choose to stay between the lines because you respect yourself, your partner, and God Himself. Yes, doing donuts in a field is fun, and maybe you won't get caught or have a negative outcome. However, when it comes to sexual activity, you choose the boundaried fun of staying between the lines because that not only honors God's healthy limits but serves you and your partner best in the long term.

Boundaries also provide safety, which is vital to healing. When we've been abused, even discussing sex and sexual activity can feel radically unsafe. What God made to be an amazing way to connect with a lifelong partner was polluted and sullied. Before we can ever feel safe with another human, we have to recover a sense of safety in ourselves with this topic.

And we need to do it nonjudgmentally.

Observing without judgment

In my experience, one of the hardest concepts for survivors to grasp is identifying and suspending judgment. We are queens of being judgmental. Lest you clutch your pearls and call me a heretic, hear me out. Judgment is not necessarily a bad thing—but only if we're mindful and intentional. We make judgments all the time. They can be helpful and used as a form of shorthand so we don't have to add extra words. For example, "We should go to bed early" might be shorthand for "We have an early flight and have to leave for the airport by 4 a.m. We need to get some sleep." If folks are on the same page, this judgment makes sense and has eliminated a whole sentence. However, judgments also can be less effective and sometimes harmful.

One way to evaluate a judgment is to listen for the word *should* or *must*:

"I *should* drive on the right side of the road."

"I *must* be on time."

"I never *should* have said that."

"I *should* get it together."

"I *must* figure this out."

Judgments also often use sweeping language:

"It's *never* going to be any different."

"I'll *never* heal."

"Things are *always* this way."

"I *hate* pizza."

"I *love* ice cream."

We often just make statements like these as if they are facts. Maybe we are stating a fact—but ideally we do so intentionally. For example, "I *must* be on time to court" is both a judgment and based in fact. If you're late to a court proceeding, there will be consequences like not having your case heard or being deemed in contempt. So this judgment is accurate and helpful. On the other hand, the declaration "I *must* be home on time from book club or my husband will be angry and punish me" is quite different. When I hear statements like that, I want to ask some clarifying questions: What is "on time," and how long would "late" be? Has he made it clear that he does not want you at book club as it is so you're only allowed to be gone a certain amount of time?

There's a reason I know to ask questions like these. It wasn't a book club, but I've swallowed someone else's judgments as my own without even realizing that's what I'd done.

I was twenty-one years old and had been married about a year. At the time, I was working with a great group of people in my first job in corporate America. We all got along so well that we often hung out after work. One of my friends and colleagues, Brent, was in a band with his brother. A group of us made plans to see them play at a local club.

I drove by myself to the club downtown, listening to a CD of the band's music that Brent had created. When I finally pulled up to the hole-in-the-wall venue, where I'd seen many bands play in the past, I carefully parked and went in. The show was great, and I had so much fun seeing Brent play and meeting the other band members and several of his family members.

Shortly after eleven, I left the club with two female coworkers because we were close friends and friends don't let friends walk alone. When we got to the place where my friend Sharla had parked her car, there was no car there. We panicked. Sharla and Kelly had ridden together because they were roommates. At first we thought their car may have been stolen. Then we noticed a small sign that said it was illegal to park there and listed the number of a towing company. Our hearts sank.

Because cell phones weren't common back then, I still dutifully carried a shiny quarter and dime to ensure I could call for help if I ever needed it. We found a pay phone and I handed Sharla my thirty-five cents so she could call the towing company. Her car was indeed there. "I guess I'll call a taxi," Sharla said. By now it was close to midnight. I said, "Absolutely not. I'll drive you guys there so you can pick up your car." So I did.

After making sure they could get Sharla's vehicle, I drove home, grateful I'd been there to help. I pulled up at our house around 1 a.m. It was dark, so I assumed my husband had gone to bed. I unlocked the door and went inside. As I stepped into the foyer facing the living room, I saw the red glow from a cigarette illuminating my husband's face as he took a deep drag. His scowl was so deep that in the amber light it seemed etched into his face. His eyes were narrowed and dark. As he slowly exhaled, the smoke curled upward. Quietly and in a menacing voice I will never forget, he said, "Where the h— have you been? Did you have fun cheating on me? Was it a good time?"

I froze, still holding on to my purse. What was he talking about? I was exactly where I said I'd be. Cheating? Where did he get that? Never in my life was that something I'd do.

I tried reasoning with him, but he wouldn't even hear me out. For the next two hours, he accused me of all manner of unfaithfulness. I cried and told him I would never be unfaithful. I encouraged him to call Sharla and Kelly to ask about the car being towed. He yelled at me for not calling him when I'd be later than I *should* have been. When I explained that I'd given Sharla the only thirty-five cents I had, he scoffed and called me a liar. He said I *should* have found a way to call him. At one point, he got so close to my face that I could feel his saliva hit me when he spat out words.

Finally, around 3 a.m., he allowed me to go to bed. As I lay there, tears streaming down my face, I thought, *I should have come home on time.* In that moment, his judgments became my own.

How judgments are formed

Many people coming out of abusive situations don't realize when they're making judgments. That's why just noticing or observing when we make one is helpful. Most people are honestly stunned by how often they judge. Again, judgments aren't necessarily problematic, but it's helpful to know when we're making one and whether or not we should stand by it.

We form judgments in a variety of ways. One is from the way we were raised. We gather information, whether explicit or implicit, from our parents and caregivers. They tell us this thing or that thing is right or wrong. We are judged right or good if we obey them. We are judged bad or wicked if we "talk back." But even what "talking back" means becomes a matter of judgment—your caregiver's. For some abusive caregivers "talking back" could be as simple as asking a question about an unclear standard.

We also develop judgments from society and workplace rules. For example, in the workplace, sanctions and the embarrassment that results from breaking them are theorized to influence our behavior on the job.[11] We may overlook a fair amount of external influence on our judgments if we aren't paying attention.

Ultimately, as we age and develop discernment, we make judgments based on our values system. We judge something good or bad based on what we believe to be good or bad.

When I judged myself for coming home late, I had been influenced by my upbringing, church doctrine on submission I'd heard for years, and my husband's anger. That powerful combination—as well as not questioning my conclusion—led me to determine that "I should have come home on time."

I often hear clients say things like, "My yes was at the altar so I can't say no" or "I have to have sex with him at least every seventy-two hours or he'll turn to porn" or "I must have a Jezebel spirit because I didn't submit." Like me, they are combining the many voices they've heard about how to be a "good" person into an absolute statement.

Learning to critically evaluate the judgments we make—about ourselves and our situation—is a critical part of healing.

Before you panic, what I'm not saying is we make it up as we go. I'm saying we start with a standard, then evaluate what we believe against that standard, and let that standard bear weight on us. And where there is gray, we look for additional information that is consistent with what we know to be truth. This isn't confirmation bias as some would say. This is consistent thinking.

My standard is God's Word. That is ultimately what sets my moral compass. It's my baseline, and it's what I compare other statements to. So when making a judgment, I ask myself, *Is this consistent with God's Word and His heart?* That helps me assess and refine my judgments. Because spiritual abuse is part of my story, I also ask "Does God's Word really say that?" And then I go look for myself. I am big on interpreting God's Word using all of God's Word. I'm not a fan of proof texting—taking a verse out of context to make it validate something you want it to say. I've found that when I'm wrestling through something, I come to a much more balanced take on things when I look at Scripture in its entirety.

Self-care

As a kid, when I expressed a need—a legitimate need—I was often told I was being selfish. I heard sermons in church that told me I was never to think of myself, only others. I stayed in abusive situations far too long because I believed my heart was desperately wicked and could not be trusted; therefore, any intuitive feelings that something was wrong must be inaccurate. As I was recovering from trauma, I was encouraged for the first time to practice self-care. It took me a while not to falsely equate self-care with self-indulgence. Let's talk a moment about that here. What is the difference between them?

Self-indulgence is "excessive or unrestrained gratification of one's own appetites, desires, or whims."[12] It doesn't give a rat's rear end about someone else. It's thinking, *I'm gonna get mine. My wants and needs are all that matter.* I'd also call it selfishness, which is also rooted in pride. That's not where we want to be, and the Bible speaks against it.

Self-care is wholly different. Self-care encompasses all aspects of caring well and stewarding ourselves physically, mentally, spiritually. We could say it encompasses every part of who we are—body, mind, spirit. Self-care can look like getting our nails done or going to a hair salon. It also can look like body movement and exercise. It can look like doing the laundry so your environment feels more peaceful. It can look like entering into healthy relationships and being known by others. It can also look like taking care of medical issues. It can look like giving space for healing traumatic events. It looks like engaging in Bible study and journaling and spending time with God. Self-care is learning to enter into Sabbath rest. Self-care gives us the capacity to care well for others. We put on our oxygen mask first so we have the capacity to help and give to others.

I'll be honest: I often struggle with self-care. It's an area I'm growing in and I think that's okay. It's hard when you've had a lifetime of being told you were never allowed to think of yourself. The road to balance and health has been a long one for me, like it is for so many women I talk to. We have to give ourselves enormous grace as we learn new things and build new neural pathways that include balance of self and others. And we need to do it nonjudgmentally.

The essential need for grace

As survivors of deep trauma, we often just want to "get it right." It's extremely helpful to be paying attention to what we think "right" or "wrong" is and how we got there.

Grace is key. Because we've so often been told we're to blame for literally everything, that becomes our default starting position. This is the story of nearly every woman who comes into my office, and Addison is a great example.

Addison looked at me as if I'd called her an alien when I asked her, "Is it possible you really didn't have a choice?"

"Of course it's my fault," she said. "I wouldn't have this stupid porn addiction if I had just said no. I got myself here."

"I hear you," I told her. "It feels like you should have just said no to him when he first insisted porn was part of your sex life. He talked you into believing it was healthy and you had to submit. Now you blame yourself. But I'm wondering, is it possible you really didn't have a safe alternative choice at the time?"

It was hard for Addison to see that her addiction started through no fault of her own. Now that she was out of the relationship, it was harder for her to understand why she just didn't quit watching. I knew she wanted to stop, but pornography had been fused to her arousal template. Now zoning out to porn was a way to tolerate what was happening to her marriage. She was judging herself so harshly.

"Are you willing to consider that this judgment is too harsh?" I asked. "I'm not saying you need to be okay about feeling enslaved to porn. Not at all. But could we have some grace for how you got here? Can we consider that it was a life preserver for you in some ways?"

It took some time, but Addison was able to move toward being nonjudgmental of herself. This gave her much more space to be able to heal and let go of pornography completely. Being nonjudgmental doesn't mean condoning thoughts or behaviors that aren't good for us, but it does help us better understand how we got there.

Being nonjudgmental also lets us let go of any faulty doctrine that doesn't truly reflect what God says. Learning to critically evaluate the judgments we've made and how they were formed really does allow us to hear from Him directly rather than just blindly accept what people say about Him. This is vital as we establish a biblical sexual ethic.

INVITING YOUR BODY TO SOMETHING DIFFERENT

Let's get practical. What do you do if, after carefully comparing what you judge to be contrary to a healthy sexual ethic to Scripture, you determine that a behavior *is* out of bounds? How do you know what choices to make to stay within your sexual boundaries? Keep in mind that no one does everything perfectly, but you can be mindful and intentional in your sexual expression—including and maybe especially in your thought life.

For example, when you find that your arousal template has been fused to something that doesn't fit within the boundary lines, *you can gently, kindly, and without judgment invite your body to something different.* Addison's outlook started to shift when she gave herself grace and compassion about how she'd gotten addicted to porn. Then she put tools in place to help make it more challenging to access. We developed a solid recovery plan. And when she was struggling with being drawn to porn for comfort or pleasure, she invited her body to something different.

She did this through mindful self-talk. She'd start with grace. "I know this has been a life preserver for me at times, but it's not anymore. Thank you, body, for trying to cope with really awful stuff as best you knew how. I'd like to try something different." Then she would take a look at her recovery plan and use a skill we'd worked on. Sometimes, she'd name out loud that she really didn't want to do something new in that moment because the urge she had was so strong. In those moments, she'd acknowledge that and reach out to a trusted friend for support. And sometimes she'd do none of that and engage in old behaviors. She learned to be gracious to herself in the moment of failure and then review her recovery plan with me to see where we needed to make an adjustment. Over time, her activity moved back between the boundary lines. No amount of shame would have been successful. She already felt shame. That caused hiding. The keys to her healing and recovery were nonjudgment; a commitment to honor God, herself, and others; and a gentle invitation to herself to try something different.

This also isn't a one-and-done situation. I'll say it again, because we really want it to be one and done, and it just can't be.

Between our highly sexualized culture, the dictates of purity culture, any abuse, and unwanted practices that have been fused to our arousal template, living within a biblical sexual ethic can be really hard. The good news is we can get there. It's a journey and a process, but one worth taking.

Celebrate the progress you make along the way! At the same time, remember that the harm you endured likely goes deep—and so your work will be intense too. For instance, you likely have questions about whether specific sexual activities—such as masturbation—have a place in a healthy, biblical sexual ethic. So many women are longing for a place to ask these hard questions but just don't feel like they can walk up to their women's ministry leader and say, "Hi, I need to talk about masturbation. Could we meet for coffee on Tuesday?" We're going to ask them in our next chapter and wrestle a few things out together.

REORIENTING TO PLAY

So many survivors have lost the ability to play due to the trauma they experienced. Many of the women I work with describe play as something that was either ripped from them or so subtly taken that it was just *gone*. Even as kids, they may have struggled with playtime. Survival took its place, and a part of them went missing. Yet I have seen how profoundly healing reengaging with play can be for my clients.

This exercise is your invitation to reorient to play. Take a moment and think about the fun activities you enjoyed as a child. If you can't think of anything specific, that's okay. You could also consider what types of play you might like today. I recently spoke to a group of women and asked them to consider this question. Their answers included playing hopscotch or pickleball, drawing with sidewalk chalk, swimming, and coloring. My personal favorite is blowing bubbles outside and seeing how many I can catch.

Once you pick your favorite or one you want to try, gather what you need and set aside time to engage in that activity. It doesn't have to be a long time if this feels a bit anxiety-provoking for you. As you engage in the activity, do your best to let yourself be all in—just doing the activity without thinking about tasks you may need to do later. Approach it as if you were a wide-eyed child and look for moments of wonder as you play. Afterward, consider journaling what you noticed in your body and mind.

11

TOO AFRAID TO ASK

Answers to Questions about Sexuality

Your questions can't stop His compassion.
JENNIFER TUCKER, *Breath as Prayer*

Many of us grew up in environments where we weren't permitted to ask questions. And if we were, they certainly weren't allowed to be about sex. Now as adults who have been through some unspeakable things, our questions are likely deeper and feel scarier and more vulnerable. So many women I meet during therapy or speaking at conferences want to know about topics like masturbation, pornography, kink, addictions and compulsions, and what to do if they have no desire at all (sexual anorexia).

I'm glad you're here. We're going to talk about all those things together. There can be so much shame wrapped up in each topic. What happened to you marked you and left scars. We've talked about how parts of that abuse can end up interwoven into your arousal template. So let's dive in together. There is no shame here. Remember that there is no shame for those of us in Christ Jesus (Romans 8:1). He already knows everything, even the parts that are hard for you to verbalize. If something inside you needs to shift, He's going to help you with that. He is not like your abuser who looks at you with disgust. He looks at you with nothing but love.

MASTURBATION

I'm sitting in my hotel room staring at a pile of papers in front of me. I just finished a Q & A session after my presentation at a conference of domestic abuse survivors, which drew more than three hundred women. I've taught this material a number of times, and I always invite the women to write down anonymous questions. I know how tough it can be to ask sensitive things in a room full of people. I'd rather they ask than not, so I give them a way to do so safely. Though I've already addressed their questions, now I have the chance to consider the questions they'd submitted as a whole.

Hands down, despite the venue, the question I get asked the most is this one: "Is masturbation sinful?" As I sorted through this batch of questions, I could see it was no different at this retreat. The debate around masturbation has raged in churches as long as I can remember, and likely long before I was even a thought.

Let's start with what masturbation actually is. Merriam-Webster defines *masturbation* this way: "erotic stimulation especially of one's own genital organs commonly resulting in orgasm and achieved by manual or other bodily contact exclusive of sexual intercourse, by instrumental manipulation, occasionally by sexual fantasies, or by various combinations of these agencies."[1] "Instrumental manipulation" refers to something like a vibrator, and masturbation can happen with or without sexual fantasies.

When I once did a simple Google search of "is masturbation sinful," all manner of articles turned up. Some articles were downright shaming of anyone even asking the question and concluded it's always sinful; others said it was sinful only if done to avoid sex with one's spouse, and still others said the activity was fine and nothing to worry about. How are we supposed to know what is accurate?

As usual, I like to start by seeing what the Bible says. Every article I read pointed out that the Bible does not mention masturbation, and that is accurate. What the Bible does talk about is sexual immorality and sexual morality. It discusses sexual union between women and men. It presents sex in marriage as something of a picture of Christ and the church. Masturbation itself is not mentioned. So if we can't point to a specific chapter and verse to answer this question, where do we start?

Healthy sexuality is a holistic concept that begins with a biblical sexual ethic, as we previously noted. Healthy sexual activity fits within the biblical sexual ethic. We steer clear of sexual immorality. We walk in the bounds of God's wisdom for us.

That then begs the question as to whether masturbation is sexually immoral. So many of the articles I read said unequivocally yes, and some were pretty scathing and shaming. The reasoning behind this is the assumption that masturbation includes lust—which is sexually immoral and thus problematic. But what if lust isn't present? What if masturbation involves simple physical pleasure? What if it is actually helpful to a survivor? Is it a sin then?

Before someone panics and assumes I'm just looking for a loophole so I can sin or let someone else sin and gratify fleshly desires, I actually think the issue is fairly nuanced. Instead of simply offering a blanket response, we need to look at what is happening for the person asking the question. Where her heart and mind are when she asks the question matters a great deal.

When masturbation is problematic

Masturbation is possibly sinful and definitely problematic in certain situations. The first, as we've said, is when it includes lust. Are you fantasizing when you masturbate, and if so, what are you fantasizing about? We've talked about the arousal template and how things like violence can get fused to it. If masturbation includes pornographic images, strangers (i.e., not your spouse), violence, or anything destructive or demeaning to yourself or another person, it is problematic.

It also is an issue when it deprives your spouse—meaning you don't want to engage in sexual activity with your spouse because you prefer self-stimulation. To be clear, I'm talking about a nonabusive spouse here. In a healthy marital relationship, sex involves mutual pleasure between the two parties. Ideally, sexual activity in marriage leads to deeper connection and intimacy. If masturbation—regardless of what you're thinking about—is getting in the way of that, you need to ask yourself some questions.

Masturbation is also problematic when it becomes compulsive. Whenever you are compulsively seeking out sexual gratification, there is an underlying issue. The apostle Paul's caution comes to mind for me here: "All things are lawful for me, but not all things are profitable. All things are lawful for me, but I will not be mastered by anything" (1 Corinthians 6:12, NASB). When we are not in balance or in control of what we are doing, we are in dangerous territory and must be curious as to why.

Consider Annabelle's story.

Annabelle started masturbating at around age eleven after being sexually abused by a teacher. Though she did not fully understand why, she felt in her heart and mind that pleasuring herself was wrong. She tried to stop but couldn't. Eventually as a teen, she had a name for what she was doing when it was discussed in her school's sex education program. She was aghast and vowed to stop. She struggled but eventually did.

Years later, she married an abusive man. Over the course of the nearly two decades they were married, he deeply sexually harmed her. He was cruel and forced her to do things sexually she did not enjoy. She was able to get free and began to heal.

As she put her life back together, she began masturbating again. She was scared because it was happening with alarming frequency and she felt unable to stop. When she finally told me about it in therapy, she said she was doing it several times per day, sometimes excusing herself to the bathroom at gatherings.

Even if Annabelle had not been sinful in masturbating, she was definitely out of balance. She did not feel as if she were in control. Masturbation was taking over her life. For Annabelle, it had become problematic.

Engaging in masturbation may also be an issue if it results in self-harm. An employee who once worked for me also worked part-time in an emergency department at a hospital. She told story after story of women who came in because they had used an object for self-gratification, and it became stuck or otherwise harmed them. Accidents can happen, but I would advocate for a serious reevaluation if you may harm yourself. It may be wise to ask yourself why you are choosing to do that. Abuse harms our sense of self and sexuality, so it is wise to consider why you are making the choice you are making.

When masturbation may not be problematic

Masturbation may not be problematic during sexual activity with your spouse. In the bedroom, self-stimulation is a way you may show your spouse how to please you and bring you to orgasm. Again, I am speaking about a healthy sexual relationship in which both parties are on equal footing. No one should feel demeaned by their spouse in the bedroom. Mutuality is vitally important to a healthy relationship, especially a healthy sexual one.

In what other scenarios, besides the marriage bed, could masturbation be acceptable? It may be in the learning of healthy touch. I had just finished speaking about healthy sexuality at a conference when a lovely woman came up to me. Answering questions and hearing stories after I speak is a highlight, so I looked forward to hearing what she might have to say.

"Thank you," she said as tears began welling up in her eyes. "Thank you for not saying it's always sinful to masturbate."

I looked at her with compassion, knowing she wanted to share her story and waited for her to continue.

As she wiped away her tears, she said, "I was abused and raped over and over in my marriage. I didn't know what gentle sexual touch was. I didn't know orgasms could be pleasurable. Once I was free, as I was healing, I wondered if it was even possible to feel anything good. I prayed a lot about it. After a ton of prayer and talking to my own therapist, I tried masturbating. I was mindful of my thoughts. There was no fantasy, just a consideration of what my body felt and what touch felt good or not good. It helped me determine what I was okay with and what actually felt good. For me, it was an important part of healing, but I can never talk about it because so many people are dogmatically against it!"

She let out an exasperated sigh. "Anyway," she said, "I'm so happy you said it's not always sinful."

If you still wonder where I stand on this issue, here it is: I don't think masturbation is always sinful. I do think it's a matter of where your heart and mind are and what your conscience says. After that, it's between you and God. If you are not lusting, if you are not compulsive or seeking it out above your spouse (if you're married), if you have truly prayed about it and are willing to surrender this to God just as we are called to surrender our whole lives to Him, then masturbation may not be sinful for you.

I'm profoundly curious about how my single friends view this aspect of sexuality, so I've been asking them. It's amazing how many awkward conversations you start when you're writing about sex. So much in the church talks about married sexuality only. Single people, however, are also sexual beings.

I asked a fellow single friend who told me she doesn't masturbate why she chose not to. She told me she did not feel it was permissible to her. She had prayed about it—truly prayed it through without a legalistic bent or some vestige of purity culture—and determined it was something she did not feel God was okay with in her life. Another single friend felt differently. While she said she doesn't engage in it often, she is mindful of her thought life and feels that God does not deem it sinful for her. Both women were profoundly intentional as they considered its place in their lives.

If you wonder about your own situation, I encourage you to read multiple sources, both for and against. Look at the Scriptures cited in those sources and then pray. Hold the question with an open hand, ready to be okay whether God says yes or no for you. And proceed with caution. We never want to be in a place where we aren't asking for His direction. What's permissible in one season of life may not be beneficial in another. There isn't a black-and-white, all-or-nothing here.

OTHER SEXUAL ACTIVITIES

As you've seen, any time a woman asks me about masturbation, there is some nuance in my answer. They ask me about many other sexual activities as well—and often that feels very threatening to them. When we've been sexually harmed, talking about sex at all can be super hard. I know something of the difficulty that comes with sharing deep sexual harm with another human for the first time. I'd shared my own words with my therapist at one point in my healing journey. There is a halting hesitation followed by a tsunami of shame the first time a survivor tries to utter the words for the darkest parts of abuse. I remember his compassion well as I said words out loud I swore I'd take to my grave.

Pornography

Whereas I hold an open view of masturbation, I don't feel the same way about pornography. I think it is deeply harmful to people and falls in the realm of sexual immorality. First, it involves engaging in lust. We don't know the women and men who are participating, and we are literally consuming another person for our pleasure. Additionally, many participants are being trafficked or exploited.

While some actors may consent to their involvement, many do not. In fact, some videos involving women and girls on one particularly large site were taken secretly by abusive men.

Pornography also glorifies violence, particularly violence against women. One study found that 88.2 percent of pornography contained violence against the partner—and the perpetrators of the aggression were largely male.[2] In a study on teen dating violence the researchers noted that both girls and boys were more likely to be violent toward their partner if they had been consuming violent porn.[3] As we talked about in the chapter on arousal structures, we can become habituated to what we consistently experience. If we are watching violent pornography that depicts violence against women, we are more likely to accept such behavior as "normal" when it is anything but.

Erotic fiction also falls into this category. Many years ago the book *50 Shades of Grey* was all the rage among women—even some Christian women. Though I never read the books or watched the movies, I did look to see what it was about. The plot included a man dominating and controlling a woman. In short, it depicted abuse and sexual coercion. It was not a healthy depiction of sexual intimacy at all. That, of course, was only the most famous of the books in recent years. Erotic romance novels remain popular—in fact, supermodel Fabio was made famous because he was the cover model for many such books.[4] Erotic fiction is no different from pornography, though some may include more elements of consent. Reading them still leads to lust—the consumption of another human for our pleasure.[5] The author of *Dopamine Nation* discusses her compulsive use of erotic fiction and how it took over her life for a season.[6] These books are not innocent.

I'll also note that few women would be okay with their spouses or significant others consuming pornography, even through the medium of erotic fiction. Yet are they holding themselves to the same standard? I'm not at all trying to shame here. I know many rationalize it and don't consider it as problematic as other forms of pornography.

Even if it's not being consumed compulsively, however, that does not mean it's innocuous. In my opinion, erotic fiction does not fit into a biblical sexual ethic.

Consuming pornography—whether in video or book form— harms sexual function and mood.[7] The website Fight the New Drug, a source of helpful, easy-to-read articles, details the many ways that pornography harms health.[8] Rather than enhancing our sex lives or sense of sexuality, it can become addictive. More on that below.

Kink

A woman was trying to flag me down after a conference. "Hey! Can I talk to you?"

I stopped walking. "Of course!"

"What are your thoughts . . . on BDSM?" she asked pensively.

I looked at her and gave her a kind smile. I knew it took her a great deal of courage to ask this question. This topic is not often talked about in Christian circles, but it should be. I am so glad she asked me about it.

Let's start by defining *kink*. Merriam-Webster defines it as "unconventional sexual taste or behavior."[9] In my practice, I've noticed that *kink* is often synonymous with *BDSM* for my clients. *BDSM* is defined as "sexual activity involving such practices as the use of physical restraints, the granting and relinquishing of control, and the infliction of pain."[10]

We all have preferences in sexual activity. Some things turn us on and are arousing to us. As we've discussed, our arousal templates were formed in a variety of ways, and many details—such as whether you're attracted to people of a certain hair color, size, or other physical characteristic—are not problematic. When violence is fused to that template, however, we have stepped away from the goodness God designed us for.

I'm going to offer some considerations here. Are themes of dominance and control—regardless of who is dominant and who is submissive—honoring to God and how He created us to be in partnership? BDSM often includes humiliation from the dominant partner to the submissive one. God would not have us dominate one another. We don't see that in Scripture in any context. From the beginning, women and men were created in equal partnership. In Genesis, God tells the man and woman to subdue the earth and have dominion over it (1:28). What they are not told is to have dominion over *each other*. Even the concept of submission, which is often taught in a distorted way, is always to be mutual. When speaking to husbands and wives, the apostle Paul said to "submit to one another out of reverence for Christ" (Ephesians 5:21).

I want to make a particular note about strangulation. First, I'll differentiate between the terms *choking* and *strangulation*. Choking is what I do on chicken that went down the wrong pipe. Strangulation is when my airway is blocked in any way, from hands around my neck, to a bed sheet, to a body being pressed on mine so I can't breathe.

Strangulation has been somewhat normalized by pornography. The more frequently women viewed pornography, the more often they were exposed to pornographic depictions of sexual strangulation. Exposure to sexual strangulation, in turn, was associated with being strangled by men, but not strangling men themselves.[11] That normalization sets up women for this sort of violence being perpetrated against them. Again, we go back to habituation.

Strangulation is extremely serious. You can lose consciousness in as little as five seconds, and there may be no external signs of injury from strangulation. Nonetheless, strangulation can cause traumatic brain injuries, and death may not happen immediately.[12] It can occur days or even weeks later. Let that register: You could think it's all good until you die well after the event. Strangulation is highly dangerous. While some of my colleagues in sex addiction treatment may not agree with me, I cannot find any circumstance in which strangulation is an appropriate part of healthy sexuality (whether you engage in it with a partner or on your own).

Addictions/Compulsions

"I can't stop."

Alex looked at me with a mix of shame and fear.

"I want to stop masturbating and watching porn. I tell myself *This is the last time*. I'm done. I'm done."

She took a deep breath before continuing. "Then after a hard day at work or when someone hurts my feelings or I have a stupid trauma trigger, it's like I have no self-control. I do it anyway. Then it's just so much shame. *So. Much. Shame.*" She emphasized each word and I could see the pain etching across her face.

"How can a Christian woman even be in this place?" she lamented. "If anyone knew . . ." Her voice trailed off and she looked out my window.

Alex is not alone in this struggle or the feelings of shame.

Sex addiction is a bit of a colloquial term to describe what many practitioners and researchers refer to as compulsive sexual behavior, which is basically defined as excessive and uncontrollable sexual behavior that causes trouble in other life areas. Research around this topic has led to a classification in the ICD-11 (the list of all possible disorders and diagnoses a person may have) to a diagnosis of compulsive sexual behavior disorder.[13] I'm not a fan of pathologizing something I believe is largely caused by traumatic experiences (more on that in a moment), so I'll stick to calling it compulsive sexual behavior, or CSB, and forgo the disorder part. Both women and men can experience CSB (or *problematic sexual behavior*, which is the term many professionals are moving toward in discussions of this topic).

While there aren't great numbers on this, I've seen a rise in the number of females struggling with sexual compulsion in my time as a therapist. Research from 2018 found that approximately 7 percent of women struggle with it.[14] While I wasn't able to find any research about this, I'd like to see a study that looks at the prevalence among women who have experienced sexual abuse or sexual assault. I wonder if the numbers among survivors might be higher. Regardless of the actual numbers, dealing with CSB as a female can be difficult. Being a Christian woman and dealing with CSB can be utterly awful and feel extremely isolating. If you are steeped in purity culture beliefs, you may have difficulty understanding how a woman could end up struggling with sexual compulsivity. Often when we hear about compulsive sexual behavior, we think about men being unable to manage their eyes and assume that women don't wrestle with it at all. That isn't true, but it leads to hiding and shame for women who are struggling.

Studies show that sexual compulsivity is often accompanied by adverse childhood experiences that lead to an anxious attachment style.[15] (An anxious attachment style forms because you wanted to experience relational intimacy but feared you'd be abandoned instead.[16]) According to the psychologist Erin L. McKeague, "Data show that women experience more childhood traumas and damage from attachment ruptures. Shame is the core affect [emotion] of sex addiction and is compounded for women by negative cultural messages. Women's sexually addictive behaviors are more relationally motivated."[17] We were made for secure attachment, but when we don't get that as kids, we may be set up to struggle as adults. Abuse exacerbates this struggle. I'd also note that attachment ruptures come from abusive relationships as well.

There are few resources for women, especially Christian women, who struggle with compulsive sexual behavior. Pure Desire Ministries does have a women's curriculum; however, though I live in a large metropolitan area, the closest group to me is nearly ninety miles away.[18] Some churches also have recovery groups that may include a focus on sexually compulsive behavior. Because in-person support groups focusing only on CSB are rare, finding support in the Christian community may be difficult.

If you find yourself in this situation, I want to encourage you. First, God is not mad at you. He knows how you got here. He does want to set you free. He doesn't want you or me in bondage to anything. If you belong to a safe church, see if there are resources for you there. I also encourage you to find a trauma-trained Christian therapist who specializes in sexual compulsivity. You can start by looking for someone who is a certified sex addiction therapist (CSAT).[19] Look into joining a Pure Desire Unraveled group that meets near you, or join an online option. I recommend Jay Stringer's book *Unwanted* [20] if you'd like to take a deeper dive into this issue.

Alex desperately wanted her CSB to stop running her life, and she wanted to live from a biblical sexual ethic. We worked together in therapy to help her find a different path and heal the trauma that was causing her compulsivity. Alex and I started by exploring how her addiction played out for her. Then we put together a recovery plan that included some good coping skills and worked on reprocessing the underlying trauma using EMDR. The road was not easy at times, but she is now living a healed and healthy life in this arena.

Alex, like many of the women I work with, is not married. Single women can heal outside of marriage. This is important to note because so many resources for Christians speak to married people. Healthy sexuality and a biblical sexual ethic are for everyone, regardless of relationship status. And, no, Alex did not become asexual and just forego desire. She still has desire; she has just learned to keep it in its proper place. She is able to bless her body's desire now while walking a healthy path.

Desire can be a tricky thing for any survivor, especially if it can't be fulfilled. We may desire sexual connection and pleasure even though we are unmarried. What do we do? I don't recommend picking up men at a bar; that doesn't go with our biblical sexual ethic (and also isn't particularly wise). Sometimes we have to acknowledge that desire exists and feel the grief that we can't fulfill it.

If you have already experienced so much grief in the abuse you endured, this likely feels really rough. I know. I hear you. I feel this with you as a single woman myself. There are things that we submit to God and trust Him for and with. Lament is far more common (and far more needed) than the modern church acknowledges. We can bless that we feel desire and lament that it is not fulfilled.

No desire (sexual anorexia)

Whereas sexual compulsivity is too much, sexual anorexia is too little. I'm not talking about a lower sex drive. I'm talking about shutting down any thoughts of sexuality or sexual desires. After being abused, many women decide that no one will touch them ever again. They effectively shut down their sexual selves.

This was my story.

The harm that happened to me was so bad that when I was finally free, I swore I was done. No man would ever touch me again.

We all have a "people picker"—it's the way we pick friends and romantic partners. When we've experienced trauma, our people-picking skills can get a little wonky. That can be especially true if we have developmental trauma—the trauma that happened to us as kids and that may have led to attachment issues, the way we bond with other humans. That can make healthy people picking a challenge. I'll also note, predatory persons look for folks with attachment issues so they can exploit them for their own gain.

Because I'd chosen an abuser as a husband, I figured my people picker was broken. So I decided never to have to use it again. At the time, this coping mechanism probably did protect me. However, as the years progressed and I began the healing process, the one area of my life I never broached was my sexuality. At one point, God told me it was time to deal with it. I was terrified. As it is for so many women, the harm to my sexuality had been enormous. I remember saying to my therapist, "I think this is so broken I'll never be healed." But our merciful God knew I needed this piece healed, just like I needed the rest of my soul healed from abuse.

If you're in this place too, I want to say God desires to heal you. Moving past sexual anorexia does not mean you'll suddenly go out and find sexual partners or engage in sexual activity. It just means that the part of you that was closed off after being abused will start to open. You make space for blessing desire. You make space for the fact that you are a sexual being. You make space for *something* other than *nothing*.

Entering into intimate, nonsexual friendships with both same and opposite sex individuals is a way to begin moving into this space. We learn healthy intimacy in relationships that are neither exploitive or abusive. For me, the first people to touch me in intimate nonsexual ways were my female friends. Over time I allowed my male friends to touch me in intimate, nonsexual ways too. As I learned what healthy intimacy looked like, I began to relax. (For a refresher, see chapters 5 and 6.)

I also became more embodied and sensual. Remembering that sensuality is not exclusive to sexual behavior or interaction, I began allowing myself to notice and feel in deep, nonsexual ways. I became (and am becoming) more comfortable in my own skin. This included feeling wonder at creation, enjoying a good meal with my whole self, and being completely present with friends instead of allowing myself to be distracted by my phone. I learned to allow pleasure into my life and to experience it in a full way. I learned to let go of foreboding joy—the joy around something good happening even as you're convinced that the other shoe will drop at some point. Now I can experience an unfiltered joy. Recovering from sexual anorexia is an imperfect and sometimes longer-than-we'd-like process, but it's such a good and rich one.

If you are married, overcoming sexual anorexia will mean re-engaging or engaging differently with your safe spouse. (I can't say this enough: This is not applicable if you are in an abusive marriage.) If you do have a safe and loving spouse, I encourage you to talk with them about what's happening for you. The book *Non-Toxic Masculinity*[21] may help your spouse understand what it's like to be with a wife who's been harmed sexually and how to navigate your relationship gently. Couples counseling with a trauma-trained counselor who specializes in working with spouses (when one or both have experienced sexual harm) can help greatly. You might also read and discuss several helpful books together, including *She Deserves Better* and *The Great Sex Rescue*. The book *Hold Me Tight* by Sue Johnson can help you talk through issues from an attachment-based lens.[22]

For anyone struggling with absent desire or sexual anorexia, skilled counseling with a trauma-trained counselor can be incredibly helpful. It certainly was for me. I found a Christian therapist who did not shame me and was not steeped in purity culture. It gave me a safe place to wrestle through the harm and the healing. Don't let a counselor's gender hold you back. If you find an ethical male counselor who is skilled in this area and he's a good fit for you, go with him! I've had amazing male counselors who walked beside me in this space. They were skilled trauma therapists and were excellent guides in my healing process.

In this time and space I would say that I've embraced being a sexual being with sexual desires, created by a good and wonderful God. I do choose to follow a biblical sexual ethic. As of this writing, I'm not married, which means sexual activity is off the table for me.

I was talking to a friend about this not too long ago. We were chatting about whether we were sad that we can't have sexual intercourse. Realistically, sometimes yes. Orgasms are fun; I'd like to have a partner whom I could both enjoy and be enjoyed by. I'm also okay with following God's rhythm and respecting both myself and others. At one time, I never thought I'd even have a sexuality to speak of, so on the hard days when I do feel grief over not having a spouse, I remind myself of how far I've come.

You, too, have come a long way. I'm so glad you are asking these questions with me!

Bestiality

Most people would never even consider engaging in sexual behavior with an animal. However, for some survivors of sexual abuse, bestiality was part of how they were harmed.

Amelia sat stone-faced as she told me with no emotion, "He raped me all the time. Then, one night, he brought the dog into the bed. At first I was confused. Then I realized what he wanted. I vomited, and he laughed. From then on, it was part of what was normal for him to require of me."

My heart ached as Amelia looked down at the floor after this heartbreaking revelation. She seemed sure I'd finally seen enough and would reject her and call her wicked. I softly said, "Amelia, I am so, so sorry. That was so horrible for you, and it shouldn't have happened. It wasn't your fault."

She looked up at me, her face incredulous. "Aren't you going to tell me that I'm damaged forever? Aren't you going to tell me that no one will ever want me again?"

"No. I'm not telling you any of those things because they aren't true," I said. "That's not how God sees the situation at all. He knows you are a victim of that man's wickedness. And He wants to heal you."

Amelia's body relaxed, and for the first time in our work together, she cried. Her tears were the beginning of the release and healing of more than two decades of horror and grief and harm. She had held it all in her body due to what an evil man had done to her and forced her to do. In the presence of an empathic witness, she no longer had to hold this alone. Shame thrives in the darkness, but it dies in the light.

While bestiality is biblically immoral, you may have been forced into it like Amelia was. This is *not your fault*, and it is *not your fault* if it is still woven into your arousal template. But as we know, whatever is woven in can be unwoven. This is part of reclaiming or establishing healthy sexuality.

Incest

Incest is generally considered to be sexual activity, including but not exclusively sexual intercourse, between two persons whose family relationship would prevent them from being married, including step-relatives.[23]

For some survivors, incest is part of their story of abuse. In fact, one patient's experience of incest led to research on adverse childhood experiences and their impact on things like obesity, launching Dr. Felitti's landmark ACEs study.[24] He accidentally asked a patient how much she weighed—rather than how old she was—when she became sexually active. Her answer—forty pounds—changed the course of what we know about trauma and physical health. Felitti was taken aback when she disclosed that she'd first been molested by her father when she was four. However, he soon discovered how common incest was among his obese patients. Sadly, incest isn't confined to a single demographic—it's a problem across all social classes and all societies. Father-daughter incest is the most common form.[25]

Incest ravages victims. The people who were supposed to care for and protect them most were the ones actively harming them. It creates deep confusion. On the one hand, abused children need their caregivers to live; on the other hand, they are being deeply harmed by them. The father-child incest I've observed also deeply harms the victim's view of God as Father. It is so wicked and so harmful.

Of course, incest perpetrated by another family member also creates confusion. Victims were almost certainly groomed by the perpetrators and may feel complicit in the harm because the attention felt good or their body responded to sexual touch. Because I have seen firsthand the harm done to women at the hands of family members, it makes so much sense to me that God calls this behavior sexually immoral.

If you were abused in your home, this was not your fault. Your abuse does not make *you* sexually immoral. The family member who abused you is sexually immoral, and what they did was wicked and wrong. This is a very important distinction.

And honestly, I'll just say this here: The term *sexually immoral* probably doesn't feel heavy enough. God calls it wicked. He loathes oppression and harm. He says that anyone who harms a child would be better off putting a millstone around their neck and "drowned in the depths of the sea" (Matthew 18:6).

Prostitution and sexual exploitation

Prostitution, or being paid to engage in sexual behavior, is also destructive. The Bible references temple prostitutes, who engaged in sexual activity as a form of worship of the temple gods (2 Kings 23:7).

Sex trafficking is a form of forced commercial sex acts. Someone more powerful than the victims forces them to complete sex acts with or for another person or persons. This could take place in a number of ways (this list is not exhaustive):

- Being taken to a location (house, hotel, nightclub) and being forced to complete sex acts with another person or persons
- Being forced to complete sex acts while being filmed, and the video is later posted to a pornographic website
- Being forced to complete sex acts while being filmed, and the video is live broadcast on a voyeuristic or social media website
- Finding out that sex acts between you and your spouse were secretly filmed and shared or sold

We often think of these things as being done to young girls who are runaways or drug addicts. While it does happen in that context, it isn't always that blatant.

Like many of my clients who wrestle with disclosing what happened to them sexually, Nancy started with the sentence, "I don't know if I can say it out loud."

I took a breath as the sensation of deep compassion and a knowing ache filled my chest and moved through my body. I invited Nancy to take her time and reminded her I was there with her. Stumbling over the words, she said, "I was shocked. Shocked. I walked into the bedroom, and his friend was there. This guy had come over for football games and stuff, so I knew who he was. But I was so confused as to why he was in our bedroom. And why he was looking at me the way he was. I looked at my husband with a confused look, I'm sure." She paused, playing with the fidget toy in her hands, not able to make eye contact with me in that moment.

I sat quietly in the tension with her. I knew she needed space, my presence, and my silence to continue forward.

She finally began speaking again. "My husband told me to undress and lie down on the bed and then do whatever this friend told me to do. I said no at first. The anger on my husband's face was new, and I was terrified. He grabbed me by my wrists and threw me on the bed. He told me I would do what I was told, or I would regret it. I didn't ask another question. In that moment, I was certain he'd hurt or kill me. This man did what he wanted while my husband watched. When it was over and I was left crying on the bed, I watched as this man paid my husband for using me. I realized then he'd sold me."

Her voice trailed off as fresh tears came. I leaned in a bit closer to her so she could better feel my presence with her as she told me this harrowing story. Taking a deep breath, she said, "And he did that for the next ten years until I could get out. I was a money maker for him . . ."

I leaned in a little closer. I gently put my hand on her arm and said, "I am so, so sorry."

Nancy's story is heartrending. Unfortunately, she's not alone. Sexual exploitation can come to us through no fault of our own. Sometimes, women are sold electronically, with or without their knowledge.

There are countless pornographic sites. These sites electronically distribute pornographic content all over the world to whoever will consume it. There have been many articles about one of the largest sites at the time of this writing *knowingly* leaving up videos to which at least one participant—often a woman—did not consent. This includes videos of children, or child sexual abuse material (CSAM). Though the site did purge millions of videos at one point in 2020,[26] victims still struggle to get illegal content removed.[27] Videos may have been taken in secret or by force, then uploaded for sale.

Some users of voyeuristic sites force women into prostitution against their will and are populated by "performers" who post videos or livestreams. Sadly, sometimes spouses or significant others force victims to create content or post it without their knowledge. Exploitation is an equal-opportunity offender, and race, ethnicity, and socioeconomic status do not matter. I've worked with women across all strata who have been forced into this sort of evil.

Often, I think we view prostitution or sex trafficking as something that happens in dark alleys with sketchy women of dubious moral fortitude. But when someone is trafficked, it often looks much different. If these horrors resonate with you, please know that what happened to you is sexually immoral. You are not. If you've been trafficked—whether that is through secretive recording or coercion to participate in it—that sin isn't yours.

Adultery

If your spouse was unfaithful to you, whether through physical infidelity, pornography, or any other way, that is not your fault. We cannot make someone else sin—even if we are the worst partner or spouse on the planet.

This form of sexual immorality is frequently discussed in both the Old and New Testaments. In the English Standard Version, the word *adultery* appears 19 times in the Old Testament and 20 times in the New Testament.[28] The first time it appears in the Old Testament is in the Ten Commandments: "You shall not commit adultery" (Exodus 20:14).[29]

The first time it appears in the New Testament is Matthew 5:27-28, "You have heard that it was said, 'You shall not commit adultery.' But I say to you that everyone who looks at a woman with lustful intent has already committed adultery with her in his heart" (ESV). Here we see Jesus look at adultery, not merely as a physical act, but also as a heart issue.

Lust is consumptive. When we lust after someone, we are not honoring them as a fellow image bearer of the Living God. We are looking at them as a commodity to be used for our pleasure. That's really demeaning. If we've been on the receiving end of this through our partner's sexual immorality, we know how awful it feels. We know how it messes with our self-concept. We wonder, *Is it me? Am I not enough?* It is also terrible when we're on the *giving* end of lust. Even if no one knows, God knows our hearts.

Hear me out here. This is an area I see many women fall into when they exit an abusive relationship. We've talked about what can get woven into our arousal templates. When our bodies responded with arousal even as we were being harmed, it can be so confusing. We may end up functioning in ways that are ultimately not God's best for us and harmful in the long run. Sometimes after we feel we played by the rules only to get hurt, we decide there are no rules. We decided we'll live like the world lives. This reaction neither honors God nor serves us.

Amber shared this with me in a session: "For years he went to strip clubs and watched porn. I had done everything right. All of it. Waited till marriage for sex. Only had eyes for him. And what did I get? Nothing. Not a d— thing. I was betrayed and abused." Her anger was intense as she wrestled with the betrayal—and rightly so.

"So you know what?" she continued. "Now is my time. Yeah, I read erotic fiction and I think about those delicious men described on those pages. I have gone to see male exotic dancers. What did being a good girl get me? Nothing. So now, screw it. I'm going to have my fun." She looked at me with total defiance.

I get it. She did what she'd been admonished to do by her church. Waiting for sexual intercourse until marriage is good, but sadly her husband was wicked. She had been deeply harmed.

Amber also told me that she did want to follow God. She struggled with her faith at times, but she wanted to follow Him. As a therapist, I know to give space for anger and to walk carefully as I work with a client who is trying to make sense of a shattered life. Amber's way of throwing aside all sexual restraint ultimately would not serve her well. And it did not fit with the overall values she had shared with me in past sessions. Sometimes defiance is a coping strategy to keep out pain—a bit of a "You didn't really hurt me, and I'll show you just how fine I am!"

Please know I'm not trying to shame anyone here. This is an easy trap for us, especially when we've been hurt and harmed. Reclaiming healthy sexuality while reckoning with big (or no) feelings and trauma's impact is difficult. As survivors, we had our voice and volition taken away. Our abusers thrived on our silence and their domination of us. Part of healing is reclaiming our God-given voices and our autonomy.

I'm guessing you picked up this book because you want a healthy, God-honoring sexuality. Part of the hard (and sometimes brutal) work of healing involves looking at the difficulties we endured *and* the unhealthy ways we may be trying to cope. Remember, this does not mean that you are responsible for your abuse. *YOU ARE NOT.* You are responsible for your healing, though, and that can be empowered by the Holy Spirit.

So what happened to Amber? As we worked together, we were eventually able to work through the pain and damage done in abuse. She chose to set down the I-can-if-I-want-to approach and live out of her actual values instead. It wasn't easy for her. She had to allow herself to feel the deep grief of what had been taken from her.

It's important to remember God isn't a giant buzzkill keeping us from having a good life and experiencing pleasure. Ultimately, His rhythms and boundaries are for our good. I've had to hold on to this truth over the course of my own healing: God is good. He loves me. He desires the best for me. So, if He's directing me to lay something down, I choose to trust those three things.

I also take comfort in remembering what the author of Hebrews 12:1-2 calls the "great cloud of witnesses":

> Therefore, since we are surrounded by so great a cloud of witnesses, let us also lay aside every weight, and sin which clings so closely, and let us run with endurance the race that is set before us, looking to Jesus, the founder and perfecter of our faith, who for the joy that was set before him endured the cross, despising the shame, and is seated at the right hand of the throne of God.
> HEBREWS 12:1-2, ESV

Who are those witnesses? Does it include those in the Hall of Faith, listed in Hebrews 11? Yes, but it's not only them. It's all those who've gone before us and lived for Christ. Many don't do it perfectly. I mean, some heroes of the faith were hot messes at points, like Rahab, who was a prostitute. Yet she was also brought into the family of faith and is in the lineage of Jesus. That's quite a redemption arc, if you ask me.

Then there are people like Joy Forrest, the founder and executive director of Called to Peace Ministries. Joy has been through it, and her book *Called to Peace*[30] tells her survivor story. She took that pain to Jesus and said, "Lord, the church needs to do better here!" She then created what is now an international ministry that trains faith-based domestic abuse advocates and churches to properly identify and handle abuse. There are men like Chris Moles, author of *The Heart of Domestic Abuse*,[31] the seminal book for pastors and churches on understanding abusive men and the dynamics they use. And I surely cannot forget Leslie Vernick, author of *The Emotionally Destructive Marriage*.[32] Leslie was one of the first authors and speakers to educate the church on this important topic. She paved the way for women like me.

These are just a few of the "great cloud" you might have heard of. There are thousands more—therapists and coaches like me who have lived experience and are helping women heal and pointing our sisters to Christ. There are pastors who humbled themselves so they could learn how to lead safer churches and took time to put in processes to protect the oppressed and call oppressors to accountability. When we look around, we see many who have gone before us, who stand with us, and who are trustworthy witnesses of God's faithfulness, goodness, and trustworthiness.

THE BEAUTY OF QUESTIONS

Asking questions about or struggling with some sexual behaviors doesn't make you perverted. It makes you honest. While some people may not understand why we need to talk about these topics, we are only as sick as our secrets. Healing happens when we drag things into the light so they are no longer allowed to have power over us. We need more places for these discussions, and I sincerely hope we can talk more about them in our churches and women's ministries. I hope this chapter is the start.

LAMENT

In my opinion, we underestimate the need for lament and grief as trauma survivors. Part of healing is grieving the loss of what we had, wished we had, or could have had apart from the abuse. Lest anyone think lament is unbiblical, I'll note that there is a whole book in the Bible called Lamentations, and a lot of the psalms are cries of lament. From them, we know that God hears and welcomes us when we cry out to Him: "God did listen! He paid attention to my prayer. Praise God, who did not ignore my prayer or withdraw his unfailing love from me" (Psalm 66:19-20, NLT).

Here is a useful framework for practicing lament.

> *Step 1:* Cry out to God. You don't have to use fancy words. Sometimes your words might even be colorful. God already knows your heart, and you can pour out your heart to Him however you need to. Be real, be raw. He can handle all of it.

> *Step 2:* Tell God about your pain. Again, real is best here. You don't have to sanitize it to bring it to God—even if your abuser said you can't. Your abuser doesn't get to control your relationship with God anymore. Bring it all. God knows.

Note: It's so important not to short-circuit this part. It may take five minutes, five days, or five weeks. You may have to revisit this part again and again while it all empties out, or as different waves of grief come. It's completely okay. You aren't broken or irredeemable because you come back with new or deeper waves of grief.

> *Step 3:* Ask God for help. Be direct. You're allowed to go before Him boldly. He already knows your heart, and He deeply cares for you.

> *Step 4:* Affirm your trust in God. Basically this means reminding yourself of who God is. You can do this by using His various names—like Jehovah Rapha (the God who heals), Jehovah Jireh (the God who provides) or El Roi (the God who sees). There are some fabulous resources that outline the names of God and that can really help you out here.[33]

12

INTENTION

Enjoying the Hopeful Path

We are all on a journey, and we are all in process.

TABITHA WESTBROOK

We've been on quite the journey together. I hope you've learned about your sexuality, the ways it was harmed, and a way forward to healing. At this point you may be ready to go even deeper or you may be scared witless—or be somewhere in between. That's all perfectly normal. You don't have to arrive at some magical place before you can move toward healing. One single step is enough to get you started. Just reading this book is an act of holy courage!

So now, as you consider your personal path forward, what feels kind and good to you? Where do you sense God leading your healing journey? You may decide that you need to set this aside for a season while you work on something else or that what you most need now is simply rest. The next step in your recovery would be a great conversation to have with your community, your therapist, or someone trusted in your life.

Imagine a life where you are walking in healing. In this scenario, your sexuality is nothing to fear but everything to celebrate—whether you are single or married. Living this out in real life and not just imagination is the very purpose of this book.

You may be at the beginning stages of healing or further along, but wherever you are, you are invited to something different.

PRACTICAL INVITATIONS

We are inviting our bodies to something different. Different from the abuse we suffered. Different from the harm that was woven into our arousal structures.

We are inviting our bodies to learn to rest and to embrace being sexual beings in the way that God created us to be. We are being invited into pleasure and sensuality. We are being invited to sexual healing and wholeness. We are being invited to healing in deep places where we may still feel shame. We are inviting our whole selves to healing, including the parts we're afraid to talk about. Here in this place, nothing is hidden. God delights in all our parts.

The healing of our bodies and souls is active. It's intentional. That doesn't mean it takes us over. We're walking the middle path together. We're healing but at the same time remembering that our sexuality isn't the sum total of who we are. As we move toward healing, let's remember to keep this balance.

As we close our time in this space together, let's look at some practical invitations to healing.

When I hear some teachings in the church, I often wonder about the "how." *How* do you do this thing? How do you take every thought captive? What does that mean? Without some practical steps, concepts are just conceptual. We need to live into healing by *doing* things differently.

Embodiment

How are you doing with your embodied practice? Have you developed a rhythm for getting into and living from your whole self—mind, body, and soul? Remember that part of our healing process is inviting our bodies to something different. The sin against us took place in our bodies. It wasn't just our minds that were harmed. Our physical self was ravaged by what was done to us sexually. Healing, therefore, happens in both our bodies and our minds.

If you haven't yet practiced being embodied, there is no shame at all here. It's *simple* but these things are not always *easy*.

I was at dinner with a group of therapists and was totally called out on one of my own embodied practice goals that I was not doing: slowing down and taking more time to ground into my body. I'm driven and very much type A. I was talking about yet another thing I'd added to my to-do list. My therapist friends know me and my junk. One of them asked, "Are you supposed to be saying yes to anything new right now?" *Oof.* I was busted. I had committed to checking in with them to consider my capacity and commitments before committing to something new. And I hadn't done that. Yes, I felt an initial burst of shame when someone noticed and pointed it out to me, but then I recognized that someone in my trusted community was inviting me to reset. These colleagues have earned the right to press in. Learning something new, especially as a trauma survivor who had to stay outside her body because being inside was too risky, can be tough. Extending ourselves grace and consciously being aware of those places in which we still have vows with the enemy are crucial.

Vows and curses

Speaking of vows, where are you holding on to them? Writing them down and then declaring war against each one can be so powerful. If you have a safe place to journal, I strongly encourage writing them out by hand. I know it sounds old school, but research shows that our brains retain information better when we write rather than type it.[1] I've worked with many survivors who learned after being betrayed by their abusers that writing things down could be dangerous. I get it. It can be a hard prohibition to break, but when you're in a safe environment, this practice can be a good place to stretch yourself.

Arousal template

As you've worked through this book, what have you learned about your arousal template? What is fused to it that you want to see shift? What in your sexual landscape do you think needs a remodel? Take a few minutes and write this out in a journaling space. Again, write out your thoughts by hand if you can.

One way to do this is to make a three-column list on a sheet of paper or in your journal. What is your arousal template fused to that you'd like to shift? Put that in the left column. What do you want to change in your sexual landscape? Also write that in the left column. In the center column, write out what you would like that shift to look like for each item you listed. In the right column, list the practices that will help you move toward your objective. For example, if violence is in the left column, then in the center column you might put tenderness and care. In the right column, you might write that you'll learn to engage in tender self-care practices, like massage or tender self-touch. Note that the practices in the right column don't have to be sexual in nature. Learning to experience tenderness and care in one area can be generalized to other areas.

Expressions of grief

If you've been doing some of the exercises in this book as you read, you likely have experienced grief. Don't discount it. Grief is important in healing. It's the realization of what we had and lost, what we wished we had and didn't, and what we may never have had that we needed. It's a worthwhile effort to take a moment and consider what you need to grieve. There has been so much taken from you in the course of abuse—and not just in the sexual landscape. Take time to lament and allow yourself to feel grief.

Do you need to engage in a ritual where there is a funeral for what you wish life had been? Or the innocence stolen?

Rituals can sound a bit silly, but I do them with clients all the time, and they can be enormously healing. If you have a tough time with the term *ritual*, you can call them practices. (I prefer the term *ritual* because when we practice them we are caring for ourselves in a sacred way, aligning our hearts with the heart of God.) A ritual or practice is something you set aside time to do, like a daily quiet time or engaging in exercise. We engage in many rituals in our lives. For example, a ritual or practice of waking up might be to place your feet on the floor, walk to the bathroom, use the restroom, then wash your face, brush your teeth, and shower. That would be a daily ritual.

We can use rituals and practices in healing too. I think they are helpful because they're embodied and intentional. We're using our whole selves to physically represent healing or to move from one state to the next.

I was doing an intensive with a client, and as we worked together, I could hear all the vows she had made with those who had spoken curses over her. At lunch I made little squares that said, "I do not receive that" and space for her to write down one of the vows. As we went through each one, she wrote them down, one at a time, on a little square. When it was all said and done, she had close to sixty squares. We went outside and burned each one after reading it out loud.

"I don't receive that I am worthless."

"I don't receive that I am hopeless."

"I don't receive that I am damaged goods."

"I don't receive that being a good, godly girl meant submitting to abuse."

She wept as she read each aloud, one at a time, and threw them into the fire. As we processed the exercise together, she marveled at the release she felt in her body each time she read aloud from and then burned one of the squares. "I could feel this weight lifting. I can't explain it, but I felt lighter and lighter as we burned each vow and I watched the smoke rise to heaven. I imagined giving them to Jesus and Him absorbing all the curses so I no longer had to carry them in my own body."

PRACTICAL HOPE

I know something of the weight my client carried because my own journey around grief and recovery has been so hard. I spent years wrestling with sexual abuse that had been held silently within me, finally coming out in symptoms of complex trauma that included health issues. My therapist asked me if I'd ever told anyone *in detail* the sexual harm that happened to me. I looked at him and said, "No. I've only ever shared the thirty-thousand-foot view. Never any details."

With compassion, he looked at me and said, "I think you need to. You've carried this alone. I'm happy to be that person, but I don't have to be."

At that point, I'd been working with him a long time, and I trusted him. There was no one else I'd tell, but I appreciated his grace in giving me a choice. I think the words I used to communicate that I was willing to share the details with him were, "You're fine."

We scheduled an intensive—in my case, three consecutive eight-hour days of therapy—to do the work. I felt my stomach lurch within me as we set that date. I was terrified.

Later that week, I sat on a ledge on the side of a mountain in Western North Carolina, feet dangling above a creek far below me. I couldn't see the creek, but the sound of moving water was comforting. I sobbed in fear as I prayed, "God, I don't know if I can even *say* these words. How can I share the things I swore I'd take to the grave?"

I felt God speak to my heart. *Write them first.*

So I did. I took out a notebook and wrote out by hand the stories of what had happened to me, from my childhood sexual abuse through being repeatedly raped in my abusive marriage. I sobbed, tears dripping onto the page and smudging the ink in some places.

When the effort became too much, I would listen intently to the roaring creek. *What is that water like?* I'd wonder, thankful for a moment to step outside the stories I could still feel in my body. Sometimes I'd just listen to the water moving below me and let the sound fill my whole self. Then I'd return to writing.

Finally, after several hours, I had the stories written out. The sun was starting to set. I closed the notebook and prayed God would give me the strength to actually read them to my therapist. I ended my time by taking a picture *down* toward the creek I was sitting above. Though I still couldn't see the water from there, I could hear it; I knew it was there. Having that anchor point—something other than what I could see—comforted me as I walked a path with an uncertain terrain.

A few weeks later, I was sitting again in my therapist's office. My body shook as I pulled out the notebook. He handed me a box of tissues and we got started. One by one, I read the stories to him. He held space with me as I wept. He asked questions to help me process. As I read one story after another, I started to feel my body inch toward rest. At the end of our three-day intensive I was totally spent, but in some profound way I was no longer holding these things alone.

I'd love to say I was totally healed after that intensive, but I wasn't. However, I was *more healed*. We continued the healing work in our regular sessions.

About a year later, I was hiking in those same Western North Carolina mountains. While walking beside a creek, my body had this profound sense of remembering and *knowing*. I paused. I looked around, and then I looked *up*. I was directly below the spot where I had sat the year before, writing out story after story of harm. Now I was standing along the bank of the creek that I'd heard as I wrote and cried.

I smiled as I watched the sun filter through the green tree canopy. The girl who had sat up there, covered in shame not knowing if she could even speak the harm out loud, was not the same one standing beside the gurgling creek. I was so much more healed.

Yes, scars remain, but the healing far outweighs them. I never in a million years thought that this much healing was possible for me. I knew it was possible for others, but I'd made a vow I was somehow different. Thankfully, God broke through, helped me break that vow, and brought me to a space I couldn't even fathom. He really does do more than we can ask or even dream.

Before heading back down the trail, I got out my camera. This time, I took a picture looking *up*.

GOOD FRIDAY, SILENT SATURDAY, RESURRECTION SUNDAY, AND A GOOD GOD

We have a Savior who gets it. Jesus Himself was abused in His journey to the cross. Falsely accused, beaten, and then nailed to that tree. He understands suffering. In Scripture we are told we have a Great High Priest who has experienced what we do on this earth. Easter shows us just how much He understands suffering, and how much He understands redemption.

As I finish writing, it's Easter weekend. A therapist friend of mine remarked it's fitting that the final push in the birth of this book takes place on such a weekend, one that holds grief and healing and new life.

Taking Communion on Good Friday reminds me how Jesus' body was broken so my brokenness and yours could be completely healed. My body won't be healed completely this side of heaven, though I care for it now as best as I can. That may be the same for you.

That can be a heartbreaking reality.

But we have assurance that all that has been broken and ravaged by sin—including the parts that may never fully heal this side of eternity—will one day be made whole and complete.

I wish I could say all things are resolved and tied up neatly like the ending of a TV show or movie, but we know they don't. But our lives and stories *don't end here*. Thank God for that. And though we may live with some suffering until eternity, we can rest assured in a God who understands and loves us in the deepest of deepest ways.

We also continue to walk forward in the land of the living. We see God's goodness in the land of the living (Psalm 27:13). Sometimes things that *feel* hopeless are not.

That is the message of Silent Saturday—that dark day between Good Friday and Resurrection Sunday. There is no happiness, no resolution on that day—only grief. We know Sunday is coming, but the disciples of Jesus did not. I think of God's tenderness toward that grief. Nowhere in Scripture is it denigrated. God knew how hard that day was for His people. He knows how hard our Silent Saturdays are now as we grieve and wrestle with the ravage of sin and death.

The exact path of our healing isn't always clear—just as the impending resurrection wasn't clear to the disciples. I often think about Psalm 119, which compares God's word to a lamp for our feet and a light to our path. That light often illuminates just the step directly in front of us in the dark nights. We can see only a bit, but God—Who has no darkness in Him and to Whom darkness is not dark at all—goes before me and you. He knows the mountains and valleys ahead. He is trustworthy, even when our trust in Him feels shaky. I wish sometimes (maybe a lot of times) that He gave us a GPS like Google Maps so we could see the whole journey laid out, but He doesn't. We get the lamp and light illuminating just our next steps, and sometimes that seems murky. But we can trust that our story will not be complete until we're home with Him.

But then the gloom and confusion of Silent Saturday is followed by Resurrection Sunday—which we meet with disbelief (at first), wonder, and joy. What was broken did not stay broken, and Jesus' resurrection once and for all means we don't stay broken either. And the first to hear this amazing news were women, at least one of whom, like us, had been broken through deep harm and abuse (yes, I'd count demon possession as being abused). I wonder what it was like for Mary Magdalene, grieving the loss of her friend Jesus who had saved her from such a horrible situation, to suddenly recognize Him and realize He was alive. I can't wait to ask her in heaven!

In our healing journey, we have Good Friday moments when we grieve the harm done and brokenness and loss. We have Silent Saturday moments when we sit in darkness wondering when, or even if, the light will break through. And then, blessed be our God, we have Resurrection Sunday moments when there is victory and the light pours forth. We can hold on to the fact that we are steadily moving toward the final Resurrection Sunday when we'll be with Christ and all that is broken will be healed and every tear wiped away.

God wants this hope for you too. If you're like me and think healing applies to everyone but *you,* please think again. If you're here, I believe God wants it for *you* too.

I'm proud of you for reading this book. I'm proud of you for daring to read words that may have scared or challenged you. I'm so grateful you took this journey with me. I know you can't see my face, but if you could, you'd see that I'm smiling when I think of you. I have a hug ready for you (or if you're not a hugger, I have a high five, a comforting gaze, and a wave) for all you have faced in these pages.

You, dear sister, are on a path to goodness and wholeness. You have invited your body, mind, and soul to something new and different. I am so excited for what God will continue to do! I hope that one day not too long from now, you are able to look *up* from a new vantage point of healing!

Acknowledgments

In so many ways this book has written me. I know what it's like to be a survivor of horrific things, and writing my own story in these pages was both liberating and terrifying. I'm first and foremost thankful to God for saving me—first from myself, then from abuse. He continues to grow me daily. Some days it feels agonizingly slow, if I'm being honest! Yet His timing is always the best. I'm grateful for the gifts He's given me, including the ability to write. He's also given me the most amazing community. This book would not be here without them.

Michelle and Mom2 have been around for what feels like my whole life. Since age fourteen, Michelle and I have been friends, and her mom was such a key champion when I was in some of the darkest of dark times. I am so grateful for them both. God knew what was needed when He dropped me and Michelle in chemistry together. I'm so dang thankful she and Mom2 never gave up on me!

Way back, when I was just a wee twenty-five-year-old lass, I walked into my church to help create skit materials for a women's retreat— my very first women's retreat ever. The only other person there was Linda Sonnendecker. That day, we painted and talked about God's grace. Little did I know we'd become family to each other. Now, more than twenty years later, I cannot imagine my life without her. Sometimes Linda knows me better than I know myself. She's been there through so much of life—the highs and the lows. And, man, some of those lows were *low*. Together we've faced the joys of new life and the immeasurable grief of loss. She saw me leave an abusive marriage, work through healing with God, and become a helper of others. She helped keep me grounded in Christ along the way. Linda headed up our women's ministry at that church long ago, and she also took a chance on letting me teach. I'd love to say my first teachings were the stuff of legends. They were not. They were anxious and spoken too quickly and full of every public speaking mistake ever. But she let me learn. She let me wrestle with Scripture and learn the process. The speaker I am today was honed in that place with loads of God's grace. Words are not enough when it comes to Linda. I am beyond grateful that she is in my life, and I can't imagine it without her.

In so much of the women's ministry leading and serving I did, I was so blessed to get to do it alongside Terri Meyers and Jennifer Hoffert. They are incredible women who showed me love beyond measure as I walked through divorce. The number of times they helped me as a single parent, reminded me I was worthy of love and care, and prayed for and with me is beyond count. It is a gift to have friends who have known both your good and your messy for more than two decades and still stick around. Linda, Terri, Jennifer, and I have been in the four musketeers in so many ways for a long, long time. Many years ago I heard a pastor say "families are formed at the Cross" and I could not agree more. These women are family.

In 2017 I walked into a conference to hand out snacks. I was a licensed therapist working with abuse survivors and felt so alone in this deep work. Little did I know that Jesus was wooing me to a community that would change my life. I happened to be serving at the very first Called to Peace Ministries conference. There I finally heard people in the church saying what I had known for decades. That night I met Joy Forrest, the ministry's founder and executive director, and we became friends and ministry partners. It's a relationship I cherish. This book would not exist without Joy. She asked me to talk about sex at a Called to Peace women's retreat: "Our women need to talk about sex, Tabitha. God said you're the one I should ask." Sneaky Jesus. This book came from that talk.

At that same conference in 2017 I heard a pastor say the things about abuse and how God sees it that I'd always longed for a pastor to say. That man was Chris Moles. I promptly walked up to him after his talk and said, "Hi, my name is Tabitha, and we're going to be friends." Over the years we've become not only friends, but also colaborers in this work. I am grateful for the work of Peaceworks and for Chris's steady guidance on batterer intervention work. I'm trained in his Men of Peace batterer intervention program, and I'm grateful for his wise counsel as I work with both survivors and abusers (though not together!), both as a clinician and a batterer intervention group cofacilitator.

Through Chris, I met someone who became a very precious friend and mentor to me. There would be no book at all without my dear friend Leslie Vernick. She was the original counselor speaking about abuse dynamics in the church, and boy, did she take heat for it. Yet, through the grace of God, people started to listen. Survivors started to break free from abuse. Were it not for her tireless efforts, I would not be able to do the work I have, nor would I have been given a voice to speak these words. She paved the way for women like me, and I could not be more thankful. Her friendship and mentorship mean the world to me, and she was the first person to encourage me to write a book. She then introduced me to my publisher. She's been a tireless champion and encourager as I've gone through the writing process.

All good therapists should have therapist besties, and I'm grateful to have three. Cyndi Doyle, Lynn McLean, and Dr. Gina Aguayo are enormous blessings in my life. Not only are they colleagues, but they are friends. We laugh together, dream together, grieve together, and everything in between. Any time I was feeling imposter syndrome as I wrote, they'd give me a loving and swift kick in the tush and help me get back to it. They were privy to some of the content as I wrote, and they gave me feedback. I am so glad to have them in my life!

The crew at The Finding Place Counseling and Recovery in

Little Rock, Arkansas—especially Ryan and Emily Russ and Dr. Dan Hunt—are the best. I've lost count of how many days I've worked from their office when I've been in Arkansas. They always make space for me there, not only in the office but in their lives. We've had deep conversations, laughter, tears, and snacks (seriously, they have the best snacks). I'm so grateful to them for being on this journey with me, challenging me, encouraging me, and—most of all—believing in me!

To my beta reading team—Dr. Kendra Thurmon, Brooke Eggen, Dr. Michael Ramsey, Matt Chandler, Dr. Dan Hunt, and Ruth Buchanan—thank you for your feedback and wisdom to help ensure I wrote clearly. I am so grateful!

Bob Goff has also been a tireless encourager. If I'm being real, I think Bob is the actual definition of both *tireless* and *encourager*. He has been a gift in my life in a million different ways, and I'm so thankful for him! I am grateful for him answering all my calls and questions, and for believing in me in such a ferocious and full-tilt way!

I also want to thank LeAnne Parsons and Colleen Ramser. They have been such great encouragers and pray-ers as I've been on this writing journey. There is so much more I'd love to say about each of them, but I'll sum it up with this: I'm so grateful to call them my friends!

Dr. Debra Wingfield has been an immeasurable gift. Her ability to find research articles amazes me, as does her passion for training the best advocates on the planet. It is a pleasure to be part of an amazing teaching team with her at the helm. Along with Dr. Jessica Evans and Joy Forrest, we help victims find their voices and break free from oppression.

My team at Tyndale—wow. What a group! I'm so thankful to Jan, Jillian, Kim, Lindsey, and Kristen for their hard work and dedication to making this book the best it can be. Thank you for being a great team. The grace and kindness you all have had as we worked through these tender topics is a total treasure. Thank you for always being so willing to answer questions and hear me as we went through this process.

I also want to thank my agent, Don Gates! His encouragement along the way has been a gift. He helped me understand the process, championed me, and was so gracious with my zillions of questions. I never in a million years dreamed I'd have an agent, and God gave me the absolute best one.

My team at The Journey and The Process is the best. Each of the incredible therapists is changing the world one client at a time. There are so many days when we have belly laughs (Norma Digeso and I are the chief laugh team, I think), days when we wrestle with darkness so we can help lead our clients to light, and every sort of day in between. I am so grateful to be on a healing mission with each of them.

Finally, thanks to my amazing son, Isaiah. He is a light in my life—the most fun human who makes me laugh often. I'm grateful for him and the gift he is. He is so deeply loved. I'm grateful to him for being patient when I had to step away to write and for listening to me read each chapter to him. I am grateful God chose me to be Isaiah's mama.

911 Card

I carefully studied Lynette and saw how dysregulated she was becoming, noting she was on the verge of dissociation. We'd worked together for some time by this point, and I could see signs that she was struggling to stay present. We were doing deep trauma work around her story of sexual harm. I noted how brave she was that day as we faced down those demons of the past. I thought, *Okay, let's keep you here and in your good body.*

Her eyes were pointed at the floor, and her breath had quickened and become more shallow. I softly said, "Lynette, can you look up at me?" She seemed to exert enormous effort to meet my gaze, but she was able to. *Good, she is still partly here.*

I smiled gently at her. "Where are you going? I feel you leaving."

She smiled ruefully as tears started to well up in her eyes. "I . . . I'm not sure." This was Lynette's language for, "I'm stuck in a memory, and I can't quite get back."

"It's okay not to be sure. Let's get you *here*. All the way here and inside your body," I said. She nodded, a flicker of relief on her face. I pulled out the copy of her 911 card and selected an exercise I knew worked well for her. "Ready?"

Lynette nodded, and I started walking her through the exercise.

BREAK (OUT) IN THE EVENT OF AN EMERGENCY

Throughout this book, we talked about how important it is to have a sense of embodiment—to be in our own bodies—as we heal. As trauma survivors, we tend to disconnect from our bodies, our *soma*. Dissociation is part of that disconnect. Though dissociation helped us survive our past, it now keeps us from being in the present and in our bodies at times. Adding in somatic practices can help us get reconnected.

While I'm teaching coping and emotion regulation skills to clients like Lynette, we develop a 911 card—a list of their favorite skills. They can go to these exercises in the moments when they feel themselves dysregulate and start to leave their bodies.

When we get dysregulated, our thinking brain shuts down. We aren't thinking, *You know, my therapist taught me this amazing skill I should use.* We literally cannot think of it in that moment. Having it written down for those moments is so helpful. In my own practice, we have created a physical card that clients can carry with them, take a picture of and save to their phone, or do both so they have easy access when things get hard.

From the exercises throughout this book, and ones you may already know, I encourage you to create your own 911 card. Copy the template below and record your top five preferred practices there. Remember to keep your list with you so you can refer to it and come back to yourself whenever needed.

911 Card—for When It All Hits the Fan

5 TOOLS THAT WORK FOR ME

1. _____

2. _____

3. _____

4. _____

5. _____

I am allowed to use these skills to care for myself.
I am worth caring for.   *With love, Me*

Selected Resources

I love a good tool. So do my clients. These are some selected resources that may be helpful on your journey and that I often recommend to my clients. Though I think these are helpful resources, that doesn't mean I agree with every single word in them or all the ideas the authors hold. I recommend these because they have helpful information. I always encourage my clients—and now you—to review them with discernment based on your values.

BOOKS

Allender, Dan B. *Healing the Wounded Heart: The Heartache of Sexual Abuse and the Hope of Transformation*. Grand Rapids: Baker Books, 2016.

Bancroft, Lundy, and JAC Patrissi. *Should I Stay or Should I Go?: A Guide to Knowing if Your Relationship Can—and Should—Be Saved*. New York: Berkley, 2011.

Burke Harris, Nadine. *The Deepest Well: Healing the Long-Term Effects of Childhood Adversity*. Boston: Houghton Mifflin Harcourt, 2018.

Byrd, Aimee. *Why Can't We Be Friends?: Avoidance Is Not Purity*. Phillipsburg, NJ: P&R Publishing, 2018.

Forrest, Joy. *Called to Peace: A Survivor's Guide to Finding Peace and Healing After Domestic Abuse*. Raleigh: Blue Ink Press, 2018.

Forrest, Joy. *Called to Peace: Companion Workbook*. Raleigh: Blue Ink Press, 2019.

DeGroat, Chuck. *Healing What's Within: Coming Home to Yourself—and to God—When You're Wounded, Weary, and Wandering*. Carol Stream, IL: Tyndale Refresh, an imprint of Tyndale House Publishers, 2024.

Gregoire, Sheila Wray, Rebecca Gregoire Lindenbach, and Joanna Sawatsky. *The Great Sex Rescue: The Lies You've Been Taught and How to Recover What God Intended*. Grand Rapids: Baker Books, 2021.

Gregoire, Sheila Wray, Rebecca Gregoire Lindenbach, and Joanna Sawatsky. *She Deserves Better: Raising Girls to Resist Toxic Teachings on Sex, Self, and Speaking Up*. Grand Rapids: Baker Books, 2023.

Hennessy, Don. *How He Gets into Her Head: The Mind of the Male Intimate Abuser*. Cork, Ireland: Atrium, an imprint of Cork University Press, 2012.

Jolman, Sam. *The Sex Talk You Never Got: Reclaiming the Heart of Masculine Sexuality*. Nashville: Nelson Books, 2024.

Johnson, Susan M. *Hold Me Tight: Seven Conversations for a Lifetime of Love*. New York: Little, Brown and Company, 2008.

Lembke, Anna. *Dopamine Nation: Finding Balance in the Age of Indulgence*. New York: Dutton, 2021.

Linehan, Marsha M. *DBT Skills Training Handouts and Worksheets*. 2nd ed. New York: The Guilford Press, 2015.

McBride, Hillary L. *Practices for Embodied Living: Experiencing the Wisdom of Your Body*. Grand Rapids: Brazos Press, 2024.

McLaughlin, Rebecca. *Jesus Through the Eyes of Women: How the First Female Disciples Help Us Know and Love the Lord*. Austin: The Gospel Coalition, 2022.

Moles, Chris. *The Heart of Domestic Abuse: Gospel Solutions for Men Who Use Control and Violence in the Home*. Bemidji, MN: Focus Publishing, 2015.

Moles, Chris, ed. *Caring for Families Caught in Domestic Abuse: A Guide toward Protection, Refuge, and Hope*. Greensboro, NC: New Growth Press, 2023.

Pierre, Jeremy, and Greg Wilson. *When Home Hurts: A Guide for Responding Wisely to Domestic Abuse in Your Church*. Fearn, Tain, Scotland: Christian Focus Publications, 2021.

Stringer, Jay. *Unwanted: How Sexual Brokenness Reveals Our Way to Healing*. Colorado Springs, CO: NavPress, 2018.

Thompson, Curt. *The Soul of Shame: Retelling the Stories We Believe about Ourselves*. Downers Grove, IL: InterVarsity Press, 2015.

Tracy, Steven R. *Mending the Soul: Understanding and Healing Abuse*. Grand Rapids: Zondervan, 2005.

van der Kolk, Bessel. *The Body Keeps the Score: Brain, Mind, and Body in the Healing of Trauma*. New York: Penguin Books, 2015.

Vernick, Leslie. *The Emotionally Destructive Marriage: How to Find Your Voice and Reclaim Your Hope*. Colorado Springs, CO: WaterBrook Press, 2013.

Wagner, Zachary. *Non-Toxic Masculinity: Recovering Healthy Male Sexuality*. Downers Grove, IL: IVP, an imprint of InterVarsity Press, 2023.

Wilbert, Lore Ferguson. *Handle with Care: How Jesus Redeems the Power of Touch in Life and Ministry*. Nashville: B&H Publishing, 2020.

ORGANIZATIONS

The Allender Center
theallendercenter.org
Provides training and immersion in story work as a means of helping people heal from trauma

Called to Peace Ministries
calledtopeace.org
Provides advocacy, support groups, and practical assistance to individuals affected by domestic abuse; offers education and mentoring to churches and organizations wanting to respond better to abuse survivors

Fight the New Drug
fightthenewdrug.org
Raises awareness and offers resources to help combat the dangers of pornography

Gottman Institute
gottman.com
Offers supports to couples and families seeking to enhance relationship dynamics

International Institute for Trauma and Addiction Professionals
iitap.com/page/Resources
Provides a directory of therapists and pastoral professionals who are equipped to work with individuals and families dealing with trauma and addiction, particularly compulsive and addictive sexual behaviors

National Domestic Violence Hotline
thehotline.org
Provides help and support 24/7 for victims of domestic abuse and those who want to help them

National Sexual Violence Resource Center
www.nsvrc.org
Provides information and tools to prevent and respond to sexual violence

Pure Desire Ministries
puredesire.org
A biblically based and clinically informed ministry dedicated to helping individuals struggling with sexual addiction; offers online and in-person support groups, counseling, and other tools

APPENDIX 3

How to Find the Right Therapy and Therapist for You

First, I want to commend you for considering therapy. I know how hard it is to begin looking for a therapist or consider changing therapists. It takes so much courage, especially when you need to talk about tender topics and harm. Finding a therapist whose approach, values, and style match your own is important. *In fact, fit is the most important aspect.* They can know all sorts of things and have all kinds of education, but if you don't have a good match, none of that will matter. In reality, they need to have both—be a great fit for you and be highly skilled. To help ensure a good fit, I offer some suggestions on what to look for in a therapist.

You want to start by asking yourself what you need the most help with. Are you struggling with depression or anxiety because of what happened to you? Think about what you may want to tackle first.

If you have friends who love their therapist, ask them who they see and what they appreciate most. Also ask if there is anything they don't like about their therapy or therapist. I encourage writing all this down because it can get overwhelming and confusing if you don't actually make a list!

If you have identified the type of therapy you're interested in (see the following pages for brief introductions to various forms of therapy), you can google "trauma therapist near me," "EMDR therapist near me," "Brainspotting therapist near me," etc. See who comes up. Look at websites and read what they say. Make a list of possible therapists to explore further.

Check directories provided by organizations like Psychology Today, Good Therapy, and Therapy for Black Girls. Not all therapists are on directories for various reasons, which is why I suggest starting with friends and an online search. I don't recommend using therapy platforms. They may seem to be cost-effective and to offer flexibility, but some platforms have faced hefty fines for selling data, and I have heard about bad therapy experiences on them. If you need online therapy, I recommend asking the therapists you are considering whether they do virtual sessions. If you'd like a deeper dive on the topic of finding a therapist, some fellow therapists and I made a video that may be helpful.[1]

Once you have a list of therapists you're considering, you have to reach out. I strongly recommend a phone call. I know that can be really hard for some people, but you need to talk to prospective therapists, and you need to pay attention to how your body feels as you do. Here are some questions you can ask.[2]

1. **"How often do you work with clients who have experienced traumatic events? What training have you had? What outcomes have you had?"**

   You want to hear that they do this often and have specific training. One trauma class or continuing education credit is not sufficient. You need someone who really understands traumatic experience and how it impacts the brain, body, and soul. You also want to hear that they have good outcomes—that the people they work with are healing.

2. **"What is your understanding of complex trauma and chronic trauma?"**

   You want to hear that they understand your experience and your world. There is a big difference between processing the fallout from a single car accident and systemic sexual abuse and assault.

3. **"Are you more directive or less directive?"**

This is really going to be your personal preference. No therapist should tell you what to do. They can give you options, but no one should ever tell you that you have to do something. Being more directive may mean offering more tools or more suggestions—but it should never mean giving you directives. Less directive will feel more open-handed with fewer direct suggestions.

4. **"How often are appointments?"**

This is a key question. I strongly recommend a therapist who sees clients weekly at least to start. You're building a new relationship and need that momentum. At our practice, we see far better outcomes for our clients who come weekly. Consistency often helps with healing. We also try to schedule clients at the same time every week to ensure they can fit appointments into their schedules, which makes regularity easier. Some therapists may do it differently, so be sure to ask how they schedule.

5. **"What is a typical session like, and how long does each last?"**

This is a great question to get some idea of what it will be like to work with this therapist. You also may want to ask if they ever do longer sessions. My practice offers custom therapy intensives because sometimes clients want to keep the momentum going and need a longer session for deeper work.

6. **"How, if at all, do you incorporate Christian faith?"**

The best answer: whatever is best for you. Some clients want to incorporate their faith in their sessions. They want a therapist who will quote Scripture and pray with them.

Most, however, were so harmed through spiritual abuse that they aren't sure where their faith is at, so a therapist who prays with every client and quotes Scripture would not be a good fit. I will say, if you have been deeply harmed through spiritual abuse, finding a therapist who can help you disentangle from faulty doctrine may be very helpful. Even so, that therapist should be gentle and follow your healing pace at all times, addressing disentanglement only when you're ready. I've had so many clients sit in front of me with their faith in tatters. My first job isn't to "fix" their faith; it's to understand their world and help them heal from the horrific harm they've experienced.

As you talk with the therapist, determine whether you feel like they're a good fit for you. If you don't feel heard and understood, or if you just don't vibe with the therapist, then they are not for you. It doesn't matter if the therapist has four hundred credentials; if they aren't a good fit, working with them will not be helpful to your healing.

As you go through this process, explore your budget. If you have insurance you want to use, call your insurance company or consult your plan documents to see if they are in your network. When your budget is a consideration, here are some other questions to ask your therapist or insurance company:

"Do you have out-of-network coverage? If so, what is your deductible?"

"What is your in-network copayment?"

"Will CPT code 90837 be covered by my insurer?" (This code is for fifty-three minutes or more of therapy.) Good trauma therapy should never be a forty-five-minute session. In my opinion, that simply isn't enough time to do the needed work.

You may also want to note whether you have a health savings account (HSA) or a flexible spending account (FSA). These can be used to pay for therapy.

Also consider whether you can pay out of pocket for therapy. A number of excellent therapists are not in-network with insurers. Many clients rework their budget to afford the therapist who works best for them. You also can ask if a therapist offers sliding scale slots. Some do and some do not, but it never hurts to ask.

Another option is to work with an intern. Our practice does not offer a sliding scale, but we do have amazing interns who see clients at a significantly reduced cost. Interns have completed most or all of their coursework for their master's degree or doctorate and are doing their fieldwork under a fully licensed therapist with supervision experience. In many ways, at a good practice, you're getting a two-for-one—the benefit of the years of experience and expertise of the supervisor and the reduced cost of the intern.

If you need additional financial support for therapy, consider asking for support from family (if they are safe to ask) or your church. Some churches have funds to help members with therapy.

WHAT THERAPIES DO YOU NEED?

This is probably the million-dollar question. You need the one that is best for you! Some work better with trauma than others, but again it's largely dependent on you as a person. I've listed a few below that have good evidence when it comes to helping heal trauma. I offer these brief descriptions for educational purposes only; I encourage you to do some research and talk with your (current or prospective) therapist to see what might work best for you.

Eye Movement Desensitization and Reprocessing (EMDR)

EMDRIA.ORG/ABOUT-EMDR-THERAPY

EMDR was a treatment developed in the 1980s by psychologist Francine Shapiro, who researched it extensively. EMDR is a structured therapy, which means that it follows a particular process and rhythm. However, it is not directive, so therapists do not guide the therapy in the same way as other therapies. There is a free association element to EMDR, which allows the client to access the trauma briefly and reprocess it.

Basically, when we're traumatized, it's as if that situation took the filing cabinet of our brain and body, shook it, and then dumped everything out everywhere. EMDR can help you pick up the papers and refile them. With EMDR you don't necessarily have to talk about the trauma you experienced, but rather this therapy can help your brain heal using the systems God created to help you process your experiences. Often when you have been traumatized, you believe things about yourself that are not true. EMDR helps replace those inaccurate negative beliefs with more accurate positive beliefs.

EMDR employs bilateral stimulation, using eye movements, tappers that vibrate alternately while being held in each hand, self-tapping, or headphones with alternating sounds to help the brain and body reprocess the trauma. EMDR has been well-researched for addressing post-traumatic stress disorder, anxiety, obsessive-compulsive disorder, sexual assault, depression, and a number of other issues. Many clients I've worked with have found it helpful in their healing process.

Brainspotting

BRAINSPOTTING.COM/ABOUT-BSP/WHAT-IS-BRAINSPOTTING

Psychotherapist David Grand developed Brainspotting from EMDR. Instead of using bilateral movements, it uses a single point in the visual field, which allows access to the trauma. From there, you're able to allow your brain and body to digest the traumatic experience. Much like EMDR, it's a bottom-up approach, engaging the autonomic and limbic systems to allow healing. Unlike EMDR, there is not a specific negative belief being targeted. Practitioners take a less-structured approach, staying in the "tail of the comet" with clients, allowing their brains to lead the way. Like EMDR, you don't necessarily have to provide details of the trauma in the sessions. For clients where bilateral stimulation is difficult or not tolerable, Brainspotting can be a great option.

Accelerated Resolution Therapy (ART)

ACCELERATEDRESOLUTIONTHERAPY.COM/WHAT-IS-ART/

ART uses eye movements exclusively to help clients replace negative images with more positive images that they choose. It's believed that the eye movements in ART are calming and help the nervous system process and replace negative images with positive ones. Some therapists use it in conjunction with other therapy modalities. ART is a more directive approach than either EMDR or Brainspotting. Some clients really benefit from that structure. It's also considered a briefer therapy, though duration depends on the client and the trauma being addressed. There is less research than there is for EMDR; however, there are promising studies with regard to its effectiveness.

Somatic Experiencing (SE)

TRAUMAHEALING.ORG/SE-101/

Somatic experiencing was developed by psychotherapist Peter Levine and uses the sensations of the body to help you "digest" traumatic experiences. SE focuses on how the traumatic experience registers or is evident in the nervous system, and it then helps clients process through it. This approach is very body oriented. The premise of SE is that your body didn't get to complete the full response to a traumatic situation—you never were able to resolve it. SE, a body-based therapy, is designed to help you do exactly that.

Art Therapy

This approach uses the creation of art during therapy to help clients process trauma. Art therapists may use painting, drawing, modeling clay, coloring, or any other artistic expression. It is often used in conjunction with other therapies.

Dialectical Behavioral Therapy (DBT) Skills

Skills training can help clients learn and practice skills related to mindfulness, distress tolerance, emotion regulation, and interpersonal effectiveness. This can help when you haven't learned some of these skills or when these skills were systematically destroyed during abuse. I often use these skills with clients. Some therapists run groups in which they teach these skills. They may be helpful in allowing space for the deeper work of trauma healing.

Narrative Focused Trauma Care

This model uses your story to help you explore the harm done to you and to help you process the traumatic experiences.[3] You may see things in your story that you had not realized in the past. This method also may help you notice body sensations that occur in the course of sharing your story. This approach is often called "story work" and can be done individually or in groups.

Internal Family Systems (IFS)

Developed by Richard Schwartz, IFS focuses on different aspects inside of us.[4] In this model, these are called "parts," and each serves a different role—for example, as a manager, firefighter, or protector to protect your core self.

Many therapists combine different modalities that are tailored to the client. For example, I often use a combination of EMDR, Brainspotting, Narrative Focused Trauma Care, IFS, and SE.

As you can see, there are a whole lot of options. That can feel overwhelming at times. Does one type of therapy resonate with you? That might be a good place to start! The healing journey isn't an easy one, but it's worth it because *you* are worth it.

Notes

INTRODUCTION: MY INVITATION TO YOU

1. I've completed extensive training on treating trauma. I'm certified in
Eye Movement Desensitization and Reprocessing (EMDR), and I'm also
an EMDR approved consultant. I'm trained in Developmental Trauma
Brainspotting, Narrative Focused Trauma Care, Gottman Method Couples
Therapy, Emotionally Focused Couples Therapy, Emotionally Focused
Individual Therapy, and Dialectical Behavioral Therapy. I'm also a certified
clinical trauma specialist and a certified Christian trauma care provider.

CHAPTER 1: ASSAULT ON THE SOUL

1. National Sexual Violence Resource Center, "Sexual Assault Statistics,"
accessed May 31, 2024, https://www.nsvrc.org/statistics.
2. Meredith Somers, "More Than Half of Christian Men Admit to Watching
Pornography," *The Washington Times,* August 24, 2014, https://www
.washingtontimes.com/news/2014/aug/24/more-than-half-of-christian
-men-admit-to-watching-/.
3. Bessel van der Kolk, *The Body Keeps the Score: Brain, Mind, and Body in the
Healing of Trauma* (New York: Penguin, 2015).
4. Brené Brown, interview by Oprah Winfrey, *Super Soul Sunday,* Season 4,
episode 13, "Daring Greatly," aired March 17, 2013, on OWN, video clip,
https://www.oprah.com/own-super-soul-sunday/dr-brene-brown-on-joy
-its-terrifying-video.

CHAPTER 2: RELATIONSHIPS START HERE

1. I refer to my inner critical voice as "she." It reminds me that her words are
not truth and not how God sees me. It helps me separate my true identity
from the one that was marred by abuse.

2. I know there are those out there that are adding more *F*s to this, but we're going to stick to these. See, for example, Ara Munir, "The 6Fs of Trauma Responses," NeuroClastic, September 28, 2021, https://neuroclastic.com/the-6fs-of-trauma-responses/.

3. Dan Allender, *Healing the Wounded Heart: The Heartache of Sexual Abuse and the Hope of Transformation* (Grand Rapids: Baker Books, 2016), 32.

4. It is imperative that all mandated reporters know the laws in their area and whether such a disclosure made by an adult of past childhood abuse must be reported to the relevant authorities. If a minor discloses that such abuse is taking place, it must be reported in accordance with local laws.

5. Jonathan Lambert, "Why Writing by Hand Beats Typing for Thinking and Learning," NPR, May 11, 2024, https://www.npr.org/sections/health-shots/2024/05/11/1250529661/handwriting-cursive-typing-schools-learning-brain.

CHAPTER 3: YES, WE CAN BE FRIENDS

1. Brené Brown, "Dare to Lead: The BRAVING Inventory," accessed May 30, 2024, https://brenebrown.com/resources/the-braving-inventory/.

2. Henry Cloud and John Townsend, *Boundaries: When to Say Yes, How to Say No to Take Control of Your Life* (Grand Rapids: Zondervan, 1992), 31–32. Italics in the original.

3. Brené Brown, *Atlas of the Heart: Mapping Meaningful Connection and the Language of Human Experience* (New York: Random House, 2021), 128.

4. Victoria Ellis, "Three Simple Rules of Boundaries: Expert Guidance from a Therapist," The Journey and the Process, YouTube video, March 21, 2024, https://www.youtube.com/watch?v=scr8RamCXOA.

5. E. L. Machtinger et al., "From Treatment to Healing: Inquiry and Response to Recent and Past Trauma in Adult Health Care," *Women's Health Issues* 29, no. 2 (March–April 2019): 97–102, https://doi.org/10.1016/j.whi.2018.11.003.

6. Susanne M. Dillmann, "Phases of Trauma Healing: Part I, Establishing Safety," GoodTherapy Blog, October 7, 2010, https://www.goodtherapy.org/blog/phases-of-trauma-healing-part-i-establishing-safety.

7. Louise C. Hawkley and John T. Cacioppo, "Loneliness Matters: A Theoretical and Empirical Review of Consequences and Mechanisms," *Annals of Behavioral Medicine* 40, no. 2 (October 2010): 218–227, https://www.ncbi.nlm.nih.gov/pmc/articles/PMC3874845/.

8. Jen Wilkin, J. T. English, and Kyle Worley, "Brothers and Sisters: More than a Metaphor," March 2, 2023, *Knowing Faith*, podcast, https://www.trainingthechurch.com/episodes/brothers-and-sisters-more-than-a-metaphor1.

9. This is not a slam on my Pentecostal brothers and sisters. I love the concept of a victory lap when God has done amazing things!

10. Author and therapist John Gottman uses the illustration of what he calls

the Sound Relationship House to show how friendship is the foundation of strong marital relationships. See "What Is the Sound Relationship House?" The Gottman Institute, https://www.gottman.com/blog/what-is-the-sound-relationship-house/; see also Zach Brittle, "F Is for Friendship," The Gottman Institute, https://www.gottman.com/blog/f-is-for-friendship/.

11. Josh Squires, "Sister, Friend, or Threat?: How Men and Women Relate in the Church," Desiring God, July 25, 2020, https://www.desiringgod.org/articles/sister-friend-or-threat.

12. Squires, "Sister, Friend, or Threat?"

13. William J. Doherty et al., "How Long Do People Wait Before Seeking Couples Therapy? A Research Note," *Journal of Marital and Family Therapy* 47, no. 4 (October 2021): 882–890, https://doi.org/10.1111/jmft.12479.

14. There are many authors that take on this topic and do it far more justice than we can for the purpose of this book. I'd encourage you to read Sheila Wray Gregoire's *The Great Sex Rescue* and *She Deserves Better*, along with Aimee Byrd's *Why Can't We Be Friends?*

15. Rebecca McLaughlin, *Jesus Through the Eyes of Women: How the First Female Disciples Help Us Know and Love the Lord* (Austin, TX: The Gospel Coalition, 2022).

16. Aimee Byrd, *Why Can't We Be Friends?: Avoidance Is Not Purity* (Phillipsburg, NJ: P&R Publishing, 2018).

CHAPTER 4: ALL OF ME, FULLY PRESENT

1. Stephen A. Wonderlich et al., "Relationship of Childhood Sexual Abuse and Eating Disorders," *Journal of the American Academy of Child and Adolescent Psychiatry* 36, no. 8 (August 1997): 1107–1115, https://doi.org/10.1097/00004583-199708000-00018; David A. Wiss, Timothy D. Brewerton, and A. Janet Tomiyama, "Limitations of the Protective Measure Theory in Explaining the Role of Childhood Sexual Abuse in Eating Disorders, Addictions, and Obesity: An Updated Model with Emphasis on Biological Embedding," *Eating and Weight Disorders—Studies on Anorexia, Bulimia and Obesity* 27, no. 4 (May 2022): 1249–1267, https://doi.org/10.1007/s40519-021-01293-3.

2. For more on the connection between sexual abuse and disordered eating, see Laura Palumbo, "The Connection between Eating Disorders and Sexual Violence," National Sexual Violence Resource Center, February 26, 2018, https://www.nsvrc.org/blogs/connection-between-eating-disorders-and-sexual-violence; and Mary Anne Cohen, "Sexual Abuse and Eating Disorders: What's the Connection?," PsychCentral, June 25, 2020, https://psychcentral.com/blog/sexual-abuse-and-eating-disorders-whats-the-connection#1.

3. U.S. Centers for Disease Control and Prevention, "About Adverse Childhood Experiences," last modified April 8, 2024, https://www.cdc.gov/aces/about/index.html.

4. Compassion Prison Project, "Fritzi Horstman Interviews Dr. Vincent Felitti, Co-Creator of the Adverse Childhood Experiences (ACEs) Quiz," February 1, 2024, https://compassionprisonproject.org/fritzi-horstman -interviews-dr-vincent-felitti-co-creator-of-the-adverse-childhood -experiences-aces-quiz/.

5. My ACE score is 8, by the way. If you want to know yours, you can go to a site like https://www.mdcalc.com/calc/10464/adverse-childhood-experiences -ace-score. Special note here: If you find the questions dysregulating or painful to answer, you don't have to answer them alone. You can always take the test with a safe, supportive friend or therapist.

6. Shanta R. Dube et al., "Cumulative Childhood Stress and Autoimmune Diseases in Adults," *Psychosomatic Medicine* 71, no. 2 (February 2009): 243–250, https://doi.org/10.1097/PSY.0b013e3181907888.

7. Bessel van der Kolk, *The Body Keeps the Score: Brain, Mind, and Body in the Healing of Trauma* (New York: Penguin, 2015).

8. Martin Huecker et al., "Domestic Violence," StatPearls [Internet] (Treasure Island, FL: StatPearls Publishing, January 2024), https://www.ncbi.nlm.nih .gov/books/NBK499891/; Emma K. Adam et al., "Diurnal Cortisol Slopes and Mental and Physical Health Outcomes: A Systematic Review and Meta-Analysis," *Psychoneuroendocrinology* 83, September 2017, 25–41, https://doi.org/10.1016/j.psyneuen.2017.05.018; Preethi Kandhalu, "Effects of Cortisol on Physical and Psychological Aspects of the Body and Effective Ways by Which One Can Reduce Stress," *Berkeley Scientific Journal* 18, no. 1 (2013): 14–16, https://doi.org/10.5070/BS3181020644; Kavita Alejo, "Long-Term Physical and Mental Health Effects of Domestic Violence," *Themis* 2, no. 1 (2014), https://doi.org/10.31979/THEMIS.2014.0205.

9. National Sexual Violence Resource Center, "Sexual Assault Statistics," accessed May 31, 2024, https://www.nsvrc.org/statistics.

10. Jake Dorothy and Emily Hughes, "The Death of the Self in Posttraumatic Experience," *Philosophical Psychology* (December 21, 2023), 1–21, https:// doi.org/10.1080/09515089.2023.2294776. Italics in the original.

11. Dorothy and Hughes, "The Death of the Self in Posttraumatic Experience."

12. Dorothy and Hughes, "The Death of the Self in Posttraumatic Experience."

13. Tyler Staton, "Theology of the Body," filmed March 26, 2023 in Portland, OR, Sunday teaching video, https://bridgetown.church/teachings/god -the-whole-person/theology-of-the-body.

14. Dan Allender, "Narrative Focused Trauma Care Level I," accessed May 29, 2024, https://theallendercenter.org/offerings/trainings/training-certificate -level-one/.

15. Ellie Lisitsa, "The Four Horsemen: Criticism, Contempt, Defensiveness, and Stonewalling," *Gottman Relationship Blog*, Gottman Institute, accessed May 31, 2024, https://www.gottman.com/blog/the-four-horsemen -recognizing-criticism-contempt-defensiveness-and-stonewalling/;

Ellie Lisitsa, "The Trouble with Contempt," The Gottman Institute, accessed July 31, 2024, https://www.gottman.com/blog/self-care-contempt/.

16. Karen Sosnoski, "Present Tense: 9 Ways to Get Out of Your Head and Live an Embodied Life," Healthline, October 25, 2021, https://www.healthline .com/health/mental-health/live-an-embodied-life#What-is-conscious -embodiment?

CHAPTER 5: COMING HOME TO YOU

1. Britney Benoit et al., "The Power of Human Touch for Babies" (paper prepared for Canadian Association of Paediatric Health Centres), 2016.

2. Ann E. Bigelow and Lela Rankin Williams, "To Have and to Hold: Effects of Physical Contact on Infants and Their Caregivers," *Infant Behavior and Development* 61 (November 2020): 101494, https://doi.org/10.1016 /j.infbeh.2020.101494.

3. Elizabeth Bush, "The Use of Human Touch to Improve the Well-Being of Older Adults: A Holistic Nursing Intervention," *Journal of Holistic Nursing* 19, no. 3 (September 2001): 256–270, https://doi.org/10.1177 /089801010101900306.

4. Oliver J. Bosch and Larry J. Young, "Oxytocin and Social Relationships: From Attachment to Bond Disruption," in *Behavioral Pharmacology of Neuropeptides: Oxytocin*, vol. 35 of *Current Topics in Behavioral Neurosciences* (Cham, Switzerland: Springer, 2018), 97–117, https://doi.org/10.1007 /7854_2017_10.

5. Harvard Health Publishing, "Oxytocin: The Love Hormone," June 13, 2023, https://www.health.harvard.edu/mind-and-mood/oxytocin-the -love-hormone.

6. Gary Chapman, *The 5 Love Languages: The Secret to Love That Lasts* (Chicago: Northfield Publishing, 1992). The love languages, like many things, are useful tools. I know they can be misused, and abusive people will use them—like so many things—to mask real issues like harmful treatment of their partner. If that happened to you and referencing this particular resource is tough for you, I'm truly sorry it was used to abuse you. Love languages do not mean your partner gets whatever they want when they want it. Mutuality and kindness should always prevail.

7. Lore Ferguson Wilbert, *Handle with Care: How Jesus Redeems the Power of Touch in Life and Ministry* (Nashville: B&H Publishing Group, 2020), 32. Italics in the original.

8. Wilbert, *Handle with Care*, 65.

9. One of the ways I've learned to process trauma with both myself and my clients is story work. Story work is a way of taking a narrative of harm and looking at it in a deeper way and searching for themes within the experience. Through that, additional insights and nuances are gained and processing is done. It's facilitated by a trained story coach. I am trained in Narrative

Focused Trauma Care by the Allender Center, and as with anything we therapists learn, we do it first before we do it with a client. We can't take anyone where we won't go ourselves.

10. Karrie Osborn, "Trauma Touch Therapy," MassageTherapy.com, originally published in *Massage & Bodywork* magazine, accessed May 31, 2024, https://www.massagetherapy.com/articles/trauma-touch-therapy.

11. Amen Clinics, "The Simplest Anxiety-Soothing Technique You've Never Heard Of," August 12, 2020, https://www.amenclinics.com/blog/the -simplest-anxiety-soothing-technique-youve-never-heard-of/.

CHAPTER 6: WHY TOUCHY-FEELY CAN BE A GOOD THING

1. Lindsay Kellner, "Repattern Your Hormones with the 20-Second Hug," mindbodygreen, October 7, 2019, https://www.mindbodygreen.com/articles /20-second-hug-releases-neurotransmitter.

2. Adapted from Marsha M. Linehan, "Interpersonal Effectiveness Handout 8" in *DBT Skills Training Manual* (New York: Guilford Publications, 2014), 63.

3. *Merriam-Webster*, online ed., s.v. "attune," https://www.merriam-webster .com/dictionary/attune.

4. Complex Trauma Resources, "Co-Regulation," August 26, 2020, https:// www.complextrauma.org/glossary/co-regulation/; Adam Young, "Attachment: What It Is and Why It Matters," Adam Young Counseling, May 19, 2020, https://adamyoungcounseling.com/attachment-what-it-is/.

5. Curt Thompson, *The Soul of Shame: Retelling the Stories We Believe about Ourselves* (Downers Grove, IL: InterVarsity Press, 2015), 138.

6. Thompson, *The Soul of Shame*, 14.

7. Richard Cook et al., "Mirror Neurons: From Origin to Function," *Behavioral and Brain Sciences* 37, no. 2 (April 2014): 177–192, https://doi.org/10.1017 /s0140525x13000903.

CHAPTER 7: WHAT TURNS YOU ON

1. Donald Pfaff, *How Brain Arousal Mechanisms Work: Volume 1: Paths Toward Consciousness* (Cambridge University Press, 2018).

2. Ajay B. Satpute et al., "Deconstructing Arousal into Wakeful, Autonomic and Affective Varieties," *Neuroscience Letters* 693 (February 6, 2019): 19–28, https://doi.org/10.1016/j.neulet.2018.01.042.

3. Dan Allender, "Narrative Focused Trauma Care Level 1," *The Allender Center*, January 26, 2023, Seattle, https://theallendercenter.org/offerings/trainings /training-certificate-level-one/.

4. Deb Dana, "What Is a Glimmer?," Rhythm of Regulation, accessed July 31, 2024, https://www.rhythmofregulation.com/glimmers.

5. Alexandra Katehakis, "Arousal Templates in Sex Addiction," Psychology Today, posted May 4, 2011, https://www.psychologytoday.com/us/blog /sex-lies-trauma/201105/arousal-templates-in-sex-addiction.

6. Katehakis, "Arousal Templates in Sex Addiction."
7. LifeWorks Recovery, "Sexual Addiction—Understanding Sexual Arousal Templates," accessed May 31, 2024, https://lifeworksrecovery.com/sexual-addiction-understanding-sexual-arousal-templates/.
8. Josephine Ensign, "Understanding 'Trauma Mastery,'" Psychology Today, August 24, 2018, https://www.psychologytoday.com/us/blog/catching-homelessness/201808/understanding-trauma-mastery.
9. Michael S. Levy, "A Helpful Way to Conceptualize and Understand Reenactments," *Journal of Psychotherapy Practice and Research* 7, no. 3 (Summer 1998): 227–235, https://www.ncbi.nlm.nih.gov/pmc/articles/PMC3330499/.
10. Annie Tanasugarn, "Trauma Reenactment in Our Intimate Relationships," Psychology Today, posted January 8, 2023, https://www.psychologytoday.com/intl/blog/understanding-ptsd/202301/trauma-reenactment-in-our-intimate-relationships.
11. Lois Zoppi, "Trauma Bonding Explained," Medical News Today, updated April 25, 2023, https://www.medicalnewstoday.com/articles/trauma-bonding.
12. Harvard Health Publishing, "A 20-Minute Nature Break Relieves Stress," July 1, 2019, https://www.health.harvard.edu/mind-and-mood/a-20-minute-nature-break-relieves-stress.
13. Erik Gustafsson et al., "Visual Exploration in Adults: Habituation, Mere Exposure, or Optimal Level of Arousal?," *Learning & Behavior* 50, no. 2 (June 2022): 233–241, https://doi.org/10.3758/s13420-021-00484-3.
14. William J. Cromie, "Pleasure, Pain Activate Same Part of Brain," *Harvard Gazette*, January 31, 2002, https://news.harvard.edu/gazette/story/2002/01/pleasure-pain-activate-same-part-of-brain/.
15. Siri Leknes and Irene Tracey, "A Common Neurobiology for Pain and Pleasure," *Nature Reviews Neuroscience* 9, no. 4 (April 2008): 314–320, https://doi.org/10.1038/nrn2333.
16. Colin Schultz, "There's a Scientific Reason Why Self-Harm Makes Some People Feel Better," *Smithsonian Magazine*, October 16, 2014, https://www.smithsonianmag.com/smart-news/theres-scientific-reason-why-self-harm-makes-some-people-feel-better-180953062/.
17. Kristen Neff, *Self-Compassion: The Proven Power of Being Kind to Yourself* (New York: William Morrow, 2011), 125. Italics in the original.
18. Harvard Health Publishing, "A 20-Minute Nature Break Relieves Stress."

CHAPTER 8: DISENTANGLING

1. Walter DeKeseredy and Marilyn Corsianos, *Violence against Women in Pornography* (New York: Routledge, an imprint of Taylor & Francis Group, 2016).
2. Kathleen C. Basile, "Prevalence of Wife Rape and Other Intimate Partner Sexual Coercion in a Nationally Representative Sample of Women," *Violence*

and Victims 17, no. 5 (October 2002): 511–524, https://doi.org/10.1891 /vivi.17.5.511.33717.

3. Hope's Door New Beginning Center. (n.d.). The formula for domestic violence: Digital media, sexual violence and our youth [Conference Presentation]. Trauma Support Services' Trauma Care Institute 2023 Female Survivors of Violence Conference, Plano, Texas, United States of America.

4. Rita C. Seabrook, L. Monique Ward, and Soraya Giaccardi, "Less Than Human? Media Use, Objectification of Women, and Men's Acceptance of Sexual Aggression," *Psychology of Violence* 9, no. 5 (September 2019): 536–545, https://doi.org/10.1037/vio0000198.

5. Michael Chancellor, "The Ongoing Epidemic of Pornography in the Church," Baptist News Global, January 27, 2021, https://baptistnews .com/article/the-ongoing-epidemic-of-pornography-in-the-church/.

6. Sheila Wray Gregoire, Rebecca Gregoire Lindenbach, and Joanna Sawatsky talk about this phenomenon at length in their book *She Deserves Better: Raising Girls to Resist Toxic Teachings on Sex, Self, and Speaking Up* (Grand Rapids: Baker Books, 2023).

7. Jay Stringer, *Unwanted: How Sexual Brokenness Reveals Our Way to Healing* (Colorado Springs, CO: NavPress, 2018), 7.

8. Dan Allender, "Narrative Focused Trauma Care Level 1," *The Allender Center*, January 26–29, 2023, Seattle, https://theallendercenter.org/offerings /trainings/training-certificate-level-one/.

9. Dan Allender, "Narrative Focused Trauma Care Level 1," *The Allender Center*, January 26, 2023, Seattle, https://theallendercenter.org/offerings/trainings /training-certificate-level-one/. See also Dan Allender, "God Loves Sex," Key Life Network, November 30, 2023, https://www.keylife.org/articles /god-loves-sex/.

10. Rachael Clinton Chen, "Narrative Focused Trauma Care Level 1," *The Allender Center*, January 26, 2023, Seattle, https://theallendercenter .org/offerings/trainings/training-certificate-level-one/.

11. Adapted from Patrick Carnes, *Facing the Shadow: Starting Sexual and Relationship Recovery*, 3rd ed. (Carefree, AZ: Gentle Path Press, 2015), 351.

12. Samantha Bickham, "Arousal Non-Concordance: What It Is & Why It Happens," ChoosingTherapy.com, September 27, 2023, https://www .choosingtherapy.com/arousal-non-concordance/; Jon Finch, *Arousal Non-Concordance and Involuntary Sexual Response*, PsychPD, March 15, 2023, https://psychpd.com.au/arousal-non-concordance-and-involuntary -sexual-response/; Meredith L. Chivers et al., "Agreement of Self-Reported and Genital Measures of Sexual Arousal in Men and Women: A Meta-Analysis," *Archives of Sexual Behavior* 39, no. 1 (February 2010): 5–56, https://doi.org/10.1007/s10508-009-9556-9.

CHAPTER 9: WHO'S REALLY TALKING HERE?

1. Deinera Exner-Cortens, John Eckenrode, and Emily Rothman, "Longitudinal Associations Between Teen Dating Violence Victimization and Adverse Health Outcomes," *Pediatrics* 131, no. 1 (January 2013): 71–78, https://doi.org/10.1542/peds.2012-1029; Katherine Wincentak, Jennifer Connolly, and Noel Card, "Teen Dating Violence: A Meta-Analytic Review of Prevalence Rates," *Psychology of Violence* 7, no. 2 (April 2017): 224–241, https://doi.org/10.1037/a0040194.
2. Dan Allender, *Healing the Wounded Heart: The Heartache of Sexual Abuse and the Hope of Transformation* (Grand Rapids: Baker, 2016), 81.
3. Dan Allender, *Healing the Wounded Heart*, 79.
4. Allender, *Healing the Wounded Heart*, 81.
5. Ruth A. Lanius, Braeden A. Terpou, and Margaret C. McKinnon, "The Sense of Self in the Aftermath of Trauma: Lessons from the Default Mode Network in Posttraumatic Stress Disorder," *European Journal of Psychotraumatology* 11, no. 1 (2020): 1807703, https://doi.org/10.1080/20008198.2020.1807703.
6. Lily A. Brown et al., "A Review of the Role of Negative Cognitions about Oneself, Others, and the World in the Treatment of PTSD," *Cognitive Therapy and Research* 43, no. 1 (February 2019): 143–173, https://doi.org/10.1007/s10608-018-9938-1.
7. Junhyung Kim et al., "The Effects of Positive or Negative Self-Talk on the Alteration of Brain Functional Connectivity by Performing Cognitive Tasks," *Scientific Reports* 11 (July 21, 2021): 14873, https://doi.org/10.1038/s41598-021-94328-9.
8. David A. Wolfe, Robert J. McMahon, and Ray DeV. Peters, eds., *Child Abuse: New Directions in Prevention and Treatment across the Lifespan* (Thousand Oaks, CA: SAGE Publications, 1997), 88.
9. Wolfe, McMahon, and DeV. Peters, eds., *Child Abuse*.
10. Neil Anderson, "Who I Am in Christ," Freedom In Christ Ministries, accessed May 29, 2024, https://www.ficm.org/about-us/who-i-am-in-christ/.
11. Dan Allender, *Healing the Wounded Heart: The Heartache of Sexual Abuse and the Hope of Transformation.* (Baker Books, 2016).
12. Allender, *Healing the Wounded Heart*, 86.

CHAPTER 10: HEALTHY SEX AMIDST SORROW

1. Beth Moore, "Thinking about Death and Healing," The LPM Blog, April 10, 2009, https://blog.lproof.org/2009/04/thinking-about-death-and-healing.html.
2. "Blessing for a Broken Vessel" (excerpt) © Jan Richardson from *Circle of Grace: A Book of Blessings for the Seasons.* Used by permission. janrichardson.com
3. Joe Carter, "The FAQs: What You Should Know about Purity Culture," The

Gospel Coalition, July 24, 2019, https://www.thegospelcoalition.org/article /faqs-know-purity-culture/.

4. *Merriam-Webster*, online ed., s.v. "pure," https://www.merriam-webster .com/dictionary/pure.

5. *Merriam-Webster*, online ed., s.v. "chaste," https://www.merriam-webster .com/dictionary/chaste.

6. *Merriam-Webster*, online ed., s.v. "chastity belt," https://www.merriam -webster.com/dictionary/chastity%20belt; Maris Fessenden, "Medieval Chastity Belts Are a Myth," Smithsonian Magazine, August 20, 2015, https://www.smithsonianmag.com/smart-news/medieval-chastity-belts -are-myth-180956341/.

7. Cleveland Clinic, "Clitoris," Cleveland Clinic Health Library, last reviewed April 25, 2022, https://my.clevelandclinic.org/health/body/22823-clitoris.

8. Is it any wonder? Just look at the Pharisees. Jesus had a whole lot to say about their extra rules, which they made others follow but didn't necessarily follow themselves.

9. Sheila Wray Gregoire, Rebecca Gregoire Lindenbach, and Joanna Sawatsky, *She Deserves Better: Raising Girls to Resist Toxic Teachings on Sex, Self, and Speaking Up* (Grand Rapids: Baker, 2023), 171. Emphasis added.

10. Gregoire, Lindenbach, and Sawatsky, *She Deserves Better*, emphasis added.

11. Danielle E. Warren and Kristin Smith-Crowe, "Deciding What's Right: The Role of External Sanctions and Embarrassment in Shaping Moral Judgments in the Workplace," *Research in Organizational Behavior* 28 (2008): 81–105, https://doi.org/10.1016/j.riob.2008.04.004.

12. *Merriam-Webster*, online ed., s.v. "self-indulgence," https://www.merriam -webster.com/dictionary/self-indulgence.

CHAPTER 11: TOO AFRAID TO ASK

1. *Merriam-Webster*, online ed., s.v. "masturbation," https://www.merriam -webster.com/dictionary/masturbation.

2. Laura Tarzia and Meagan Tyler, "Recognizing Connections Between Intimate Partner Sexual Violence and Pornography," *Violence Against Women* 27, no. 14 (2021): 2687–2708, https://doi.org/10.1177/1077801220971352; Gert Martin Hald, Neil M. Malamuth, and Carlin Yuen, "Pornography and Attitudes Supporting Violence against Women: Revisiting the Relationship in Nonexperimental Studies," *Aggressive Behavior* 36, no. 1 (January/February 2010): 14–20, https://doi.org/10.1002/ab.20328.

3. Whitney L. Rostad et al., "The Association between Exposure to Violent Pornography and Teen Dating Violence in Grade 10 High School Students," *Archives of Sexual Behavior* 48, no. 7 (October 2019): 2137–2147, https:// doi.org/10.1007/s10508-019-1435-4.

4. Michael Small, "Love for Sale," *People*, October 4, 1993, https://people .com/archive/cover-story-love-for-sale-vol-40-no-14/.

5. I purposely keep defining *lust* and noting its consumptive nature. When we hear words like this used in church, they feel rote and maybe even sanitized, so they lose the impact they need to have. Lust is a problem because it consumes another person made in the image and likeness of God. That devalues someone God has called inherently valuable.

6. Anna Lembke, *Dopamine Nation: Finding Balance in the Age of Indulgence* (New York: Dutton, 2021).

7. Haseeb Mehmood Qadri et al., "Physiological, Psychosocial and Substance Abuse Effects of Pornography Addiction: A Narrative Review," *Cureus: Journal of Medical Science* 15, no. 1 (January 2023): e33703, https://doi .org/10.7759/cureus.33703.

8. Fight the New Drug. Blog. https://fightthenewdrug.org/blog/.

9. *Merriam-Webster*, online ed., s.v. "kink," https://www.merriam-webster .com/dictionary/kink.

10. *Merriam-Webster*, online ed., s.v. "BDSM," https://www.merriam-webster .com/dictionary/BDSM.

11. Paul J. Wright, Debby Herbenick, and Robert S. Tokunaga, "Pornography and Women's Experience of Mixed-Gender Sexual Choking/Strangulation: Eroticization Mediates, Perceived Similarity Moderates," *Journal of Health Communication* 27, no. 3 (May 2022): 173–182, https://doi.org/10.1080 /10810730.2022.2073406.

12. Training Institute on Strangulation Prevention, "Strangulation in Intimate Partner Violence Fact Sheet," accessed May 31, 2024, https://www .familyjusticecenter.org/wp-content/uploads/2017/11/Strangulation -in-Intimate-Partner-Violence-Fact-Sheet-2017-1.pdf.

13. Laura Kürbitz and Peer Briken, "Is Compulsive Sexual Behavior Different in Women Compared to Men?," *Journal of Clinical Medicine* 10, no. 15 (July 21, 2021): 3205, https://doi.org/10.3390/jcm10153205.

14. Janna A. Dickenson et al., "Prevalence of Distress Associated with Difficulty Controlling Sexual Urges, Feelings, and Behaviors in the United States," *JAMA Network Open* 1, no. 7 (November 2018): e184468, https://doi .org/10.1001/jamanetworkopen.2018.4468.

15. Yasuhiro Kotera and Christine Rhodes, "Pathways to Sex Addiction: Relationships with Adverse Childhood Experience, Attachment, Narcissism, Self-Compassion and Motivation in a Gender-Balanced Sample," *Sexual Addiction and Compulsivity* 26, no. 1–2 (2019): 54–76, https://doi .org/10.1080/10720162.2019.1615585.

16. Hilary I. Lebow, "Anxious Attachment Style: Signs, Causes, and How to Change," Psych Central, June 22, 2022, https://psychcentral.com/health /anxious-attachment-style-signs.

17. Erin L. McKeague, "Differentiating the Female Sex Addict: A Literature Review Focused on Themes of Gender Difference Used to Inform Recommendations for Treating Women with Sex Addiction," *Sexual*

Addiction & Compulsivity 21, no. 3 (September 2014): 203–224, https://doi.org/10.1080/10720162.2014.931266.

18. Nick Stumbo and Trevor Winsor, "The Female Addict & Unraveled," October 20, 2020, *Pure Desire Podcast*, https://puredesire.org/podcast/the-female-addict-unraveled/.

19. International Institute for Trauma & Addiction Professionals, Document and Resource Library, https://iitap.com/page/Resources.

20. Pure Desire Ministries, "Join a Group," accessed July 30, 2024, https://puredesire.org/join-a-group/; Jay Stringer, *Unwanted: How Sexual Brokenness Reveals Our Way to Healing* (Colorado Springs, CO: NavPress, 2018).

21. Zachary Wagner, *Non-Toxic Masculinity: Recovering Healthy Male Sexuality* (Downers Grove, IL: IVP, an imprint of InterVarsity Press, 2023).

22. Sheila Wray Gregoire, Rebecca Gregoire Lindenbach, and Joanna Sawatsky, *She Deserves Better: Raising Girls to Resist Toxic Teachings on Sex, Self, and Speaking Up* (Grand Rapids: Baker Books, 2023); Sheila Wray Gregoire, Rebecca Gregoire Lindenbach, and Joanna Sawatsky, *The Great Sex Rescue: The Lies You've Been Taught and How to Recover What God Intended* (Grand Rapids: Baker Books, 2021); Susan M. Johnson, *Hold Me Tight: Seven Conversations for a Lifetime of Love* (New York: Little, Brown and Company, 2008).

23. Ali Yildirim et al., "Evaluation of Social and Demographic Characteristics of Incest Cases in a University Hospital in Turkey," *Medical Science Monitor* 20 (2014): 693–697, https://doi.org/10.12659/msm.890361.

24. Nadine Burke Harris, *The Deepest Well: Healing the Long-Term Effects of Childhood Adversity* (Boston: Houghton Mifflin Harcourt, 2018), 34.

25. Ali Yildirim et al., "Evaluation of Social and Demographic Characteristics of Incest Cases in a University Hospital in Turkey."

26. Kari Paul, "Pornhub Removes Millions of Videos after Investigation Finds Child Abuse Content," *The Guardian*, December 14, 2020, https://www.theguardian.com/technology/2020/dec/14/pornhub-purge-removes-unverified-videos-investigation-child-abuse.

27. Mairead McArdle, "Pornhub's System for Removing Nonconsensual Content Doesn't Work, Investigation Finds," Yahoo News, February 6, 2020, https://www.yahoo.com/news/pornhub-system-removing-nonconsensual-content-192027176.html.

28. Bible Gateway, keyword search "adultery," https://www.biblegateway.com/quicksearch/?quicksearch=adultery&version=ESV.

29. Yes, some of the folks in the Bible had more than one wife. It never went well. It's why in the New Testament Paul talks about elders/pastors being the husband of one wife (see 1 Timothy 3:2).

30. Joy Forrest, *Called to Peace: A Survivor's Guide to Finding Peace and Healing After Domestic Abuse* (Raleigh: Blue Ink Press, 2018).

31. Chris Moles, *The Heart of Domestic Abuse: Gospel Solutions for Men Who Use Control and Violence in the Home* (Bemidji, MN: Focus Publishing, 2015).
32. Leslie Vernick, *The Emotionally Destructive Marriage: How to Find Your Voice and Reclaim Your Hope* (Colorado Springs, CO: WaterBrook Press, 2013).
33. See, for example, Bible Facts Press, "32 Names of God and Their Meaning," accessed July 30, 2024, https://www.biblefactspress.com/bible-facts/names-of-god/.

CHAPTER 12: INTENTION

1. Timothy J. Smoker, Carrie E. Murphy, and Alison K. Rockwell, "Comparing Memory for Handwriting versus Typing," *Human Factors and Ergonomics Society* 53, no. 22 (October 2009): 1744–1747, https://doi.org/10.1177/154193120905302218.

APPENDIX 3: HOW TO FIND THE RIGHT THERAPY AND THERAPIST FOR YOU

1. The Journey and The Process, "Status of Mental Health Round Table," March 23, 2023, YouTube video, 54:07, https://www.youtube.com/watch?v=_pR72VsFulY.
2. Adapted from Tabitha Westbrook, "How to Find a Trauma Therapist in Wake Forest," The Journey and the Process blog, May 7, 2023, https://thejourneyandtheprocess.com/how-to-find-a-trauma-therapist-in-wake-forest/.
3. For more information, see The Allender Center, "The Foundations of Narrative Focused Trauma Care," March 1, 2024, https://theallendercenter.org/2024/03/the-foundations-of-narrative-focused-trauma-care/.
4. See Psychology Today, "Internal Family Systems Therapy," last updated May 20, 2022, https://www.psychologytoday.com/us/therapy-types/internal-family-systems therapy

About the Author

TABITHA K. WESTBROOK, LMFT-S, LCMHC-QS, LPC-S, LPC, is a licensed therapist who helps people who have messy, funky pasts (and sometimes messy, funky presents) live amazing, empowered lives. Tabitha graduated with her bachelor's in psychology from North Carolina Central University and her master's in professional counseling from Liberty University. In addition to being a licensed counselor and supervisor, Tabitha is an EMDRIA Certified Therapist, EMDR Approved Consultant, Certified Sex Addiction Therapist (CSAT), Certified Clinical Trauma Professional (CCTP), and Certified Christian Trauma Care Provider (CCTCP).

She is the founder and CEO of The Journey & The Process, a private practice with offices in North Carolina and Texas. Tabitha and her team specialize in complex trauma, with a focus on domestic abuse and coercive control. A nationally known expert and speaker, she provides training to churches, therapists, and agencies and helps train domestic abuse advocates through Called to Peace Ministries.

Tabitha is the proud mom of an adult son and lives in Dallas.